Social Finance

Neil Shenai

Social Finance

Shadow Banking During the Global Financial Crisis

Neil Shenai
Mexico City, Mexico

ISBN 978-3-030-08231-4   ISBN 978-3-319-91346-9 (eBook)
https://doi.org/10.1007/978-3-319-91346-9

© The Editor(s) (if applicable) and The Author(s) 2018
Softcover re-print of the Hardcover 1st edition 2018
This work is subject to copyright. All rights are solely and exclusively licensed by the Publisher, whether the whole or part of the material is concerned, specifically the rights of translation, reprinting, reuse of illustrations, recitation, broadcasting, reproduction on microfilms or in any other physical way, and transmission or information storage and retrieval, electronic adaptation, computer software, or by similar or dissimilar methodology now known or hereafter developed.
The use of general descriptive names, registered names, trademarks, service marks, etc. in this publication does not imply, even in the absence of a specific statement, that such names are exempt from the relevant protective laws and regulations and therefore free for general use.
The publisher, the authors and the editors are safe to assume that the advice and information in this book are believed to be true and accurate at the date of publication. Neither the publisher nor the authors or the editors give a warranty, express or implied, with respect to the material contained herein or for any errors or omissions that may have been made. The publisher remains neutral with regard to jurisdictional claims in published maps and institutional affiliations.

Cover illustration: kaarsten, iStock/Getty Images Plus
Cover design by Akihiro Nakayama

This Palgrave Macmillan imprint is published by the registered company Springer Nature Switzerland AG
The registered company address is: Gewerbestrasse 11, 6330 Cham, Switzerland

Preface

I started thinking about writing a book on financial crises a decade ago during my final semester as a Master's student at Johns Hopkins University School of Advanced International Studies (SAIS), where I returned, after a stint on Wall Street, to complete my Ph.D. At the time, political economists were trying to comprehend the origins and implications of the global financial crisis. There was a widespread acceptance that mainstream economics—with its focus on market efficiency, rational expectations, no-arbitrage pricing, and equilibrium—failed to foresee the crisis. Savvy analysts returned to the insights of Hyman Minsky, Charles Kindleberger, and other so-called "Post-Keynesians" to understand financial instability.

I too read Minsky and Kindleberger and soon realized that my road to a finished dissertation traveled through Post-Keynesianism. Even though Minsky and Kindleberger were broadly convincing, there were a few aspects of their theories that warranted extra attention. I was surprised to learn that the foundational texts of Post-Keynesianism omitted the epistemology of John Maynard Keynes, Minsky's intellectual father, from their theories. Nevertheless, Keynesian arguments about how agents cope with uncertainty in markets–by projecting linear trends into the future, by deferring to authoritative actors, and by trying to guess the intentions of fellow investors–described the markets that I witnessed as a junior fixed-income analyst on Wall Street. Social scientists such as international relations theorists and economic constructivists had a ready-made vocabulary for describing the social interdependencies that permeate complex environments. They had a lot to say about why crises occur and how governments respond to macroeconomic stress.

This book presents a modified Post-Keynesian model of financial crises that draws upon John Maynard Keynes' notions of conventionality, Charles Doran's power cycle theory, and economic constructivism. This model attempts to solve several empirical puzzles of financial crises, including where financial stability comes from, why crises take markets by surprise, how defied expectations trigger financial panics, why uncertainty causes market volatility, how economic elites respond to financial instability and, crucially, why some interventions are more effective than others.

Like any good compromise, this book runs the risk of leaving disciplinary partisans dissatisfied. *Social Finance* does not depend on mathematical elegance to make its points (though I encourage readers interested in such arcana to peruse the book's footnotes and references). Rather, I wrote *Social Finance* to provide a heuristic device for policymakers, students, portfolio managers, and academics to explain and forecast financial instability. Readers interested in extensions of Post-Keynesianism, the global financial crisis, and a framework for anticipating future financial crises will benefit from this book. Hopefully, this book's lack of disciplinary fidelity is compensated by its accessibility and novelty.

Once I had an idea of my theory, I needed to decide how best to illustrate its applicability to crises. Choosing a case was an easy decision. The global financial crisis was the most significant shock to the global economy since the Great Depression. It demonstrated the risks posed by shadow banking, or market-based financial intermediation, which has since become one of the most important sources of credit creation in the world. There is no shortage of excellent work on shadow banking written over the last decade, including by authors and institutions such as Gary Gorton, Perry Mehrling, Zoltan Pozsar, the Bank of International Settlements, the Federal Reserve Board of Governors, the Financial Crisis Inquiry Commission, and the International Monetary Fund, from which this book borrows liberally. *Social Finance* contributes to this literature by grounding its analysis of shadow banking within a modified Minsky-Kindleberger framework and by incorporating firsthand accounts of financial market participants into its empirical work. To write this book, I conducted interviews with hedge fund managers, market makers, private equity investors, and regulators, who oversaw over $2 trillion in annual order flows and managed over $160 billion in assets at the time of the crisis. Readers interested in learning more about how financial market participants think during crises and the fragility of shadow banking generally will benefit from *Social Finance*.

I close with a note about this book's cover. To state the obvious, falling dominoes are an apt metaphor for markets in crisis. The book's cover should serve as a gentle reminder about the critical role that financial crisis fighters play in stopping crises. Because of the nature of their work, these men and women do not always receive the credit they deserve. Granted, society is right to question their bureaucrats and the mistakes of financiers—we should not take the bailouts lying down. But things could have been much worse. Hopefully this book shows readers that the choices of central bankers, politicians, and regulators have generational implications on the economy, and that more timid choices could have led to a worse outcome for all. We should therefore take care to nurture our crisis-fighting institutions during quiet periods, knowing that when disaster strikes, our welfare often depends on the highly visible hand of government to save us from the abyss.

Mexico City, Mexico Neil Shenai

Acknowledgements

First, I thank my doctoral dissertation advisor from Johns Hopkins SAIS, Charles Doran, for accepting me as his Ph.D. student and lending me his bold thinking, can-do attitude, peerless advice, and steady stewardship of my project from initial concept to this finished book. Charles helped me formulate my research questions, encouraged me to use a diverse toolkit to understand the role of conventionality in financial markets, tolerated my peripatetic whims to write my dissertation on three continents, and read all iterations of my argument, making it stronger at every stage. This book would not have been possible without Charles' support.

I also thank my other doctoral dissertation advisors including Gordon Bodnar, Roger Leeds, and Matthias Matthijs at SAIS and Mark Blyth from Brown University. Each was generous with his time and criticism, shaping my malformed hunches about conventionality in financial markets into a coherent whole.

In addition to my doctoral dissertation committee, I thank my advisors, colleagues, friends, and mentors including Ines Avalos, Jonathan Bateman, Robert Barbera, Nora Cafritz, Zachary Cafritz, Ryan Connelly, Kevin Carr, Travis Crum, Steven David, Chad DeLuca, Joseph Dickson, John Driscoll, Sam duPont, Jessica Einhorn, David Elam, John Fagan, Benjamin Felt, Desh Fernando, Francis Fukuyama, Gregory Fuller, James Goldgeier, Jakub Grygiel, Tamar Gutner, Margel Highet, Jason Imbrogno, Roberta Jacobson, Bruce Jones, Erik Jones, Edward Joseph, Theodore Kahn, Matthew Kroenig, Michelle Langdon, Starr Lee, Albert Liu, Michael Mayernick, Julie Micek, Daniel Moger, Herschel Nachlis, Khalid Nadiri,

Vali Nasr, Dolly Parker, Joseph Palombo, Bruce Parrott, Megan Petry, Dori Phaff, Michael Plummer, Arturo Porzecanski, Shyla Raghav, Dan Raviv, Emma Raviv, Jon Raviv, Julie Rose, Richard Sattora, Sally Shelton-Colby, Navin Shenoy, Daleep Singh, Ed Suarez, Michelle Tellock, Kyle Thomson, Chloe Thurston, Fred Tsai, Andrew Whitworth, Bonnie Wilson, Geoffrey Underhill, Stephan Vitvitsky, and Constantino Xavier. I especially thank Shereef Elnahal for his years of friendship and support.

My research benefitted from significant institutional backing. I thank the George L. Abernethy and Hopkins Scholars fellowship committees for their funding to study at the SAIS Europe and SAIS China campuses. A grant provided by the Fred Hood Research Fund enabled me to travel to Cambridge University to present an early version of my book's theoretical chapter. I am also grateful to the George Soros-backed Institute for New Economic Thinking, especially Perry Mehrling, for selecting me as a 2012 Young Scholar and inviting me to attend their 2012 plenary in Berlin.

Tula Weis and Ruth Noble, my editors from Palgrave, deserve special thanks for answering my cold inquiry in autumn 2017 and guiding me through the publication process. They made the process easy. I am also indebted to my anonymous peer reviewers for their frank and constructive feedback. The final book is all the better for their criticism. Of course, all errors are my own.

Writing this book was much easier with the love of my family, Radhika Papandreou, Kamalakar Shenai, and Shaila Shenai. I thank Radhika for being an awesome sister and for teaching me about banking while I was still in high school. Because of her, I always felt a little bit ahead of the curve. Thanks to my father for making immense personal sacrifices to move to America to give us a better life. I am grateful to my mother for constantly putting her family first while juggling a demanding career.

Most of all, I owe thanks to my partner, Daphne Morrison, who encouraged me to pursue my goal of publishing a book. She knew my writing with a full-time job meant that I would have to spend months of mornings, nights, and weekends laboring in relative seclusion. This book bears my name but is the product of her inspiration and willing sacrifice. For that and much more, I dedicate this book to Daphne, with love.

Contents

1 McCulley's Warning 1
2 Conventions and Financial Crises 29
3 Monetary Policy and the Housing Bubble 73
4 The Rise of Fragile Finance 103
5 Regulators as Liquidity Providers of Last Resort 133
6 Markets After Lehman 155
7 Conclusions and Extensions 191
Interview Appendix 211
Index 223

Abbreviations

ABCP	Asset-backed commercial paper
ABS	Asset-backed security
A-IRB	Advanced internal ratings-based approach
AIG	American International Group
AIG-FP	American International Group Financial Products group
AMLF	Asset-Backed Commercial Paper Money Market Mutual Fund Liquidity Facility
ARM	Adjustable-rate mortgage
BLS	United States Bureau of Labor Statistics
CDO	Collateralized debt obligation
CDS	Credit default swap
CPFF	Commercial Paper Funding Facility
CPI	Consumer Price Index
CRA	Credit rating agency
DSGE	Dynamic stochastic general equilibrium
FCIC	Financial Crisis Inquiry Commission
FDIC	Federal Deposit Insurance Corporation
FHFA	Federal Housing Finance Agency
FOMC	Federal Open Market Committee
FRBNY	Federal Reserve Bank of New York
FSA	Financial Services Authority
G7/G20	Group of Seven/Group of Twenty
GSE	Government-sponsored enterprise
HERA	Housing and Economic Recovery Act
LIBOR	London Interbank Offered Rate
LOLR	Lender of last resort

LSAP	Large-scale asset purchases
LTCM	Long-Term Capital Management
MBS	Mortgage-backed security
MMIFF	Money Market Investor Funding Facility
MMMFs	Money market mutual funds
NRSRO	Nationally recognized statistical rating organization
OECD	Organization for Economic Cooperation and Development
OIS	Overnight indexed swap
PCE	Personal Consumption Expenditures
PDCF	Primary Dealer Credit Facility
PIMCO	Pacific Investment Management Company
PPIP	Public-Private Investment Program
Repo	Repurchase agreement(s)
S&P	Standard & Poor's
SEC	Securities and Exchange Commission
SIV	Structured investment vehicle
TAF	Term Auction Facility
TALF	Term Asset-Backed Securities Loan Facility
TARP	Troubled Asset Relief Program
TED spread	Difference in three-month Treasury bill rate and three-month dollar LIBOR
TIPS	Treasury Inflation Protected Security
TSLF	Term Securities Lending Facility
VaR	Value-at-risk

LIST OF FIGURES

Fig. 1.1	A visualization of Doran's model	8
Fig. 1.2	Sample schematic of shadow bank	11
Fig. 2.1	Minsky's taxonomy of financing arrangements	34
Fig. 2.2	Non-routine change triggering convention uncertainty	44
Fig. 2.3	A schematic of crises and conventions	54
Fig. 3.1	Schematic of conventions and monetary policy	74
Fig. 3.2	The NASDAQ composite boom and bust: 1998–2003	75
Fig. 3.3	US GDP growth: 1999–2003	76
Fig. 3.4	US unemployment rate and job creation: 1998–2003	77
Fig. 3.5	Monetary policy and US housing prices: 2000–2012	78
Fig. 3.6	Monetary policy and selected mortgage rates: 2000–2008	79
Fig. 3.7	Monetary policy and real interest rates: 1998–2006	80
Fig. 3.8	GDP volatility: 1969–2012	83
Fig. 3.9	Inflation volatility: 1969–2012	84
Fig. 3.10	US Treasury yield curve: December 2000 vs. August 2003	85
Fig. 3.11	CPI weights by category: 2006	88
Fig. 3.12	CPI vs. Modified CPI: 1996–2011	90
Fig. 4.1	Stylized shadow bank consolidated balance sheet with parent bank	105
Fig. 4.2	The rise and fall of ABCP: 2001–2013	109
Fig. 5.1	Maiden Lane's capital structure	142
Fig. 5.2	The TED spread: December 2006–October 2009	143
Fig. 6.1	Financial and non-financial commercial paper rates after Lehman	166
Fig. 6.2	Post-Lehman flight to quality: the dollar and short-term interest rates	168

Fig. 6.3	Global financial crisis locus of financial support	174
Fig. 6.4	US GDP growth: 2006–2011	176
Fig. 6.5	US unemployment rate and job creation: 2007–2009	177
Fig. 6.6	Federal Reserve balance sheet: 2002–2018	183

List of Tables

Table 1.1   Keynes' conventions: definitions and examples   6
Table 1.2   Orthodox model vs. Post-Keynesianism vs. *Social Finance*
            (with précis of case study)   19
Table 3.1   Average annual federal funds rate and change in housing
            prices   77
Table 3.2   Counterfactual inflation measurement   89

CHAPTER 1

McCulley's Warning

In August 2007, the United States' leading central bankers convened in Jackson Hole, Wyoming for the Federal Reserve Bank of Kansas City's annual Economic Policy Symposium. The conference's topic was the housing, housing finance, and monetary policy. Unlike the self-congratulatory mood of prior years, the 2007 meeting was downbeat and uncertain. The global economy faced the early stresses of the impending financial crisis. Housing prices were falling. "Teaser rates" on adjustable rate mortgages reset to higher levels, ballooning monthly payments and putting stress on consumers. Investors in subprime mortgages took significant losses. The investment bank BNP Paribas suspended redemptions on two housing-related hedge funds, while the Federal Reserve cut its discount rate to provide liquidity to troubled banks. Despite these early warning signs, few in attendance, including Federal Reserve Board Chairman Ben Bernanke, Federal Reserve Governor Frederic Mishkin, and former US Treasury Under Secretary John Taylor knew how bad things would get (Federal Reserve Bank of Kansas City 2007; Evans 2007).

However, Paul McCulley had a hunch. McCulley was the chief economist of Pacific Investment Management Company (PIMCO), one of the world's savviest and most influential asset managers. While many of the Jackson Hole participants concentrated on housing market vulnerabilities, McCulley focused on the overlooked plumbing of the global economy. McCulley described the mechanics of a parallel banking system that emerged in tandem with the housing bubble. Trillions of dollars flowed

© The Author(s) 2018
N. Shenai, *Social Finance*,
https://doi.org/10.1007/978-3-319-91346-9_1

through the global shadow banking system daily but fell outside the purview of regulators. Shadow banks put people in homes, gave investors a safe place to park their cash, and earned US and European banks hefty profits during the bubble years. Few economists knew much about shadow banks, let alone studied them in depth, so the audience listened to McCulley.

McCulley spoke candidly. The global shadow banking system that profited so many stood on increasingly shaky foundations. Beneath the surface of the early 2000s bull market sat a global financial system that transformed from stability to fragility. Absent more extensive support from regulators, financial strains would persist. The global economy may have even been on the verge of a "Minsky moment" in which declining asset prices sap the market's confidence, disrupting credit, and ultimately leading to a deep recession. Shadow banks put the solvency of the global financial system at risk (Lahart 2007).

McCulley's warning proved prescient. Asset prices remained volatile throughout late 2007 and early 2008. Investors lost billions of dollars on mortgage assets. Banks failed. Bear Stearns' sale to J.P. Morgan highlighted the risk of financing risky activities using short-term, runnable capital in the shadow banking markets. Lehman Brothers' bankruptcy in September 2008 shattered financial stability, threatening the solvency of all firms and requiring a theretofore unthinkable regulatory response to save the global economy. Trillions of dollars of emergency support provided by the Federal Reserve and US Treasury helped prevent a second Great Depression, though the crisis left lasting scars on the real economy. Continued economic malaise contributed to a growing sense of political dissatisfaction that challenged the legitimacy of democratic institutions.

Scholars and practitioners have caught up to the trends McCulley identified during his Jackson Hole commentary in the years since the crisis. Viral Acharya, Tobias Adrian, Cornel Ban, Gary Gorton, Eric Helleiner, Perry Mehrling, Andrew Metrick, and Zoltan Pozsar, among others, argued that shadow banking *was* banking.[1] While the term "shadow banking" has come to mean different things, for the purposes of this book, shadow banking is defined as *market-based financial intermediation* in which the core banking transformations take place outside of the formal financial system. Shadow banks engage in credit, liquidity, and maturity transformation, just like traditional banks. Whereas traditional banks lent insured deposits directly to consumers and firms, shadow banks prior to the global financial crisis borrowed funds via commercial paper and repurchase agreements and lent to borrowers via securitized assets. Shadow banks' reliance on runnable short-term capital and their lack of deposit insurance made them vulnerable to bank runs, as the global financial crisis made clear.

The crisis also popularized the work of Hyman Minsky, Charles Kindleberger, and other so-called "Post-Keynesian" asset market theorists. Post-Keynesian vocabulary of bubbles, fragility, Ponzi financing, and the "Minsky moment" entered the financial vernacular during the global financial crisis. Some of the crisis' biggest players, including former US Treasury Secretary and Federal Reserve Bank of New York President Timothy Geithner, described the global financial crisis as a quintessential "Minsky crisis" (Geithner 2014, 68). Janet Yellen, the former Federal Reserve Chair and Federal Reserve Bank of San Francisco President, said "Minsky's work has become required reading" in the wake of the crisis (Yellen 2009). Daniel Tarullo, former Federal Reserve Board Governor from 2009 to 2017 in charge of financial reform, referenced Charles Kindleberger's work in a speech shortly after the most acute phase of the crisis. Quoting Kindleberger, he noted that financial crises remained a "hardy perennial" that were "recurring stories in human history" (Tarullo 2009). In October 2017, China's former central bank governor Zhou Xiaochuan warned that without significant reform, China's economy might soon face a "Minsky moment" of its own (Reuters 2017). And in April 2018, the International Monetary Fund warned of Minsky-Kindleberger style risk-taking due to prolonged easy financial conditions in the global economy (International Monetary Fund 2018, 61).[2]

Social Finance: Shadow Banking during the Global Financial Crisis sits at the nexus of these intellectual currents. The premise of this book is that while Post-Keynesian asset market theory is broadly correct, several Post-Keynesian contentions are themselves things that need to be explained. *Social Finance* thus develops a modified Minsky model of financial crises and illustrates its applicability via a case study of the global financial crisis. This model reincorporates sociological insights from John Maynard Keynes (Minsky's intellectual father) back into the Minsky model to present a more complete account of why bubbles form, why some financing structures are more vulnerable to panics than others, and why financial crises are so hard to predict. It borrows from scholarship on crises in international relations theory to examine the triggers of financial distress and the crisis dynamic. And it draws on perspectives from international political economy, particularly economic constructivism, to show how foundational economic ideas shape elite choices prior to, during, and after financial panics and how the effectiveness of regulators' crisis responses depends on their credibility with the marketplace. This book demonstrates the utility of this new paradigm via a case study of shadow banking during the global financial crisis. It presents the results of interviews with some of the world's leading investors in London, Los Angeles, New York, and Toronto, a close examination of primary and secondary sources, and quantitative evidence to contribute to the collective understanding of shadow banking.

This chapter serves as a stand-alone summary of *Social Finance*. It describes the core arguments of the Post-Keynesian model and then outlines the book's theoretical arguments. A penultimate section explains why this book matters to both academic and policymaking audiences. The chapter concludes by setting the stage for the subsequent theoretical and empirical chapters.

BUILDING ON THE POST-KEYNESIAN MODEL: ALTERNATIVE PARADIGMS AND THE *SOCIAL FINANCE* SYNTHESIS

Post-Keynesians argue that bubbles, fragility, crises, and panics are natural features of capitalist economies. According to Post-Keynesian theory, a crisis begins with an exogenous "displacement" that changes anticipated profits in a sector of the economy. This shock then triggers a boom in credit to the displaced sector, and asset prices rise. Market participants adopt increasingly risky financing structures to take advantage of newfound profit opportunities. Investors purchase assets to flip them for a future profit rather than because of their long-term income-generating potential. Eventually, economic fundamentals cannot keep up with expectations, and sellers outnumber buyers. Prices fall, exposing the system's underlying fragility. If fragility is sufficiently widespread, prices may fall pro-cyclically, possibly leading to a panic. Banks respond by rationing credit even to healthy borrowers, making it difficult for firms to meet their maturing financial obligations. Financial distress follows. Left unchecked, a crisis can lead to a deep recession or even a depression, though countercyclical fiscal and monetary policy can help to cushion the blow to the real economy (Kindleberger and Aliber 2005, 23–30; Minsky 1982, 85–87).

Several aspects of the Post-Keynesian model aptly describe crises. Financial panics and fragility tend to follow from periods of stability, comporting with Minsky's notion that stability begets fragility over time. Importantly, there is ample precedent for financial crises to take hold without any *bolt from the blue* exogenous shock—rather they often occur because of the processes that are inherent to capitalist finance. Market participants do not live in a world where they can process perfect information, leading them to rationally identify optimal investment strategies. Financiers, awash in *pervasive uncertainty*, instead take their cue about the future from the recent past. This Keynesian convention, that tomorrow will resemble yesterday, then is married to the key Minsky assertion—that the longer the string of similar yesterdays, the more confident investors become. This epistemic blindness fuels bubbles and fragility. Methodologically, Post-Keynesian models are simple and stylistic. They are light on math and depict the market as a fully constituted whole, making the Post-Keynesian framework accessible to a wide audience.

But the Post-Keynesian paradigm, in key ways, is incomplete. Limitations include a lack of specificity about the origins of stability, an underdeveloped causal mechanism for understanding when and how stable (but fragile) financial systems erupt into crisis, and silence on how regulators react to financial instability and whether their interventions will be successful.

The chapters that follow use the solid foundation provided by the Post-Keynesian framework to advance a new, sociological view of financial crises based on Keynesian epistemology, Charles Doran's power cycle theory, and economic constructivism.

John Maynard Keynes believed uncertainty dominates economic life. To cope with this inherent uncertainty, market participants employ *economic conventions* to give them a basis of knowledge to guide their behavior. Conventions are rules of thumb, norms, or institutionalized metrics used to coordinate expectations and provide regularity to economic life. Keynes identified three types of conventions in markets: (1) the notion that the past provides a reliable guide to the future (i.e. *ergodicity*); (2) the tendency of market participants to latch onto the narratives of authoritative actors when forming their own expectations of the future and assuming that present market conditions are stationary and reflect a logical equilibrium (i.e. *expert opinion*); and (3) the habit of market participants to try to guess the expectations of *fellow* market participants when forming their own expectations (i.e. *conventional expectations* or the Keynesian beauty contest).[3] Keynes believed that collective confidence in economic conventions leads to stable markets (Keynes 1937, 214, see Table 1.1). When markets have convention certainty, forecasts become self-fulfilling, with circular reinforcement of convention construction, market outcomes, and further convention confidence (Crotty 1994, 123–124). So, when conventions are stable, markets are stable. When conventions are unstable, markets can become unstable. Over the years, iterations of Post-Keynesianism downplayed these crucial Keynesian sociological insights (or "micro-foundations") in their models.[4]

Table 1.1 Keynes' conventions: definitions and examples (Keynes 1937)

Convention and definition	Examples
Ergodicity: The belief in expectations that the future will resemble the past; therefore, market participants extrapolate linearly from past trends when forming expectations of the future	• Technical analysis in financial markets and other inductive investment theses • Federal Reserve fears of repeating Japan's history of deflation from the 1990s during the early 2000s (see Chapter 3) • Bank risk models such as value-at-risk based on historical asset price performance (see Chapter 4)
Expert opinion: Narratives of authoritative actors set the bounds of other market participants' expectations and anchor the belief that prevailing market outcomes reflect "true" asset values	• A notable investor announcing an intent to purchase shares of a company boosts market confidence in the company, leading to higher prices • Economic metric construction requires authoritative actors to determine what constitutes an underlying economic phenomenon (see Chapter 3) • Institutionalized credit ratings for corporates, governments, and households drive investment decisions (see Chapters 4–6)
Conventional expectations: Market participants consider what fellow market participants believe before making decisions; therefore, portfolio decisions are second and third order social practices rather than first order decisions based on material fundamentals. This practice is colloquially known as a "Keynesian beauty contest"	• Fiat money that retains value based on presumption of reciprocity • Counterparty confidence in unsecured shadow banking markets during global financial crisis (see Chapters 4–6) • Credibility transfer mechanisms such as deposit insurance and multilateral credit lines (see Chapter 6)

As this book contends, Keynesian notions of convention formation address how market participants collectively create narratives that support stable markets, thus facilitating the Minsky model's endogenous fragily dynamics over time.

This book also uses a model of crises in international relations to explain the triggers of financial panics. Charles Doran's power cycle theory provides a causal mechanism explaining when and how systems transformations in international politics leads to great power conflict. To Doran, much like Keynes, expectations are central to elite decision making. Doran argues that agents form expectations of the future based on linear extrapolations from past trends. If outcomes evolve in a linear fashion, as they do most of the time, then linear forecasts will provide a reliable anchor of behavior, giving agents confidence in their projections. However, when nonlinearities or shocks occur, the decision environment changes profoundly. Agents suddenly must deal with the stress of realizing that their most taken-for-granted beliefs no longer apply, triggering massive uncertainty about future security and foreign policy. Systems transformation occurs when multiple states experience such a nonlinear shock to their long-held expectations, causing uncertainty to ricochet throughout the system and greatly increasing the likelihood of violence and protracted conflict (Doran 1991, 28–30; 1999). This book analogizes Doran's model to the financial system, arguing that shocks to convention-given expectations trigger uncertainty in markets which, under certain conditions, can lead to panics. Doran's argument explaining how and why (and thus the conditions for when) shocks to expectations trigger massive uncertainty helps us come to grips with the seeds of instability in financial markets (see Fig. 1.1).

How do regulators respond once a crisis hits? Minsky argued that regulators have a choice of using countercyclical fiscal and monetary policy to cushion the blow from financial crises to the broader economy. If governments are willing to run larger deficits and the central bank serves as a lender of last resort, then regulators can restore confidence and avoid depressions after systemic crises (Minsky 1982, 11–13). Charles Kindleberger further added that lender of last resort insurance is part of the repertoire of regulators' crisis response but that the knowledge of the provision of this insurance may trigger the very behavior that the insurance was designed to prevent (i.e. moral hazard) (Kindleberger and Aliber 2005, 32–33). Neither Minsky nor Kindleberger specify the

A visualization of Doran's model

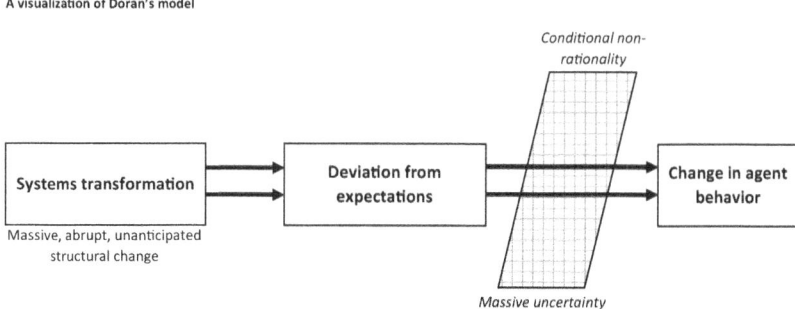

Fig. 1.1 A visualization of Doran's model (Doran 1991)

political economy channels that constrain, enable, and shape regulatory responses to crises.

But it is worth considering what determines whether states can provide support to the economy. What factors constrain and shape policy choices? When and why does the market permit crisis responses? What determines whether interventions succeed or fail?

A popular subfield of international political economy, economic constructivism, studies how economic ideas shape elite responses to economic crises. Economic constructivists believe that economic ideas reduce uncertainty and help elites diagnose the causes of crises and determine appropriate policy responses (Blyth 2002).[5] Constructivists also claim that during crises, elites can use discourse and persuasion to elevate certain policy solutions over others (Matthijs 2011). Other constructivists contend that open capital markets constrain policymakers because international investors can punish states for pursuing policies that they deem illegitimate with capital outflows while rewarding legitimate policies with capital inflows and lower borrowing costs. Critically, both borrowers and lenders socially construct legitimacy, and these notions are subject to radical change during crisis periods (Kirshner 2003). Constructivism provides an apt framework of understanding elite responses to financial instability, and this book incorporates the insights of economic constructivists to investigate how social forces shape elite responses to financial instability.

Social Finance's theory of financial crises rests on five causal propositions on the role of economic ideas in financial markets. These propositions directly address the weaknesses in the Minsky model using the aforementioned paradigms. The first two propositions describe the antecedent forces of financial instability, while the latter three propositions describe the crisis dynamic and resolution:

First, *financial stability depends on convention stability*. Agents create financial stability through social processes, chiefly through agreeing on a certain set of economic ideas that in turn reinforce their behavioral priors via market outcomes. These conventions, though self-stabilizing in the short run, paradoxically facilitate the economy's shift from stability to fragility over time. Second, as *conventions become more entrenched, agents make greater and greater wagers on the persistence of their conventions. This process blinds agents to bubbles and fragility*. In other words, the same uncertainty mitigation devices used by market participants to guide their behavior are also responsible for sowing epistemic blindness prior to crises. Conventions thus simultaneously stabilize markets, trigger endogenous fragility dynamics identified by Minsky, and blind market participants to the growing reality of financial fragility. Third, *shocks to agents' expectations catalyze uncertainty*. When market outcomes belie convention-given expectations, market participants question the truth-value of their conventions. The absence of convention certainty triggers convention uncertainty of varying degrees. Fourth and as a corollary to the third proposition, *given sufficient fragility, convention uncertainty causes agents to revert to first principles of survival, disrupting the market's normal price discovery mechanism and triggering financial instability*. At a minimum, dashed confidence reinstates the reality of pervasive uncertainly, replacing the socially agreed upon fiction that defined the previous convention. But convention uncertainty catalyzed by deep and widespread shocks to agents' expectations goes deeper and beyond the ordinary pervasive market uncertainty. Convention uncertainty causes market participants to hoard liquid capital, in turn disrupting in varying degrees the market's normal price discovery mechanism. This behavior is colloquially known as a "flight to quality" and reflects a natural defensive response of market participants to financial distress. Once the panic begins, financial elites have a menu of choices on how best to respond. The fifth proposition of *Social Finance* is that *elite responses to financial instability are a function of the economic frameworks that inform their diagnoses of the crisis and regulators' market-given leeway to intervene in the economy*. To state what should be obvious, but is mostly ignored by mainstream approaches, how financial elites conceptualize the causes and consequences of an ongoing panic determines how they respond to financial instability. The efficacy of regulators' response, in turn, depends on the latitude the market gives them to intervene as well as regulators' ability to marshal domestic and international resources to stem a panic. *Social Finance* terms regulators' degrees of freedom to respond to crises as *intervention capacity*. The higher regulators' intervention capacity, the greater their ability to stop market panics and mitigate broader deflationary impacts of falling asset prices.

A New Understanding of the Global Financial Crisis[6]

An old adage holds that theory without evidence has no legs upon which to stand, while evidence without theory has no eyes with which to see. Four empirical chapters of *Social Finance* apply the above theoretical propositions to understanding central and shadow banking prior to and during the global financial crisis.

At its core, the global financial crisis is best understood as a shadow banking bank run by commercial paper and repurchase agreement ("repo") counterparties on the global shadow banking system. Two primary asset classes, asset-backed commercial paper (ABCP) and repo, served as short-term "deposits" in the shadow banking system. Shadow banks used their proceeds from ABCP and repo to purchase long-term securitized assets, known as asset-backed securities (ABS), or bonds backed by cash flows of pooled loans from sectors such as residential real estate, credit cards receivables, and automobile loans, among other types of underlying collateral. ABCP and repo counterparties were shadow banking "depositors," while counterparties that contributed the underlying securities in ABS loan portfolios constituted the "borrowers" (see Fig. 1.2). Unlike traditional banking, shadow banks lacked sovereign-sponsored deposit insurance, so they were vulnerable to bank runs (Gorton 2010). If cash flows from long-term assets covered short-term debt servicing costs, investors would willingly refinance or "roll over" maturing shadow banking liabilities. If shadow banking counterparties doubted banks' ability to meet their maturing obligations (as they did when collateral prices fell because of the deflating housing bubble and rising mortgage delinquencies), then they could refuse to roll over maturing liabilities, causing funding costs to rise and spreading financial contagion.

Sample schematic of shadow bank

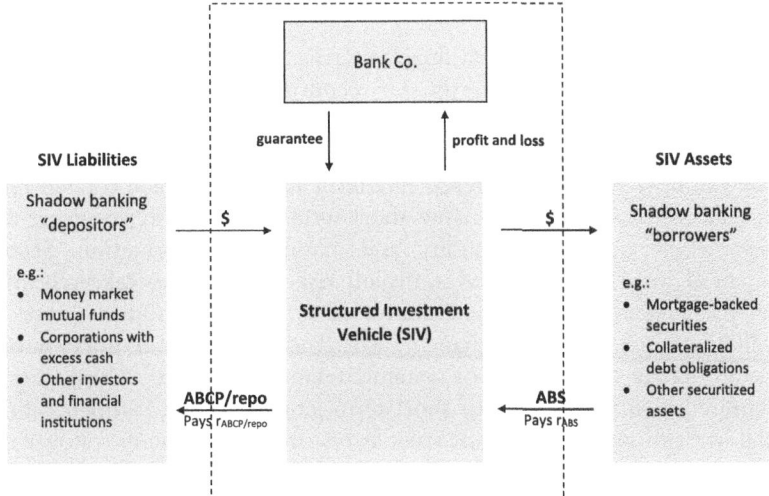

Fig. 1.2 Sample schematic of shadow bank (Author and Gorton 2010)

As the housing bubble inflated and economic boom wore on during the early 2000s, financial institutions sponsored increasingly fragile shadow banking structures in off-balance-sheet vehicles. This activity reinforced rising home prices but eventually succumbed to creditor panics when the housing bubble burst. The rise of unsecured shadow banking—via ABCP, repo, and securitization—created a systemic vulnerability to falling housing prices by predicating banks' liquidity on the continued willingness of potentially flighty counterparties to roll over maturing short-term debt. Early tremors in the shadow banking system felt from 2007 to early 2008 amplified in September 2008 with the failure of investment bank Lehman Brothers, leading to a full-scale shadow bank run in which all borrowers had trouble refinancing their maturing obligations.

Regulators' response to the global financial crisis can be interpreted as a successful attempt at providing de facto deposit insurance to shadow banking conduits.

To understand the global financial crisis, then, it is necessary to study the sources of fragility in the US economy during the early 2000s. Hyman Minsky argued that the economy's endogenous shift from stability to fragility depended on four conditions. First, the economy had to have an upward-sloping interest rate term structure, which created financial incentives for firms to issue short-term debt to purchase long-term risky assets via credit, liquidity, and maturity transformation. Second, financial institutions needed sufficient risk tolerance to take advantage of the upward-sloping yield curve. If financial institutions were not willing to adopt fragile financing structures, then asset price bubbles could deflate without risk of systemic financial collapse.[7] Third, fragility required a sufficient pool of short-term lenders willing to finance financial institutions' purchases of risky assets, thus introducing rollover risks to banks. And fourth, fragility depended on the existence of end-borrowers willing to emit risky, long-term debt to financial institutions, fueling credit and liquidity risk in the financial system.

Chapters three and four claim that all four of these factors were present in the US economy prior to the global financial crisis and that economic conventions explain the relaxation of these constraints on fragility. Chapter 3 argues that the Federal Reserve's accommodative monetary policy from 2001 to 2004 led to an upward-sloping interest rate term structure. This policy followed from several conventions, including: (1) the Fed's fears of falling into a Japan-style deflationary trap; (2) the Fed's preferred method of counting housing price inflation based on rent rather than housing prices; and (3) the widespread acceptance of the "Greenspan Doctrine" that it was better to *clean up* the aftermath of a bubble than to *lean against* its inflation. Together, these three conventions explain the Fed's accommodative monetary policy and upward-sloping yield curve that contributed to the rise in housing prices and incentives for banks to engage in interest rate term-structure arbitrage prior to the global financial crisis, thus relaxing Minsky's first constraint on fragility.

Chapter 4 argues that economic conventions facilitated the rise of fragile shadow banking prior to the global financial crisis by contributing to the relaxation of Minsky's second, third, and fourth constraints on fragility.

First, the stability of shadow banking conduits depended on counterparties' *conventional expectations* about the creditworthiness of shadow banks. Shadow banks and their sponsors remained liquid if

ABCP and repo counterparties believed that *fellow* market participants would continue to roll over maturing short-term liabilities. If counterparties doubted the intentions of fellow investors, however, they could refuse to roll over their ABCP and repo holdings, triggering a run on shadow banks.[8] Therefore, investing in shadow banking conduits was akin to a Keynesian beauty contest in which market participants had to guess the preferences of other investors before acting. Investment in shadow banks fluctuated pro-cyclically, with sentiment swings amplified due to Keynesian beauty contest dynamics. This conventional process explains the relaxation of Minsky's third condition for fragility: the presence of lenders willing to lend to financial institutions on a short-term basis.

Second, systemic fragility stemmed from financial institutions' undercapitalization, which depended on economic conventions. Prior to the global financial crisis, regulators concluded that banks were the best arbiters of their own portfolio risk and left banks to write their own regulatory capital rules. Banks assumed that future housing and securities prices would follow from their historical performance (i.e. conventions of *ergodicity*) when making regulatory capital provisions. This practice made banks susceptible to credit write downs and capital shortfalls when prices deviated from historical trends. The rise of uninsured shadow banking, coupled with bank capital inadequacy and low precautionary buffers, explains why the deflating housing bubble wreaked such havoc on the US financial system during the global financial crisis. Banks' risk management techniques enabled Minsky's second condition for fragility: sufficient risk tolerance among financial institutions.

Third, institutionalized conventions of *expert opinion* provided by credit rating agencies drove fragility in shadow banking. These ratings allowed risk-averse investors such as money market mutual funds to invest in the collateralized debt of financial institutions and helped banks mint risky securitized assets. If shadow banks posted valuable collateral in ABCP and repo transactions, then shadow banking did not face significant credit risk—in the worst-case scenario, counterparties could seize the collateral backing their transactions and sell it for its face value, recouping their original investment even if their counterparty could not meet their maturing obligations. Bond ratings gave counterparties a value anchor to gauge the creditworthiness of ABCP and repo collateral while also allowing financial institutions to tap into a deep pool of risk-averse capital to fund their shadow banking operations. Ratings thus served a mutual need for both shadow banking counterparties and financial institutions, leading both groups to believe that ABCP and repo collateral was immune to adverse selection problems due to information asymmetry. When market participants realized that bond ratings underestimated the likelihood of default of ABS, they reevaluated their assumptions about financial markets and questioned the truth-value of their governing conventions, altering market outcomes in the process. Credit ratings therefore relaxed Minsky's third and fourth constraints on fragility by permitting short-term lenders and long-term borrowers to participate in the global shadow banking system.

While useful in understanding the US economy's proneness to crisis, these economic conventions-based factors of fragility alone do not provide a point estimate about why markets suffered an acute seizure after the failure of Lehman Brothers.

To understand why Lehman Brothers' failure caused a panic in financial markets, Chapters 5 and 6 argue that regulators' repeated interventions in financial markets, including in the case of Long-Term Capital Management in 1998; the Bear Stearns sale to J.P. Morgan in March 2008; and the nationalization of Federal housing giants Fannie Mae and Freddie Mac in September 2008 created a *conventional expectation* among ABCP and repo counterparties that regulators would serve as *liquidity providers of last resort* in wholesale funding markets. These interventions led the market to believe that regulators would bail out counterparties at the face value of their loans any time a systemically important financial institution ran into trouble, thus preserving the "moneyness" of shadow banks' short-term debt and mitigating counterparty risk. This conventional expectation maintained a tenuous stability in financial markets as far as liquidity problems remained isolated to specific firms and not generalized across all short-term funding markets.

After the September 15, 2008 bankruptcy of Lehman Brothers, however, things changed. Lehman's failure eviscerated the market's belief that regulators would serve as lenders of last resort in wholesale funding markets, thus initiating a generalized bank run by all counterparties across all short-term funding markets. *Convention uncertainty* about regulators' willingness to provide deposit insurance to shadow banks caused investors to assume the worst about their counterparties and hoard liquid capital. Investors sold risky assets and purchased safe haven assets like short-term Treasury bills and the US dollar, just as Keynes would have predicted. Trading in some markets ceased, while asset prices plunged.

Faced with this banking panic in commercial paper and repo markets, regulators had a choice: allow the crisis to conclude via Schumpeterian creative destruction, or to intervene in financial markets to reestablish convention certainty by reoffering deposit insurance to the shadow banking system. As is now clear, regulators opted for the latter option, which raises two interrelated questions: first, how did conventions influence regulators' decision to grant unconditional bailouts to financial institutions after Lehman's bankruptcy, and second, how did the market's conventions about regulators implicate regulators' intervention capacity in the US financial system?

This book argues that regulators' historic memories of past crises (namely the Great Depression), coupled with the market's faith in the US's sovereign creditworthiness granted America's regulators a high degree of both willingness and policy latitude to respond to the shadow bank runs during the global financial crisis. Regulators' response to the crisis is best understood as a successful attempt to restore *convention certainty* to markets by demonstrating their commitment to guaranteeing banks' short-term liabilities, thus obviating counterparty fears in wholesale funding markets and restoring confidence to the financial system. The fact that regulators were successful reveals a great deal about the market's perception of regulators' credibility and regulators' preferences about the optimum means of restoring market confidence when faced with a panic.

Table 1.2 summarizes the theoretical and empirical arguments of *Social Finance*, which serves as a roadmap for the rest of the book.

BENEFITS OF *SOCIAL FINANCE*

Social Finance offers four benefits to its readers:

First, this book remedies some of the theoretical shortcomings of Post-Keynesianism and improves a popular model of financial instability. This book sheds light onto the social processes underpinning stability and fragility in financial markets. It offers a micro-level framework for understanding the formation of asset price bubbles and fragility; it digs into the deeper causes of the market's epistemic blindness to bubbles and fragility before crises; it specifies the intersubjective triggers under which stable (but fragile) financial systems erupt into panics and crises; and it explains how economic ideas constrain and enable policymakers' response to financial distress. Together, these theoretical insights—drawn from an eclectic mix of interdisciplinary approaches—constructively build on the Post-Keynesian model, ultimately leading to a better theory of financial instability.

Second, *Social Finance* strengthens readers' understanding of the vulnerability of shadow banking to financial instability. It builds on the work of other scholars of shadow banking to demonstrate how the global financial crisis is best understood as a bank run in shadow banking markets and adds value to the study of shadow banking by showing the conditions under which shadow banking structures are prone to triggering systemic stress and when they are relatively safe forms of financial intermediation. Given shadow banking's growing importance in the global economy, anyone interested in understanding the implications of shadow banking on financial stability will benefit from reading this book.

Third, *Social Finance* bridges the divide between theory and practice in financial markets by incorporating the insights of market practitioners into a theory of financial instability. This book draws on first-hand accounts of market participants who lived through the global financial crisis into its empirical work. These interviews allow the reader to see the analytical utility of the book's theoretical framework directly from those closest to the market during periods of stress.

Fourth, this book enhances readers' understanding of the global financial crisis and the potential for future financial distress. Much of the contemporary analysis of the crisis falls short on several axes. Many mainstream accounts of the global financial crisis tend to elevate moral and agency-based causes over more dispassionate, theory-grounded explanations. Notions of swashbuckling traders, ideological central bankers, greedy financiers, and captured regulators typify this type of analysis. And no doubt, there was no shortage of incompetence before the crisis.[9] But ex-post theorizing about the moral and intellectual flaws of market participants does not lend itself to better theory. Quite the opposite is true. For if it is accepted that the global financial crisis was caused by greedy bankers, then the policy prescription for financial stability is misleadingly simple: replace bankers with their morally circumspect counterparts, and future crises can be averted. However, the regularity of crises in capitalism should cause us to take greedy bankers as givens—most of the time, financiers will do what is in their best interest. By focusing on the general features of financial instability as illustrated by the global financial crisis, *Social Finance* transcends a mere description of events and dives deeper into generalizable causal processes at play in financial markets. Readers can then apply the framework and findings of *Social Finance* to forecast future incidences of financial instability.

CONCLUSION

The purpose of this chapter was to serve as a stand-alone summary of *Social Finance*. The chapter discussed the primary motivation of the book—that renewed interest in the Minsky-Kindleberger paradigm (i.e. Post-Keynesianism) is a step in the right direction, but the Post-Keynesian model understates the critical role that *social* factors play in setting the stage for, triggering, and resolving financial instability. The chapter delivered a precis of several alternative paradigms of understanding, including Keynesian epistemology, Doran's theory of crises in international relations, and economic constructivism. Thereafter, the chapter outlined the core propositions of *Social Finance* and the book's shadow banking case study.

The chapter situated *Social Finance* in the study of the global financial crisis by arguing that to understand the US economy's susceptibility to crisis, it was necessary to study the key pre-crisis drivers of fragility, in the Minsky sense, and how these factors followed from certain economic conventions. This rise in fragility principally stemmed from the upward-sloping yield curve and the development of a parallel, or shadow, banking system in the United States, in which financial institutions formed off-balance-sheet vehicles that issued short-term debt in ABCP and repurchase agreement ("repo") markets to purchase longer-dated securitized assets. It is proposed that the upward-sloping interest rate term structure depended on several key conventions held by Federal Reserve policymakers, including fears of falling into a deflationary trap, construction of the Fed's preferred inflation metrics, and posture toward asset price bubbles. The rise of shadow banking depended on several core economic conventions as well, including banks' risk management technologies that assumed historical asset price distributions provided a sound guide to future price movements, thus predicating bank capital adequacy on economic conventions of ergodicity, which led to banks' undercapitalization on the eve of the crisis; pro-cyclical *conventional expectations* about shadow banking conduit liquidity and solvency among ABCP and repo counterparties; and institutionalized conventions of expert opinions of bond ratings that lulled investors into a false sense of security regarding overall shadow banking asset quality.

These drivers of fragility set the stage for the financial collapse witnessed in September 2008. But they alone do not give a point estimate for understanding when and why markets seized after the failure of Lehman Brothers. To understand this panic triggers, this chapter argued that it is necessary to study the drivers of confidence in short-term money markets. Regulators' repeated interventions in financial markets beginning with the orchestration of the bailout of hedge fund Long-Term Capital Management in 1998 and continuing through the bailouts of investment bank Bear Stearns in March 2008 and the Federal housing giants, Fannie Mae and Freddie Mac, in early September 2008 maintained a fragile but stable confidence in short-term funding markets. However, Lehman Brothers' failure eviscerated this confidence and triggered a system-wide bank run on all short-term funding markets, leading investors to shun nearly all unsecured short-term asset classes and purchasing perceived safe havens in a flight to quality. Regulators' response to this panic and generalized contagion is best understood as a successful attempt to restore *convention certainty* to markets by providing de facto lender of last resort provisions to short-term funding markets for all bank and nonbank institutions. Regulators chose to intervene because of their historic memory of the Great Depression, and they were capable of intervening in the first place because of the United States' high degree of *intervention capacity* as sanctioned by the market.

The rest of this book fleshes out these arguments in full. Chapter 2 places *Social Finance* in the literature and presents the core theoretical propositions of the study. It also includes information for fellow academics, including a section on the operationalization of the book's model. Chapters 3–6 are the book's empirical chapters. Chapters 3 and 4 focus on the rise of the housing bubble and fragile financing structures prior to the global financial crisis and demonstrate propositions one and two of *Social Finance*'s theoretical framework. Chapters 5 and 6 describe the acute crisis interval of the global financial crisis and marshal evidence in support of propositions three, four, and five of the study. Chapter 7 concludes.

Table 1.2 Orthodox model vs. Post-Keynesianism vs. Social Finance (with précis of case study)

Concept	Neo-classical model	Post-Keynesianism	Social Finance	Social Finance case study
Stability and fragility	Self-sustaining and perpetual; natural state of affairs and does not lead to endogenous fragility; robust	Prolonged stability leads to fragility (i.e. stability is destabilizing); emphasis on financing arrangements (e.g. hedge vs. speculative vs. Ponzi)	*Proposition 1*: Financial stability depends on convention stability; conventions drive the market's shift from stability to fragility over time	• Federal Reserve accommodative monetary policy led to upward-sloping yield curve, and Fed's policy followed from several key economic conventions • The stability of shadow banking conduits followed from conventions related to conventional expectations, bank capital adequacy, and credit risk; conventions proved self-stabilizing while leading to pro-cyclical flows that sowed fragility via Minsky processes

(continued)

Table 1.2 (continued)

Concept	Neo-classical model	Post-Keynesianism	Social Finance	Social Finance case study
Blindness	Nonexistent at system-wide level; newer research affords for individual-level blindness	Pervasive prior to crisis; emphasis on blind capital investing in bubble assets due to mania	*Proposition II:* Conventions blind markets to bubbles and fragility prior to crises	• Federal Reserve reliance on conventions made Fed technocrats blind to risks of housing inflation prior to global financial crisis • Epistemic blindness followed from misplaced faith in bond ratings and bank capital adequacy models that systematically underestimated the likelihood rising defaults and crises • Regulators' repeated interventions created a *conventional expectation* about shadow banking deposit insurance, blinding market participants to the possibility of losses in wholesale funding markets

(continued)

1 MCCULLEY'S WARNING   21

Table 1.2 (continued)

Concept	Neo-classical model	Post-Keynesianism	Social Finance	Social Finance case study
Uncertainty	Conflated with risk; newer research focuses on uncertainty due to asymmetric information	Rises during crises, instability increases uncertainty	*Proposition III:* Shocks to agents' convention-given expectations catalyze uncertainty	• The failure of Lehman Brothers eviscerated market's *conventional expectation* that regulators would serve as regulators of last resort in shadow banking markets, triggering Knightian uncertainty in markets
Flight to quality	Presumes markets self-stabilize and that flight to quality reflects changing relative prices based on fundamentals; subsequent work in macroeconomics acknowledges flight to quality as pro-cyclical risk but is less concerned about loss of expectational anchors	Acknowledges existence of the phenomena in further research (i.e. not in seminal works); recognizes disruption of normal price discovery mechanism but does not identify structural uncertainty as a cause of the loss of conventional anchors	*Proposition IV:* Given sufficient fragility, uncertainty causes agents to revert to first principles of survival; market participants hoard liquid capital; loss of conventional anchors triggers flight from risky assets in markets	• During financial crisis market participants refused to roll over maturing short-term shadow banking obligations in ABCP and repo markets, triggering a run on all short-term money markets. This run was caused by a loss of perceived lender of last resort protection among shadow banking conduits • The flight to quality during the global financial crisis was a symptom of convention uncertainty

(continued)

Table 1.2 (continued)

Concept	Neo-classical model	Post-Keynesianism	Social Finance	Social Finance case study
Elite responses	Unspecified; extensions of mainstream work focus on rational choice political economy drivers of political outcomes	Frames choice as 2 × 2 options matrix of fiscal and monetary expansion; does not study political economy mechanisms that shape interventions systematically	*Proposition V*: Elite responses to financial instability are a function of their economic ideas and intervention capacity, which in turn determines efficacy of their crisis response	• Regulators' response to the crisis depended on their historical memory and fears of repeating the Great Depression; • The market sanctioned use of public balance sheet in United States to underwrite bailouts of short-term money markets due to the United States' high degree of sovereign creditworthiness

Notes

1. Acharya and Richardson (2011), Ban and Gabor (2017), Gorton (2010), Gorton and Metrick (2010), McCulley (2009), Mehrling (2011), Mehrling et al. (2013), Pozsar (2014), and Pozsar et al. (2010).
2. Examples of Post-Keynesian postcrisis scholarship include Barbera (2009), Geithner (2014), McCulley (2009), Wolf (2014), Wray (2012), and Wray (2015). The Federal Reserve also began to appreciate the insights of Charles Kindleberger and Hyman Minsky after the crisis (Dokko et al. 2009). For a commentary on the Fed's rediscovery of Minsky, see *The Economist* (2010).
3. See also Keynes (1936, 148), Crotty (1994), and Runde and Mizuhara (2003), among others.
4. Neither Hyman Minsky in *Stabilizing the Unstable Economy* nor Robert Aliber and Charles Kindleberger in *Manias, Panics, and Crashes*, two foundational Post-Keynesian asset market texts, include *conventional judgment* in their descriptions of financial instability (Minsky 2008; Kindleberger and Aliber 2005).
5. See also Abdelal et al. (2010), Kirshner (2003), and Matthijs (2011).
6. The global financial crisis was an overdetermined phenomenon for which there existed many plausible and confounding causes. It is difficult to isolate specific factors, consider natural experiments, and identify which of these causes are necessary, necessary but insufficient, necessary and sufficient, and simply epiphenomenal to financial instability. By now, nearly a decade since the crisis, there is no shortage of explanations for why the global financial crisis occurred. Analysts have blamed, inter alia, greedy financiers for defrauding borrowers and taking outsized risks (Johnson and Kwak 2010); the government-sponsored housing entities Fannie Mae and Freddie Mac for subsidizing homeownership and fueling the housing bubble (The Financial Crisis Inquiry Commission 2011, 411–529); the Federal Reserve for keeping interest rates "too low for too long" and turning a blind eye to risks in the financial system (Taylor 2007); free market ideologues in government and the private sector that pushed for deregulation of the financial system after 1980, including the repeal of the Glass-Steagall Act that separated commercial and investment banking in 1999, further fueling the financialization of the US economy and susceptibility to financial collapse (Crotty 2009); global financial market imbalances, which saw the surge of large precautionary savings in Asia and recycled petrodollars into the US economy after 1998 and accelerating after 2001, depressing risk-free US interest rates and leading market participants to take more risk (Wolf 2014); a loss of risk control by financial institutions' risk committees and poor corporate governance (Erkens et al. 2012); and the

development of a parallel "shadow banking" system that allowed financial institutions to sponsor banking-like off-balance-sheet structures that fell out of the purview of traditional bank regulation (Gorton 2010). Parsing through these myriad causes is the work of historians. Even today, scholars cannot fully agree on the causes of the Great Depression.

Rather than joining this debate, *Social Finance* instead focuses on a subset of these causes, specifically fragility in the shadow banking system. This book's explanation for the crisis is not mutually exclusive from the other accounts. For instance, Johnson and Kwak's argument fits with this book's account of financial institutions risk tolerance and Taylor's belief about Federal Reserve monetary policy comports with the main argument in Chapter 3, to name two examples.

7. These conditions explain why years of low interest rates and accommodative monetary policy in the United States have not yet triggered a crisis: banks' risk tolerance is significantly lower today than it was in 2000–2006, as evidenced by high precautionary savings in the form of excess bank reserves held at the Federal Reserve. For more, see Keister and McAndrews (2009).
8. As argued in Chapter 4, under unsecured shadow banking, rumors of insolvency could prove self-fulfilling, as demonstrated by the swift collapse of Bear Stearns and Lehman Brothers investment banks in 2008. Bank runs occurred idiosyncratically pre-Lehman and generally, across all ABCP and repo issuers, after Lehman's bankruptcy.
9. Perhaps the best articulation of this line of reasoning was Simon Johnson and James Kwak's *Thirteen Bankers*, where the authors assert that the crisis was simply the byproduct of thirty years of financial deregulation and Wall Street capture. While there is some truth to this argument, it alone does not provide a robust model of financial crises generally, nor does it explain the socially contingent processes by which authoritative actors in the financial system convinced the rest of the country to go along with the deregulation of the financial sector, see Johnson and Kwak (2010).

Works Cited

Abdelal, Rawi, Mark Blyth, and Craig Parsons. 2010. *Constructing the International Economy*. Ithaca: Cornell University Press.

Acharya, Viral, and Matthew Richardson. 2011. "How Securitization Concentrated Risk." In *What Caused the Financial Crisis*, by Jeffrey Friedman (ed.), 183–199. Philadelphia: University of Pennsylvania Press.

Acharya, Viral, Philipp Schnabl, and Gustavo Suarez. 2013. "Securitization Without Risk Transfer." *Journal of Financial Economics* 107 (3): 515–536.

Adrian, Tobias, and Hyun Song Shin. 2009. "The Shadow Banking System: Implications for Financial Regulation." *Federal Reserve Bank of New York Staff Reports* (382): 1–18.

Ban, Cornel, and Daniela Gabor. 2017. "The Political Economy of Shadow Banking." *Review of International Political Economy* 23 (6): 901–914.

Barbera, Robert J. 2009. *The Cost of Capitalism: Understanding Market Mayhem and Stabilizing our Economic Future.* New York: McGraw-Hill Company.

Blyth, Mark. 2002. *Great Transformations: Economic Ideas and Institutional Change in the Twentieth Century.* Cambridge: Cambridge University Press.

Blyth, Mark. 2013. "This Time It Really Is Different." In *The Third Globalization: Can Wealthy Nations Stay Rich in the Twenty-First Century?* by Dan Breznitz and John Zysman (eds.), 207–231. Oxford: Oxford University Press.

Colander, David, Hans Follmer, Armin Haas, Michael Goldberg, Katarina Juselius, Alan Kirman, Thomas Lux, and Brigette Sloth. 2009. "The Financial Crisis and the Systemic Failure of Academic Economics." *Kiel Working Papers*, 17. Kiel Institute for the World Economy.

Crotty, James. 1994. "Are Keynesian Uncertainty and Macrotheory Incompatible? Conventional Decision Making, Institutional Structures and Conditional Stability in Keynesian Macromodels." In *New Perspectives in Monetary Macroeconomics: Explorations in the Tradition of Hyman Minsky*, by G. Dymski and R. Pollin (eds.), 105–142. Ann Arbor: University of Michigan Press.

Crotty, James. 2009. "Structural Causes of the Global Financial Crisis: A Critical Assessment of the 'New Financial Architecture'." *Cambridge Journal of Economics* 33 (4): 563–580.

Dokko, Jane, Bryan Doyle, Michael T. Kiley, Jinill Kim, Shane Sherlund, Jae Sim, and Skander Van den Heuvel. 2009. "Monetary Policy and the Housing Bubble." *Finance and Economics Discussion Series, Divisions of Research & Statistics and Monetary Affairs* (Federal Reserve Board) (49): 1–61.

Doran, Charles F. 1991. *Systems in Crisis: New Imperatives of High Politics at Century's End.* Cambridge: Cambridge University Press.

Doran, Charles F. 1999. "Why Forecasts Fail: The Limits and Potential of Forecasting in International Relations and Economics." *International Studies Review* 1 (2): 11–41.

Erkens, David H., Jingyi Hung, and Pedro Matos. 2012. "Corporate Governance in the 2007–2008 Financial Crisis: Evidence from Financial Institutions Worldwide." *Journal of Corporate Finance* 18: 389–411.

Evans, Stephen. 2007. "Bankers Tackle the US Credit Crisis." *BBC*. September 9. Accessed April 18, 2018. http://news.bbc.co.uk/2/hi/business/6974972.stm.

Federal Reserve Bank of Kansas City. 2007. "Housing, Housing Finance, and Monetary Policy." *Federal Reserve Bank of Kansas City.* Accessed April 18, 2018. https://www.kansascityfed.org/publications/research/escp/symposiums/escp-2007.

Fligstein, Neil, and Luke Dauter. 2007. "The Sociology of Markets." *Annual Review of Sociology* 33: 105–128.
Frydman, Roman, and Michael D. Goldberg. 2011. *Beyond Mechanical Markets: Asset Price Swings, Risk, and the Role of the State*. Princeton: Princeton University Press.
Geithner, Timothy F. 2014. *Stress Test: Reflections on Financial Crises*. New York: Crown Publishers.
Gorton, Gary B. 2010. *Slapped by the Invisible Hand: The Panic of 2007*. Oxford: Oxford University Press.
Gorton, Gary B., and Andrew Metrick. 2010. "Haircuts." *Federal Reserve Bank of St. Louis Review* 92 (6): 507–519.
Helleiner, Eric. 2011. "Understanding the 2007–2008 Global Financial Crisis: Lessons for Scholars of International Political Economy." *Annual Review of Political Science* 14 (2): 67–87.
Institute for New Economic Thinking. n.d. *About the Institute*. https://www.ineteconomics.org/about/our-purpose.
International Monetary Fund. 2018. "Global Financial Stability Report: A Bumpy Road Ahead." *International Monetary Fund* 1–150.
Johnson, Simon, and James Kwak. 2010. *13 Bankers: The Wall Street Takeover and the Next Financial Meltdown*. New York: Random House.
Keister, Todd, and James McAndrews. 2009. "Why Are Banks Holding so Many Excess Reserves?" *Current Issues in Economics and Finance* 15 (8): 1–10.
Keynes, John M. 1936. *The General Theory of Employment, Interest and Money*. Cambridge: Cambridge University Press (1972).
———. 1937. "The General Theory of Employment." *The Quarterly Journal of Economics* 51 (2): 209–223.
Kindleberger, Charles P., and Robert Aliber. 2005. *Manias, Panics, and Crashes: A History of Financial Crises*. Hoboken: Wiley.
Kirshner, Jonathan. 2003. "Money Is Politics." *Review of International Political Economy* 10 (4): 645–660.
Lahart, Justin. 2007. "In Time of Tumult, Obscure Economist Gains Currency." *The Wall Street Journal*. August 18. Accessed April 18, 2018. https://www.wsj.com/articles/SB118736585456901047.
Lie, John. 1997. "Sociology of Markets." *Annual Review of Sociology* 23: 341–360.
MacKenzie, Donald. 2008. *An Engine, Not a Camera: How Financial Models Shape Markets*. Cambridge: The MIT Press.
MacKenzie, Donald, Fabian Muniesa, and Lucia Siu. 2009. *Do Economists Make Markets? On the Performativity of Economics*. Princeton: Princeton University Press.
Malkiel, Burton G. 2007. *A Random Walk Down Wall Street: The Time-Tested Strategy for Successful Investing* (Ninth Edition). New York: W. W. Norton.

Matthijs, Matthias M. 2011. *Ideas and Economic Crises in Britain from Attlee to Blair (1945–2005)*. London: Routledge.
McCulley, Paul A. 2009. *PIMCO.com*. May. Accessed December 3, 2017. https://www.pimco.com/en-us/insights/economic-and-market-commentary/global-central-bank-focus/the-shadow-banking-system-and-hyman-minskys-economic-journey/.
Mehrling, Perry. 2011. *The New Lombard Street: How the Fed Became the Dealer of Last Resort*. Princeton and Oxford: Princeton University Press.
Mehrling, Perry, Zoltan Pozsar, James Sweeney, and Daniel H. Neilson. 2013. "Bagehot Was a Shadow Banker: Shadow Banking, Central Banking, and the Future of Global Finance." *Institute for New Economic Thinking Shadow Banking Colloquium* 1–20.
Minsky, Hyman. 1982. *Can "It" Happen Again? Essays on Instability and Finance*. Armonk and New York: M. E. Sharpe.
———. 1992. "The Financial Instability Hypothesis." *Levy Economics Institute of Bard College Working Papers* 1–9.
———. 2008. *Stabilizing an Unstable Economy*. New York: McGraw-Hill.
Pozsar, Zoltan. 2014. "Shadow Banking: The Money View." *Office of Financial Research Working Paper Series* 14 (4): 1–71.
Pozsar, Zoltan, Tobias Adrian, Adam Ashcraft, and Hayley Boesky. 2010. "Shadow Banking." *Federal Reserve Bank of New York Staff Report* (458): 1–82.
Read, Carveth. 1909. *Logic, Deductive and Inductive*. London: The De La More Press.
Reuters. 2017. *Reuters.com*. October 19. https://www.reuters.com/article/us-china-congress-debt-minskymoment/china-central-bank-warns-against-minsky-moment-due-to-excessive-optimism-idUSKBN1CO0D6.
Runde, Jochen, and Sohei Mizuhara. 2003. *The Philosophy of Keynes's Economics: Probability, Uncertainty and Convention*. London: Routledge.
Song Shin, Hyun. 2011. "Global Banking Glut and Loan Risk Premium." *12th Jacques Polak Annual Research Conference*, 1–48. Washington: International Monetary Fund.
Soros, George. 2003. *The Alchemy of Finance*. Hoboken: Wiley.
———. 2009. *The Crash of 2008 and What It Means*. New York: Public Affairs.
Stiglitz, Joseph. 2010. *London Review of Books*. April 22. Accessed December 3, 2017. https://www.lrb.co.uk/v32/no8/joseph-stiglitz/the-non-existent-hand.
Taleb, Nassim. 2007. *The Black Swan: The Impact of the Highly Improbable*. New York: Random House.
Tarullo, Daniel K. 2009. "Speech: In the Wake of the Crisis." *Federal Reserve Board of Governors*. October 8. Accessed May 7, 2018. https://www.federalreserve.gov/newsevents/speech/tarullo20091008a.htm.

Taylor, John B. 2007. "Housing and Monetary Policy." *NBER Working Paper Series* (13682).
The Economist. 2016. *Minsky's Moment*. July 30. Accessed March 31, 2018. https://www.economist.com/news/economics-brief/21702740-second-article-our-series-seminal-economic-ideas-looks-hyman-minskys.
———. 2010. *The Fed Discovers Hyman Minsky: Ben Bernanke's Embrace of Realism in Regulation*. January 7. Accessed December 3, 2017. https://www.economist.com/blogs/freeexchange/2010/01/the_fed_discovers_hyman_minsky.
The Financial Crisis Inquiry Commission. 2011. *The Financial Crisis Inquiry Report: Final Report of the National Commission on the Causes of the Financial and Economic Crisis in the United States*. Washington: U.S. Government Printing Office.
Turner, Adair. 2012. *Economics After the Crisis: Objectives and Means*. Cambridge: The MIT Press.
Wolf, Martin. 2014. *The Shifts and the Shocks: What We've Learned–And Have Still to Learn–From the Financial Crisis*. New York: Penguin.
Wray, L. Randall. 2012. "Global Financial Crisis: A Minskyan Interpretation of the Causes, the Fed's Bailout, and the Future." *Levy Economics Institute of Bard College Working Paper* (711): 1–31.
———. 2015. *Why Minsky Matters: An Introduction to the Work of a Maverick Economist*. Princeton: Princeton University Press.
Yellen, Janet. 2009. "A Minsky Meltdown: Lessons for Central Bankers." *18th Annual Hyman P. Minsky Conference on the State of the U.S. and World Economies: Meeting the Challenges of the Financial Crisis*. New York: Levy Economics Institute. 1–16.

CHAPTER 2

Conventions and Financial Crises

INTRODUCTION

This chapter presents *Social Finance*'s conventions-based theoretical framework of financial instability. This framework emerges from a theoretical synthesis of several academic fields, including Post-Keynesian asset market theory, Keynesian epistemology, Charles Doran's power cycle theory, and economic constructivism. The chapter begins by explaining why neoclassical economics, the main academic paradigm of studying asset markets, fails to account for financial instability. It then provides an overview of Post-Keynesianism, with a focus on Hyman Minsky and Charles Kindleberger's core ideas. This section outlines both the benefits and drawbacks of Post-Keynesianism, from which the discussion of economic conventions, power cycle theory, and economic constructivism follows. The chapter then presents *Social Finance*'s five propositions on economic conventions and financial stability. The final chapter section addresses the operationalization of this model via the book's case study of the global financial crisis, detailing *Social Finance*'s pathway case study method and constituitive causal standards.

LIMITS OF THE ORTHODOX APPROACH

In the wake of the global financial crisis, a consensus emerged that mainstream economics failed to foresee the economic collapse. As Queen Elizabeth reportedly asked her economic advisors in November 2008, "if [financial crises] were so large, how come everyone missed it?" (Pierce 2008).

One answer, according to Nobel Memorial Prize in Economics winner Joseph Stiglitz, is that economists' models "effectively said that [the crisis] couldn't happen" by ignoring the financial system, blinding economists to financial risks (Stiglitz 2018). Dynamic stochastic general equilibrium (DSGE) models are the main tools used by macroeconomists to model the economy and gained prominence among the world's leading academic economists. These models influenced policymakers' views on asset markets and assume that financial frictions and credit intermediation were ancillary variables. They also focus on periods of equilibrium, underestimating the likelihood of tail events and crisis moments (Haldane 2012).[1]

Unlike what most DSGE models would predict, however, financial fluctuations have macroeconomic consequences. Because financial intermediaries sit between savers and borrowers, their activity has large impacts on the economy via household and firm borrowing, confidence, and systemic fragility channels (Mehrling 2011, 4–5).[2] David Colander et al. further criticize DSGE's "representative agent" micro-foundations, which presume that aggregate behavior corresponds to the behavior of component parts in the economy. Representative agent models treat the economy's components as utility maximizing agents that make rational cost-benefit optimizing decisions under perfect information. This oversight causes DSGE models to engage in what John Maynard Keynes termed the "fallacy of composition," ignoring that individually rational actions lead to system-wide negative results by overgeneralizing the consequences of individual actions to the aggregate. For example, situations in which multiple market participants convert risky asset holdings into cash at the same time may be logical on an individual level but disrupts the whole market's price discovery mechanism. Moreover, such actions may depress asset prices below their equilibrium values. Thus, individually rational behavior leads to collectively irrational results. As Colander concludes, economists ought to recognize that "any meaningful model of the macro economy must analyze not only the characteristics of the individuals but also the structure of their interactions"—something DSGE models fail to do (Colander et al. 2008, 2; Leijonhufvud 2009).[3]

The global financial crisis similarly caught neoclassical financial market theory off guard. Neoclassical finance assumes efficient markets, or that prices reflect all known public and private information. Under information efficiency, prevailing asset prices prevent arbitrage profits. Orthodox models also assume "rational expectations," in which agents' expectations reflect optimal forecasts that, crucially, follow from the supply and demand of financial assets, which themselves are derived from utility maximizing producers and consumers. Under such conditions, bubbles (or long-term deviations from intrinsic value) should not occur, since asset prices ultimately reflect supply and demand fundamentals. For this reason, neoclassical finance tends to ignore the possibility of asset price bubbles and market manias, conflate notions of uncertainty and risk, and under-specify market reflexivity (Colander et al. 2009; Lo 2017, 17–28; Soros 2003).[4]

Given the limitations of mainstream economics as a framework for understanding financial crises, scholars and practitioners began to search for alternatives.[5] Real life crises made analysts realize that market participants are not universally rational but that emotion and caprice can drive decisions. Prices are not always informationally efficient, which can lead to long-term deviations from fundamental value (e.g. bubbles). And practical factors such as market's architecture can impact market processes via liquidity and credit constraints.[6] This search for new paradigms led to a resurgence in interest in the Post-Keynesian model of financial crises in the tradition of Hyman Minsky and Charles Kindleberger. As Colander et al. argue, Post-Keynesian scholarship "had been neglected and even suppressed" among academic economists prior to the crisis (Colander et al. 2009, 2–3). But after the global financial crisis, academics and policymakers turned to Hyman Minsky and Charles Kindleberger and their intellectual progeny to provide answers about the ongoing economic dislocation (Harcourt 2008).

THE POST-KEYNESIAN ALTERNATIVE AND ITS BENEFITS

The basic Post-Keynesian story of financial crises is as follows. A crisis begins with an exogenous "displacement" that alters profit expectations in some part of the economy.[7] Improved expectations cause financial institutions to extend credit to the displaced sector, causing asset prices to rise. Positive feedback between rising prices and optimism ensues. Consumers and firms feel wealthier and finance consumption and capital expenditure via leverage. Rising economic activity causes output to expand and unemployment to fall. A euphoria may develop as investors purchase assets to flip them for short-term capital gains, rather than based on their long-term income-generating potential. Financial authorities, aware that they are facing unique circumstances, may invent reasons to explain why the traditional rules of economic gravity no longer apply. As the boom wears on, insiders sell assets to monetize paper profits, causing prices to fall. Banks realize losses and become defensive, hoarding liquid capital. Credit contagion spreads as trading in certain asset classes cease, leading investors to purchase safe havens in a flight to quality. Declining market confidence exposes the underlying fragility of the entire economy, making it difficult for all borrowers—healthy and otherwise—to meet their maturing obligations. The failure of a major financial institution, a notable investor boycotting the bubble asset class, or a sharp, unanticipated drop in the price of a security might trigger a financial panic. Absent regulatory intervention, panics can lead to cascading defaults, falling confidence, declining prices, and further credit rationing. Lenders of last resort might intervene to guarantee banks' liabilities and remove bad debts from the financial system. Governments may increase deficit spending through automatic stabilizers and discretionary fiscal stimulus to cushion the real economy, though the use of countercyclical fiscal policy depends on the ability and willingness of the authorities to dissave or to lever the public balance sheet. In some cases, the mania may consume governments themselves, leading the sovereign authorities to seek international bailouts for the official sector. If regulators are successful, interventions can restore market confidence, though the hangover from the bust could lead to decades of sub-par economic growth, anemic job creation, and hysteresis, while the hit to political legitimacy from macroeconomic malaise can challenge the very precepts of globalization and liberal markets that preceded the systemic crash (Blyth and Matthijs 2017; Davidson 1993; Kindleberger and Aliber 2005, 21–29; Minsky 1982, 2008).

Several practitioners and policymakers have extolled the benefits of Post-Keynesianism in the wake of the global financial crisis (Harcourt and Kriesler 2013).[8] But what makes Post-Keynesianism better than traditional approaches? This book identifies five advantages—four theoretical, one stylistic—of Post-Keynesianism, including: (1) the Post-Keynesian argument that stability leads to fragility over time; (2) its endogenous treatment of fragility and bubbles; (3) the dichotomous depiction of risk and uncertainty; (4) the model's emphasis on epistemic blindness prior to crises; and (5) the theory's narrative approach, which makes it accessible to non-specialist audiences.

First, one of the foundational beliefs of Post-Keynesianism is that prolonged periods of stability lead to fragility. Hyman Minsky presented this argument in his *Financial Instability Hypothesis*, which states that periods of stability tend to drive the economy toward fragile financing structures. Minsky believed that financial institutions could adopt three types of financing structures, the prevalent mix of which determined the economy's overall proneness to crises. These three structures are hedge financing, speculative financing, and Ponzi financing. Hedge financing units can meet their obligations from operating cash flows and without reliance on additional financing. Hedge financing units are thus solvent (with total assets greater than total liabilities) and liquid (i.e. having enough cash on hand to cover short-term debt). Minsky believed hedge finance units were majority equity financed, rather than financed by debt.[9] Speculative borrowers can meet their interest payments via investment income but must refinance maturing principal obligations to remain liquid. Their expected cash flows exceed total debt payments (both principal and interest) and they are therefore solvent, though they may face liquidity issues in stressed financing conditions. Ponzi borrowers can meet neither their principal nor interest payments from investment income and must rely on price appreciation, asset sales, or continued borrowing to meet maturing obligations. Without the ability to flip assets for higher prices or access to fresh market financing, Ponzi finance structures could face funding pressures. Consequently, the stability of Ponzi finance depends on the realization of continued asset price appreciation (Minsky 1982, 22–29, see Fig. 2.1).

Minsky argued that the greater the proportion of hedge finance units in the economy, the greater the likelihood an economy would be self-stabilizing and equilibrating. However, over a prolonged period of stability, the composition of financing structures in the economy gradually shifted from hedge finance toward speculative and Ponzi structures. And because speculative and Ponzi financing structures were more vulnerable to instability than hedge financing, economies tended to shift from stability to fragility over time. In this way, Minsky concluded that stability sowed the seeds of its own undoing via the capitalist economy's endogenous tendency to shift to more fragile financing structures.

Why do economies dominated by hedge finance units shift to speculative and Ponzi finance endogenously over time? According to Minsky, economies with hedge finance units tend to have an upward sloping interest rate term structure, or yield curve, in which long-term interest rates are higher than short-term interest rates. In such an environment, it is profitable for financial institutions to issue short-term liabilities to purchase longer-dated (and higher yielding) assets, in turn capturing

Hedge finance – Can meet financial obligations strictly through cash flows from operations; structures tend to be equity financed; has enough cash on hand to withstand creditor panic; both solvent and liquid	Speculative finance – Meets maturing obligation interest payments via cash flows but cannot meet principal payments without additional borrowing; solvent but under disruptive financial conditions may not be liquid	Ponzi finance – Borrowers cannot meet principal nor interest payments from investment income; must rely on asset appreciation, asset sales, or further borrowing; neither solvent nor liquid

Rising fragility

Economy self-stabilizing and equilibrium seeking; mutes shocks counter-cyclically *Prone to systemic collapse; amplifies shocks pro-cyclically*

An economy transitions from hedge to speculative to Ponzi financial structures given: 1) the existence of an upward-sloping interest rate term structure; 2) sufficient risk tolerance by financial institutions to take advantage of term structure arbitrage opportunities (i.e. borrowing short-term debt and acquiring long-term assets) to engage in credit, liquidity, and maturity transformation; 3) willing buyers of short-term, money-like liabilities (i.e. "depositors" in fragile financing structures); and 4) borrowers willing to emit longer-dated, risky debt.

Fig. 2.1 Minsky's taxonomy of financing arrangements (Minsky 1992, 7–8; 2008, 233–236; Kindleberger and Aliber 2005, 27–28; Gorton and Metrick 2010)

the yield differential or spread between short-term borrowing costs and long-term lending revenues. The market compensates financial institutions for engaging in three transformations, including liquidity transformation, credit transformation, and maturity transformation. Credit transformation describes turning deposit-like liabilities from savers seeking the safety (and seniority) of cash at par value into assets backed by different classes of borrowers that offer higher yields and fall lower down on the capital structure. This process exposes financing entities and their depositors to credit risks due to potential losses in the financial institution's loan portfolio. Liquidity transformation involves converting money-like liabilities to less liquid assets. More liquid securities tend to trade at a premium since liquidity is valued by market participants. Thus, financial institutions that create liquidity are compensated for this activity, though liquidity transformation can create liquidity risk if depositors (or holders of short-term liabilities) choose to redeem their holdings at the same time. Few banks have one hundred present liquidity coverage, so mass withdrawals can pose a risk. Therefore, governments often sponsor deposit insurance programs to hedge against redemption risk. Maturity transformation involves turning short-term liabilities into assets with long-term durations. Maturity transformation is subject to credit mismatches if the interest rate term structure inverts and the cost of financing exceeds long-term asset returns. As financial institutions increasingly engage in the above transformations, prices rise, thus fueling ever-greater adoption of speculative and eventually Ponzi financing structures.

Minsky acknowledged that an upward sloping yield curve was a necessary but insufficient condition for fragility. Other constraints on fragility include a low risk tolerance by firms who may prefer to hold money and money-like short-term assets rather than longer-dated ones; a lack of willing buyers of short-term liabilities; and insufficient borrowers willing to emit longer-dated and higher yielding speculative assets. Minsky believed that Keynesian animal spirits could relax these constraints, thus precipitating fragility. Stability could last for a long time, possibly decades, before expectations and animal spirits took over, in turn relaxing the constraints on fragility (Minsky 2008, 233–236, see Fig. 2.1).[10]

Paul McCulley, Pacific Investment Management Company (PIMCO)'s former chief economist and Post-Keynesian financial market practitioner, summarized the endogenous tendency of capitalist economies to move from fragility to stability as follows: "…stability is destabilizing because capitalists have a herding tendency to extrapolate stability into infinity, putting in place ever-more risky debt structures…that [themselves] undermine stability." In other words, stability lulls market participants into believing good times will last forever, leading them to adopt increasingly fragile financing structures to take advantage of asset price inflation (McCulley 2009). The longer stability persists, the more likely prior periods of stress fade from the market's collective memory. The lack of memory of past crises increases the economy's risk tolerance, further undermining stability.[11]

A second benefit of the Post-Keynesian model is its treatment bubbles and fragility as endogenous variables. Neoclassical economics describes bubbles and crises as the theoretical equivalent of a "meteor from space," or explained by exogenous shocks that emanate from outside of their modeled economy (Blyth 2013, 219). Bubbles contradict neoclassical notions of market efficiency, since price deviations from equilibrium in the neoclassical model are random and self-correcting.

And since equilibrium asset price values are rational, momentary deviations from equilibrium will self-correct over time, ensuring that asset mispricings do not persist. But to what extent are bubbles exogenous and self-correcting in an empirical sense? In hindsight, the rapid rise of prices in NASDAQ stocks in 1990s and housing prices in the 2000s was sustainable, at least for a few years, while simultaneously constituting a deviation from fundamental value (Fenton-O'Creevy et al. 2007, 31–35). The Post-Keynesian model remedies this theoretical oversight by problematizing the formation of bubbles and fragility and viewing them as endogenous features of capitalist economies. For instance, Hyman Minsky contended that over periods of prolonged stability, markets would endogenously move toward adopting more fragile financing structures, which could then lead to bubbles and systemic vulnerability to crises (Minsky 1992). Charles Kindleberger complemented this paradigm by arguing that displacements trigger endogenous financial instability dynamics. Provided the displacement is large enough, they set off pro-cyclical credit and asset price dynamics such as bubbles, endogenously sowing fragility over time (Kindleberger and Aliber 2005, 22–23).[12]

A third advantage of the Post-Keynesian framework is its dichotomous treatment of uncertainty and risk. Financial markets require actors to make judgments about the expected probability of future events. Some events have easily calculable probabilities, like the result of a fair coin flip, while others are less certain, such as where the stock market will close ten years hence. Neoclassical economics assumes that agents understand the probabilities of potential future states of the world, such that they have a calculable basis of their behavior. The orthodox approach also assumes future outcomes will adhere to agents' subjective probabilities, thus conflating uncertainty with risk (Lo 2017, 51–55). The ability to guess the probabilities of future outcomes describes a world of risk, since odds are strictly calculable and comport with realized outcomes.[13] However, as argued by Frank Knight and J.M. Keynes, actors might not always operate in a world of complete and knowable probabilities of future states (i.e. a world of risk), but may occasionally face situations in which there *is no measurable probability of future events* (Knight 1921).[14] Hyman Minsky believed that all investors had to deal with uncertainty and that uncertainty often drove many phases of economic booms, fragility, crises, and crises responses (Minsky 2008, 18). Charles Kindleberger noted that when euphoria metastasizes into panic, uncertainty prevails

(Kindleberger and Aliber 2005, 81). Keynes himself problematized uncertainty in financial markets and believed that agents adopted economic conventions to deal with this uncertainty (Keynes 1937a, 214).[15] Post-Keynesians thus recognized this dichotomy and emphasized uncertainty as a key variable of financial instability.[16]

A fourth benefit of the Post-Keynesian model is its recognition of epistemic blindness as a driver of pre-crisis fragility. Both Hyman Minsky and Charles Kindleberger acknowledged that blindness—or ignorance of bubbles and fragility prior to crises—was a critical component of financial instability. Without markets willing to believe that bubbles are sustainable or constitute a "new normal," bubbles could not form in the first place (Kindleberger and Aliber 2005, 75).[17] For instance, in the most recent global financial crisis, the bipartisan Financial Crisis Inquiry Commission recognized that financiers and regulators ignored the crisis' warning signs until it was too late and that blindness to risk helped inflate the housing bubble and proliferate fragility (The Financial Crisis Inquiry Commission 2011, xvii). Orthodox approaches do not discuss blindness explicitly, though they do acknowledge the role of asymmetric information in causing market failures (Akerlof 1970).[18]

The fifth advantage of the Post-Keynesian model is its accessibility to non-specialist audiences. Most academic literature on financial markets can be esoteric and inaccessible. Equations, statistical technics, and dense, jargon-filled prose fill the average research article published by the *American Economic Review*. This methodology allows economists to arrive at parsimonious, internally consistent conclusions, but offers little value to most policymakers and market participants, who lack the methodological training to interpret the mathematical and deductive approach but still have a sophisticated, inductive understanding of markets (Colander et al. 2009; Keen 2017; Krugman 2009; Soros 2003).[19] Post-Keynesianism's narrative structure allows its theories to be considered by wider audiences, providing a clear language for thinking about financial instability. While this narrative style may not make for parsimonious, mathematically elegant theory, this methodology offers greater empirical validity and provides a practical schema for foreseeing financial instability. As Martin Wolf, a regulator commentator in the *Financial Times* and former policymaker at the United Kingdom's Treasury, argues, Hyman Minsky's views are "roughly right, while many of the brightest macroeconomists proved precisely wrong" (Wolf 2018).

Limits of Post-Keynesianism

The Post-Keynesian model deserves renewed interest in the wake of the global financial crisis. Yet the Minsky–Kindleberger paradigm, while useful, rests on several concepts and arguments that themselves need to be explained. This section describes three limitations of the Post-Keynesian model, which *Social Finance*'s conventions-based theoretical framework addresses head-on in the chapter's subsequent causal propositions.

First, the Post-Keynesian model does not specify the micro-foundational causes of stability in financial markets. Although Minsky convincingly reasons that stability creates incentives for fragility, stability is just the *proximate* cause of fragility in markets. Minsky and Kindleberger's theories do not study the sociological sources of how agents construct stable markets and treat market stability as a model prior, rather than an endogenous phenomenon. While Minsky finds that economies will transition from stability to fragility over time, his model does not describe how market participants create stability and relax the constraints on fragile financing arrangements on a micro-sociological level. As this book argues, the process by which agents construct financial stability and relax the constraints on fragility is historically contingent and shapes the contours of subsequent crises. Understanding where stable markets come from can also guide policymakers' response to crises by helping them diagnose crisis causes and shape their response to market panics.[20]

Second, the Post-Keynesian model does not provide a point estimate about how and why stable but fragile financial systems erupt into crisis. Although Charles Kindleberger and Robert Aliber offer plausible crisis triggers (such as the revelation of widespread fraud in the displaced sector, a sharp price fall in a bellwether asset class, or the failure of a large financial institution), the authors do not present a generalized causal mechanism that specifies the conditions under which stable (but fragile) systems yield to instability (Kindleberger and Aliber 2005, 22–29). For his part, Minsky identified that booms would bust when Ponzi financial structures appear, though he, like Kindleberger, did not emphasize the moment at which crisis occurs (Minsky 1992).[21] By identifying the mechanisms of crisis triggers, policymakers can better forecast when panics may occur and diagnose how to stop them after they begin.[22]

Third, while the Post-Keynesian model argues that regulators will sometimes intervene to restore confidence to the financial system, it does not specify whether, when, and how regulators choose to respond to crises. Furthermore, Post-Keynesians do not offer a unified theory about how differences in the intervention capacity of regulators implicate their policy latitude to restore confidence to their financial systems. When faced with a crisis, some countries nationalize their financial systems. Others simply hope that the crisis will eventually burn itself out. Some countries lack the means to bail them out and must turn to multilateral and bilateral lenders to solve their crisis. Others have significant financial resources to deploy to save their financial systems. Post-Keynesians say little about this diversity of capabilities and outcomes. Minsky and Kindleberger present intervention as a choice of fiscal and monetary intervention. Minsky himself acknowledges that governments face choices on whether to use fiscal and monetary policy to cushion the blow from financial panics (Minsky 1982, 11–13). But why do some governments lever their sovereign balance sheets to respond to crises, while others insist on fiscal discipline? Why do some central banks opt to tighten monetary policy pro-cyclically, while others conduct large-scale asset purchases? Having guidelines for understanding regulators' crisis response can ultimately lead to better theory of financial crises.

While these limitations do not invalidate the Post-Keynesian paradigm, addressing them would lead to a better understanding of financial crises. Therefore, this chapter now presents three alternative paradigms of studying agent behavior in complex systems, including Keynesian epistemology, Doran's model of crises, and economic constructivism. These paradigms yield *Social Finance*'s five propositions on economic ideas and financial crises that build on the core model of Post-Keynesianism.

ALTERNATIVE PARADIGMS I: KEYNESIAN EPISTEMOLOGY

John Maynard Keynes believed that economic conventions dominate economic life because of the nature of knowledge in uncertain environments. Keynes claimed that contrary to utilitarian models of agent behavior, in which cost-benefit optimizing rational agents made Benthamite calculations about risk and reward under conditions of information symmetry and low transactions costs, fundamental (or "Knightian") uncertainty plagued markets (Knight 1921). Uncertainty to Keynes did not simply refer to the absence of knowledge that was, in principle, attainable. Rather, uncertainty implied that rational agents lacked a basis of predicting the probability distributions of future outcomes (Keynes 1936, 149). This uncertainty can at times inhibit agents from making informed decisions (or, as Keynes would argue, in a 'Benthamite' fashion) and prevent markets from functioning normally. Despite the inherent complexity and uncertainty of markets, however, events compel market participants to act. Economic conventions help market participants overcome this uncertainty by serving as a *substitute for knowledge*, leading agents to believe that they live in a world of calculable risk, rather than irreducible uncertainty (Boyland and O'Gorman 2013, 64–65; Keynes 1937b; Runde and Mizuhara 2003, 10–11). Keynes identified three types of conventions in financial markets: (1) the belief that the future will resemble the past; (2) the tendency of market participants to follow defer to authoritative actors; and (3) the practice of falling back on what fellow market participants believe when forming expectations (Keynes 1937a, 214).

Keynes' first convention is the belief that the future will resemble the past, which reflects the tendency of market participants to base future expectations on linear extrapolations of past trends. To Keynes, market participants believe that recent history determines the range of future outcomes. Therefore, agents often fail to consider the possibility of discontinuities and novel stimuli, leaving them surprised when tail events occur (Keynes 1937b, 14). In the parlance of statistics, agents believe that the world is *ergodic*, wherein a sampling of past data can help them reliably predict future outcomes (Blyth 2009; Taleb 2004, 50–51). The belief that stock prices converge to historically average cyclically-adjusted price-to-earnings ratios, risk models that sample past data when predicting total potential losses, or Phillips Curve estimates based on historical unemployment and inflation relationships are examples of ergodic conventions. This book refers to Keynes' first convention as *ergodicity*.

Keynes' second convention describes to the practice of conflating status quo market outcomes (as reflected in market prices) with fundamental value (i.e. an *equilibrium bias*). It also relates to agents' tendency to listen to the narratives of authoritative actors when forming their expectations (Keynes 1937a; Skidelsky 2009). Investors purchasing an asset because a credible market actor, such as Warren Buffett, has also purchased the same asset is an example of a convention of expert opinion at work. Credit ratings for corporations and households are examples of formalized conventions of expert opinion. These conventions allow lenders to assess the creditworthiness of borrowers about whom they would have little other actionable information. *Social Finance* refers to Keynes' second convention as *expert opinion*.

Keynes' third convention describes the tendency of financial market participants to consider what *fellow market participants* believe before acting. Keynes argued that portfolio allocation decisions are not based on individual calculations of risk and reward. Rather, market participants had to consider the beliefs of fellow investors before acting. Investment is thus a *social* activity that involves trying to guess the intentions of other market participants. Seen in this light, investment is not a single-iteration decision of an agent vis-à-vis the market but is an inter-subjective process in which many agents simultaneously divine the beliefs of fellow market participants (Keynes 1937a, 214). This book refers to Keynes' third convention as *conventional expectations*, which contrasts *rational expectations* from neoclassical economics. As Robert Skidelsky believes, conventional expectations are quite rational, since successful investing depends on outsmarting other market participants and adequately estimating average market opinions (Skidelsky 2009, 92–94). Conventional expectations explain phenomena such as bank runs, in which rumors of insolvency are self-fulfilling. If bank depositors believe that fellow depositors doubt the solvency of a bank, then it is rational to withdraw deposits based on the logic that fellow market participants believe the same thing. If many investors arrive at the same conclusion, then creditors will deny the bank access to credit, leading to self-fulfilling liquidity and solvency issues.[23] Conventional expectations thus explain pro-cyclical market phenomena such as herding and panic selling (Sent 2004).[24]

Together, these three conventions—ergodicity, expert opinion, and conventional expectations—serve as pillars of knowledge in the face of uncertainty.

Economic conventions are not simply individually-held biases but are constituted via social processes and are shared by the epistemic community of the market. Stable conventions can provide continuity to markets. Thus, epistemic consensus or *convention certainty* can produce financial stability (Crotty 1994, 121–124). This insight helps to understand the sociological micro-foundations of stability and endogenous fragility in the Post-Keynesian model, as described in this book's theoretical propositions.

Several scholars have featured economic conventions in their study of markets. For example, Victoria Chick noted that economic conventions impact uncertainty via reflexive processes. She finds that conventions dominate economic life in the modern payments system, in which firms accept claims on demand deposits from banks in exchange for goods and services, as well as the conventions behind fiat money, which agents accept because of expectations of reciprocal use and as a store of value (Chick 2013). Sheila Dow argued that market irrationality regarding evolving economic conventions explains financial instability. She ties economic conventions to reflexive market outcomes, in which conventions create the very outcomes they were meant to predict, thus self-stabilizing the market endogenously (Dow 2012, 8–10). Robert Skidelsky finds that economic conventions present an alternative epistemology for thinking about markets. To Skideksly, conventions *are* fundamentals, since they lead to self-fulfilling market outcomes (Skidelsky 2009, 92–94). In an edited volume of Keynesian epistemology, Jochen Runde and Sohei Mizuhara present several essays about Keynes' emphasis on uncertainty in economic life, demonstrating Keynes' contributions to methodology, ontology, and probability (Runde and Mizuhara 2003). This renewed focus on Keynesian epistemology highlights the potentially fruitful use of conventions to investigate economic phenomena, though to date no account of Keynesian conventionality has sought to reincorporate Keynesian epistemology into the Minsky-Kindleberger framework of financial instability. *Social Finance* fills this theoretical gap.

Alternative Paradigms II: Doran's Model of Crises

Markets are stable if a critical mass of market participants believes that their conventions provide a reliable basis of knowledge in the face of uncertainty in a fundamentally rational environment. But what happens when markets doubt the veracity of their conventions? James Crotty finds that when agents doubt their conventions, the uncertainty masked by conventions can reemerge and paralyze action (Crotty 1994, 124–125). Keynes himself recognized the fickleness of conventions, noting that when agents doubted their taken-for-granted conventional anchors, underlying tensions masked by stable conventions are exposed, precipitating uncertainty (Keynes 1937a, 214–215). Even though conventions might stabilize markets, they cannot stabilize markets permanently because convention-given expectations cannot account for the complete range of possible market futures. To understand the *triggers* of financial instability, then, it is necessary to study the conditions that cause agents to lose faith in their conventions.

Charles Doran provides a framework for conceptualizing how structurally-induced shocks to agents' expectations catalyze structural and behavioral uncertainty that causes crisis. Doran's model of decision-making draws on his power cycle theory, which is a dynamic theory of international relations that describes the behavior of political leaders based on the evolution of their state's relative power. Doran established the principles of a single dynamic that contours a particular non-linear pattern of change on each state's relative power trajectory, together with the expectations that each state has about its future foreign policy and security at each point along the cycle. Doran's model shows how structural change impacts agent decision-making along the cycle and ultimately causes a discontinuity in future policy expectations at the critical point of non-linearity. Note that it is the direction of the change in structure on the cycle of relative power that is transmitted to expectations (the tangent line on the curve of relative power as depicted in Fig. 2.2). Causation goes from structure to decision-making, from structure to agent. The discontinuity is in expectations (in the changing slope of the line drawn tangent to the curve of changing structure), not in terms of structure per se. This model (and its mathematical representation) came out of Doran's early work on power cycle theory dating back to the 1960s, published in *Politics of Assimilation: Hegemony and its Aftermath* (Doran 1971). Doran, like Keynes, believed that in uncertain environments, agents extrapolate from past trends when forming expectations. Since linear projections of past trends tend to be more right than wrong, they often become the preferred form of expectations for decision makers. Trouble emerges because linear extrapolations from past trends leave agents unprepared for non-linear moments that emerge.

Non-linearities produce surprises that agents' linear expectations cannot foresee. When expectations pass through a discontinuity, such as when the market realizes that wholesale funding might not always be available to shadow banks, a flood of commercial and financial uncertainty overtakes the market. Whereas Keynes described irrationality in markets in perpetuity, only to be mitigated via economic conventions, Doran stressed the existence of *conditional non-rationality* during crisis periods, meaning that markets are rational most of the time and usually contain enough information upon which firms and individuals can make appropriate decisions about the future. During a crisis, however, agents must cope with the stress associated with realizing that their extrapolative forecasts are wrong. Facing conditional non-rationality, agents

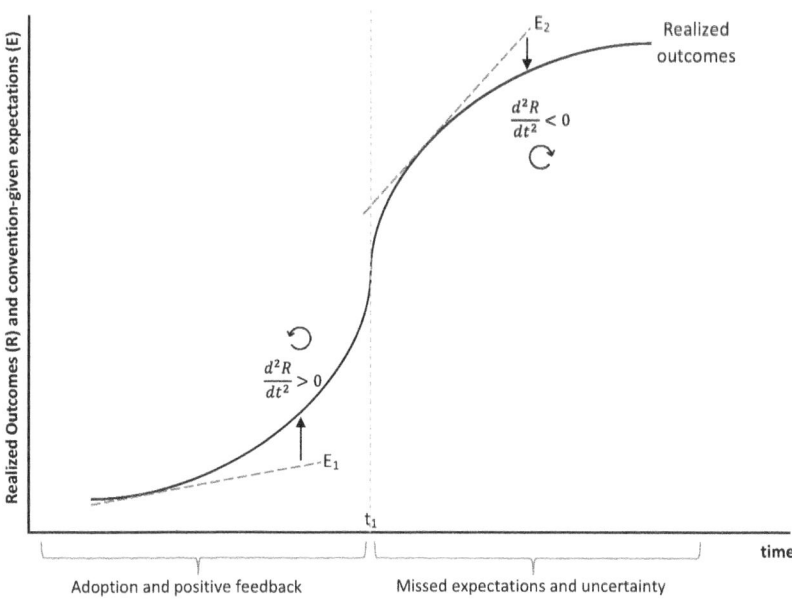

A graphical representation of Doran's ideas (and of the mathematics underpinning his analysis) depicts how the *trend of the slope* (that is, of the linear rate of change) along a state's curve of relative power yields the *trend of future expectations*. Doran shows how at a critical point (occurring at t_1 in the graph above), there occurs a shift from a concave ever-rising trend of linear expectations to a convex ever-declining trend of linear expectations. The shift in torque along the above logistic curve is represented mathematically by the second derivatives (that is, by the rates of change of the rate of change) along the Realized Outcomes curve, which abruptly shift in sign from greater than 0 (ever-rising slope) to less than 0 (a lesser-steep slope) at the inflection point. A discontinuity has occurred in the trend of future expectations. Expectations are formed by linear projections of current material trends, which are tangent to the curve of realized outcomes (e.g. E_1 and E_2). For all $t < t_1$, outcomes and expectations are congruent and self-stabilizing, such that the perceived truth-value of agents' expectations generating formation (what this book terms *conventions*) increases pro-cyclically with confirmatory data. For all $t > t_1$, however, non-ergodic deviations from agents' convention-given expectations via an inflection point at t_1 of realized outcomes is a shock that causes agents to reappraise their taken-for-granted linear expectations. Non-routine change reveals to agents the bankruptcy of their linear projections of past trends into the future, thus catalyzing a period of convention uncertainty in financial markets. Provided a sufficient number of agents must cope with the shock of missed expectations at the same time, and given the pre-existence of a fragile financial system, the likelihood of systemic crisis rises.

Fig. 2.2 Non-routine change triggering convention uncertainty (Author; Doran 1991; Doran and Parsons 1980)

adopt conventions that are rigid and inapplicable to novel circumstances, precipitating massive uncertainty. Under such conditions, trust falls to a point where mistrust paralyzes the market's core allocative functions. The moment of acknowledgement of a non-linearity, or an abrupt discontinuity in the prior trend of expectation, along with the shock of realizing that the future that does not comport with those long-held expectations, cascades uncertainty in Doran's decision-making model.[25] In this setting, uncertainty floods decision-making and hinders it. Even when decision-making is rational most of the time, and when the decision-maker is a certifiably rational agent, decision-making can and will go awry when a discontinuity in expectations occurs.

Doran provides a *probabilistic* understanding of conflict in the international system, hypothesizing that the likelihood of systemic crisis rises as more states simultaneously go through critical intervals on their power cycles (or periods when linear forecasts fail) (Doran 1991, 95–98, see Figs. 1.1 and 2.2).[26] This notion is consistent with Keynes and Crotty's belief that deviations from convention-given expectations can cause breakdowns in conventional certainty (Crotty 1994, 121–124; Keynes 1937a, 214–215). During a moment of acute, structural, or conventional uncertainty, agents realize that their prior assumptions were wrong and that they no longer face a world of risk as such, but of uncertainty as described by Knight, Keynes, and others (Doran 1991, 108–111; Knight 1921; Keynes 1937a; Blyth 2009). Learned patterns of behavior, reflected in assumptions about the future and positively reinforced during the stable period, are no longer credible. As more states experience structural uncertainty, their likelihood of over-estimating their material capabilities while underestimating the costs of violent conflict and capability of their adversaries rises (Doran 1991, 97).[27] This dynamic of systems transformation can lead to systemic conflict.

Social Finance incorporates Doran's notions of system transformations into its study of financial stability. As Doran argues, systems transformation (brought about by massive, abrupt, and unanticipated structural change) belies agents' expectations, initiating a period of *conditional non-rationality* and *massive uncertainty*, in turn leading to a change in agent behavior (see Fig. 2.2). To understand why crises emerge in financial markets, one must study the conditions under which the market's most taken-for-granted, ontological priors fail.[28] By merging Doran's insights on expectations formation and systems transformation with

Keynesian notions of conventionality, this book provides a theoretical lens of understanding how stable (but fragile) financial systems erupt into crisis, thus remedying one of the core oversights of the Post-Keynesian model: specifically, its lack of a generalized causal mechanism for understanding financial crisis triggers.

ALTERNATIVE PARADIGMS III: ECONOMIC CONSTRUCTIVISM

Keynes provides a solid understanding of how agents socially construct stability in financial markets via conventions, while Doran explains how non-routine deviations from agents' convention-given expectations catalyze uncertainty. But how do regulators respond to crises once convention uncertainty takes hold?

To answer this question, *Social Finance* draws on the insights of economic constructivists like Rawi Abdelal, Jacqueline Best, Mark Blyth, Matthias Matthijs, Kathleen McNamara, Craig Parsons, and others, who argue that scholars need to take economic ideas seriously as causal drivers of outcomes in the global economy.[29] These authors provide a framework for understanding how economic ideas influence elite responses to economic stress. For instance, in *Ideas and Economic Crises in Britain from Attlee to Blair* (1945–2005), Matthias Matthijs presents a "punctuated evolution" model of ideational change to understand economic policy in Post-War Britain. Matthijs' framework builds on Mark Blyth's work on institutional change in the United States and Sweden in the 1930s and 1970s, which he presents in his book, *Great Transformations: Economic Ideas and Institutional Change in the Twentieth Century*. While not about financial crises per se, these arguments provide several core insights that specify how regulators respond to moments of crisis, remedying some of the theoretical limitations the Post-Keynesian model (Blyth 2002; Matthijs 2011).

According to Blyth and Matthijs, economic ideas frame elite responses to crises by reducing uncertainty, giving agents cogent narratives about the causes of crises, and specifying appropriate crisis responses. Blyth argued that economic ideas help agents diagnose the causes of crises and the appropriate regulatory response to market stress. He also focuses on the role that political entrepreneurs play in employing economic ideas to set the bounds of debate about the drivers of economic stress and best way to fix them (Blyth 2002, 38).

Matthijs adds that economic ideas narrow down the universe of potential explanations for crises and shape how elites build coalitions around specific ideational scripts of behavior. As applied to moments of financial instability, economic ideas help regulators diagnose the causes of the crisis, identify potential responses, and build institutional support for intervening in markets. Moreover, in Matthijs' punctuated evolution model, which drew on the insights of Paul Pierson, ideas also have strongly path dependent tendencies, such that the idea sets that are adopted by agents after crises tend to be sticky until subsequent crises make ideational consensuses malleable once more (Matthijs 2011, 28–31; Pierson 2000).

Economic ideas explain why the market sanctions certain elite courses of action while prohibiting others. Jonathan Kirshner finds that economic ideas held by the market about regulators determine the feasibility of policy responses. Capital mobility implies that the market can punish unpopular policies via capital flight and higher interest rates, while the market rewards policies perceived to be market-friendly with continued access to international credit at lower interest rates. Abdelal et al. further add that economic ideas held by the market about regulators determine the efficacy of regulators' response to financial instability given capital mobility. How regulators are perceived by the market determines the efficacy and policy latitude of national regulators in responding to bouts of financial instability. Concepts such as market credibility are contingent and depend on the market's ideas about regulators (Abdelal et al. 2010, 9–10; Kirshner 2003).[30]

SOCIAL FINANCE: FIVE PROPOSITIONS OF ECONOMIC CONVENTIONS AND FINANCIAL INSTABILITY

Having presented an overview of the weaknesses of Post-Keynesian asset market theory, as well as the main arguments of Keynesian epistemology, Doran's power cycle theory, and economic constructivism, this chapter now introduces *Social Finance*'s five inductively derived causal propositions about conventions and financial crises. Effort is made to link this study's propositions to the Post-Keynesian model while also identifying evidence and causal indicators marshaled in the subsequent empirical chapters.

Proposition 1 *Convention stability produces financial stability and enables the economy's transition to fragility over time.*

This first proposition draws on the insights of J.M. Keynes, James Crotty, and Sheila Dow, among others, who argue that economic conventions stabilize financial markets by coordinating agents' expectations and serving as a social basis of knowledge given fundamental uncertainty about the future (Keynes 1937a; Crotty 1994; Dow 2012). Conventions are defined as *formal and informal epistemological anchors created and shared by market participants to mitigate fundamental uncertainty and coordinate expectations.* This working definition draws on Keynes' writings and other scholarship on conventions, as well as Stephen Krasner's description of regimes in international relations theory (Keynes 1937a; Crotty 1994; Dow 2013; Krasner 1982). As described earlier in the chapter, there are three types of economic conventions in markets: *ergodicity* (i.e. the belief that the past provides a reliable guide to the future), *expert opinion* (i.e. the tendency of market participants to latch onto authoritative narratives when forming their own expectations), and *conventional expectations* (i.e. guessing the average opinion of *fellow market participants* before acting). When conventions are stable and widely accepted, markets will be self-stabilizing and equilibrium seeking systems.[31]

This proposition reincorporates Keynesian insights about conventions into the Minsky model to explain how agents construct stable markets while also adopting more fragile financing structures. This book draws on Garry Schinasi's definition of stability, namely that *financial systems are stable when they allocate capital with minimal frictions* (Schinasi 2004). Minsky believed stability was a necessary but insufficient condition for an economy's endogenous shift to fragility over time. The economy's move to fragility requires an upward sloping interest rate term structure; a willing pool of buyers to purchase short-term debt issued by financial institutions; sufficient risk tolerance by financial institutions to take advantage of interest rate term structure arbitrage opportunities; and a group of borrowers willing to issue long-term assets. *Social Finance* finds that conventions explain the relaxation of Minsky's four constraints on fragility prior to the global financial crisis.

First, *Social Finance* describes how the upward sloping yield curve prior to the global financial crisis followed from economic conventions held by the Federal Reserve's interest rate setting body, the Federal

Open Market Committee (FOMC), including historic memories of Japan's experience with deflation (*ergodicity*), how Fed technocrats counted inflation (*expert opinion*), and the Fed's philosophical approach to asset price bubbles that it was better to *clean up* after a bubble burst rather than to *lean against* its inflation (*expert opinion* again). Different conventions may have led to different monetary policy choices, possibly avoiding a steeply upward sloping yield curve prior to the global financial crisis.

Second, pro-cyclical *conventional expectations* by shadow banking counterparties such as money market mutual funds enabled financial institutions to issue billions of dollars of short-term, money-like liabilities such as asset-backed commercial paper (ABCP) and repurchase agreements ("repo"). The steadiness and reliability of shadow bank deposits depended on counterparties' positive conventional expectations regarding the solvency of shadow banking conduits. These conventional expectations were both pro-cyclical and self-fulfilling, creating incentives for financial institutions to issue short-term debt in the ABCP and repo markets to profit from the housing bubble and credit boom. Provided counterparties believed that *fellow counterparties* would roll over shadow banks' maturing liabilities, then shadow banking depositors routinely rolled over banks' maturing short-term obligations, and shadow banking conduits remained liquid and stable. These conventional expectations enabled the liability side of shadow banking while making financial institutions vulnerable to rollover risks when the housing bubble burst.[32]

Third, conventions of *ergodicity*, such as bank risk management techniques like value-at-risk, made financial institutions vulnerable to declining asset prices while also increasing bank risk tolerance prior to the global financial crisis. These ergodic risk measures were self-stabilizing in the near term, as investors and regulators trusted banks to monitor their own credit risks. However, banks also took advantage of the leeway afforded to them by regulators to set their own regulatory capital rules, taking on greater risks while justifying their high leverage based on their internal methodologies. During the boom years, banks appeared well capitalized while simultaneously taking on more risk. In the Minsky context, ergodic conventions enabled banks' risk tolerance and made them apt to lever their balance sheets to take advantage of the favorable interest rate term structure.

Fourth, institutionalized conventions of *expert opinion* via bond ratings facilitated fragility in the shadow banking system. Favorable ratings on asset-backed securities (ABS) enabled capital flows into highly rated, risky securities, lowering yields and reifying the very creditworthiness that ratings were meant to reflect. Stable bond ratings allowed risk-averse investors, such as money market mutual funds, to lend to shadow banks that purchased risky (but highly rated) ABS, decreasing bond yields and incentivizing greater risk-taking by financial institutions and borrowers. Bond ratings also allowed risk-averse investors to purchase shadow banking liabilities since ostensibly high-quality debt collateralized these transactions. Ratings were critical to the development of the global securitization chain as well by allowing ABS issuers to mint risky, highly rated securities. Thus, ratings facilitated both the asset and liability sides of shadow banking prior to the global financial crisis.

Proposition 2 *Conventions blind agents to the prospect of non-routine change in financial markets.*

The premise of this proposition is that the inflation of bubbles and economy's transition to fragility require several actors to be ignorant or permissive of unsustainable economic conditions for a prolonged period. *Social Finance* defines blindness as *the failure of agents to take into account the range of potential future outcomes that, if fully considered, would lead to a different course of action*. This proposition draws on the work of Keynes and Knight, as well as economic constructivists, who argued that agents do not live in a world of risk as such, but one of uncertainty, in which both the causal generators and probability distributions of outcomes are in principle unknowable (Abdelal et al. 2010, 10–12; Keynes 1937a; Knight 1921). The inability to know the causal generators and probability distributions of future outcomes is the source of blindness in markets.

As rational actors, agents come up with different conventions that serve as a basis of social knowledge, leading to the very stability that agents end up taking for granted. Trouble emerges because no amount of past sampling yields gives agents complete knowledge of the future because markets are prone a priori unknowable shifts. As Keynes put it, "we simply do not know" (Keynes 1937a, 214). Conventions are useful because they elevate certain narratives over alternatives, such that prolonged periods of convention stability tunnel agents' expectations and sow epistemic blindness to non-routine change in financial markets. In the process of taking conventions for granted, agents become blind to futures not forecasted and considered by their animating conventions. The more stability conventions provide, the more agents will be shocked when their ontological priors fail. Long-run uncertainty mitigation via conventions cannot hold forever because markets are non-ergodic systems: no amount of past sampling of historic data will give agents' perfect foresight into *future* outcomes (Blyth 2011).

Social Finance's empirical chapters offer several examples of conventions blinding market participants prior to the global financial crisis. Chapter 3 finds that FOMC conventions blinded them to risks from the housing bubble and credit boom. FOMC members' fears of repeating Japan's experience with deflation caused the central bank to overlook the risks of prolonged easy monetary policy. Inflation metrics based on rent ignored housing price inflation. And the Greenspan Doctrine of cleaning burst bubbles rather than leaning against their inflation may have caused FOMC officials to overlook the US economy's fragility prior to the global financial crisis.

Chapter 4 shows how the institutionalization of certain economic conventions, such as bond ratings and capital adequacy metrics, created epistemic blindness among banks, their counterparties, regulators, and market participants toward non-routine change in financial markets. Assumptions of normally distributed asset price returns and low default correlations based on historical data underpinned these models. Because agents based their expectations of losses on their conventions, they underestimated the likelihood of scenarios in which realized market outcomes diverged from their convention-given expectations.

Chapters 5 and 6 discuss how shadow banks lacked deposit insurance and were thus vulnerable to bank runs. This book found evidence that regulators' successive interventions in financial markets, including during the bailouts of hedge fund Long-Term Capital Management (LTCM) in 1998, investment bank Bear Stearns in March 2008, and the Federal housing giants, Fannie Mae and Freddie Mac, in September 2008, created a conventional expectation in financial markets that regulators would serve as de facto liquidity providers of last resort in the wholesale funding markets. Agents' acceptance of this convention maintained a tenuous stability in shadow banking markets and ensured that the deflating housing bubble did not lead to a generalized panic across all shadow banking conduits. The provision of this quasi deposit insurance by regulators prior to the failure of Lehman Brothers blinded markets to the risk that shadow banking deposits would be vulnerable to bank runs (or as Gary Gorton would reason, regulatory interventions made shadow banking deposits appear *information insensitive* or immune to adverse selection problems because of information asymmetry) (Gorton 2010, 11).

Proposition 3 *Shocks to convention-given expectations catalyze convention uncertainty.*

Propositions 3 and 4 consider the conditions under which stable (but fragile) financial systems erupt into crisis. They augment the Post-Keynesian model by specifying the causal drivers under which crises occur, tying financial market panics to convention uncertainty. Proposition 3 draws on the work of Charles Doran to argue that non-linear deviations from agents' extrapolative forecasts of the future catalyze structural uncertainty. These propositions also refine the Post-Keynesian model by offering a mode of understanding how and why fragile financial systems collapse. *Social Finance* shows how this Minsky/Doran model of the discontinuity of investor expectations helps to explain shadow banking runs during the global financial crisis.

Keynes believed that conventions produced stability if they were reliable. When market participants questioned the truth-value of their conventions, convention-engendered market stability could break down, in turn triggering uncertainty in markets (Keynes 1937a, 214–215). What causes the conventional method of decision-making to break down? According to James Crotty, shocks to expectations cause agents to question their conventional method of decision making, thus catalyzing convention uncertainty (Crotty 1994, 125–126). Crotty, like Doran, argued that novel shocks, or "surprises" to agents' expectations cause them to question their most taken-for-granted ontological assumptions. Absent conventional anchors of behavior, agents must cope with acute informational uncertainty. If a majority of actors experience convention uncertainty, the likelihood of systemic crisis rises dramatically.

Chapter 6 argues that regulators' decision to allow Lehman Brothers to fail while bailing out the larger and more systemically important American International Group (AIG) negated the market's conventional expectation that regulators would serve as liquidity providers of last resort in shadow banking markets, as they had come to expect due to regulators' pre-Lehman interventions. Fears of counterparty solvency, idiosyncratically limited to specific financial institutions pre-Lehman, metastasized into a generalized bank run against all shadow bank-sponsoring financial institutions in the wholesale funding markets after Lehman. Regulators' disparate treatment of Bear Stearns, Fannie Mae, Freddie Mac, Lehman Brothers, and AIG introduced *convention uncertainty* into markets regarding regulators' commitment to backstopping shadow banking conduits, eviscerating the very stability to which markets had grown accustomed because of regulators' prior interventions. The absence of conventional anchors of behavior translated Lehman's failure into broader financial instability, as described in the following proposition.

Proposition 4 *Given sufficient financial fragility, uncertainty causes agents to revert to first principles of survival, disrupting the market's normal price discovery mechanism and triggering financial instability.*

This proposition draws on the insights of Keynes, Doran, and Frank Knight to explain how agents behave during moments of convention uncertainty (Keynes 1937a; Doran 1991; Knight 1921). Lacking conventional anchors of behavior, agents revert to "first-principles" of survival by hoarding safe assets and selling risky assets. Agents' demand for money and its equivalents increases during periods of convention uncertainty. Observed price adjustment such as the rise in the price of safe assets and fall in the price of risky assets occurs because of changes in expectations. This "flight to quality" disrupts the market's normal price discovery mechanism and can lead to adverse selection problems in markets, causing liquidity to dry up, securities prices to fall, and trading in entire asset classes to cease.

Keynes recognized that one of the main indicators of convention uncertainty in markets was elevated money demand, which he saw as a symptom of the market's degree of "disquietude" regarding conventions (Keynes 1937a, 216). Therefore, the price of safe assets (such as bank deposits, short-term US Treasury securities, and safe haven currencies) increases during periods of convention uncertainty, causing the yield on these securities to fall. Individual attempts to make portfolios liquid and less risky have the paradoxical effect of reducing the aggregate liquidity in the financial system, precipitating broader market instability (Dow 2013).[33]

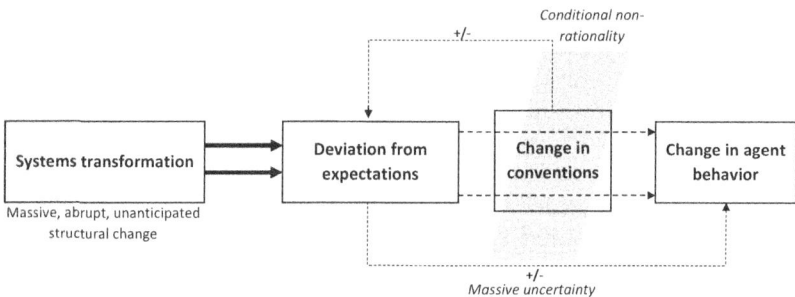

Fig. 2.3 A schematic of crises and conventions

A visualization of *Social Finance*'s crisis schematic, as described in Propositions 3 and 4, is presented in Fig. 2.3:

Figure 2.3 shows how a massive, abrupt, unanticipated structural change within fragile financial systems shocks agents' expectations of the future. Defied expectations cause agents to reappraise the applicability of their taken-for-granted conventions, and the stress associated with convention uncertainty introduces acute, structural uncertainty into agents' decision-making, causing them to revert to first principles of survival and hoard liquid capital. Convention uncertainty can cause either positive or negative feedback vis-à-vis agents' expectations. Negative feedback entails "divergent equilibria," or situations in which individually rational behavior (for instance, hoarding liquid capital) proves collectively disastrous for all market participants (e.g. by exacerbating liquidity issues for the market as a whole). The shock engendered by an unanticipated structural change defies agents' expectations and causes them to reappraise the truth-value of their dominant conventions, changing agent behavior because of convention uncertainty.

This book demonstrates how the simultaneous failure of investment bank Lehman Brothers and bailout of insurance giant AIG catalyzed convention uncertainty in financial markets regarding the willingness of regulators to act as *liquidity providers of last resort* in shadow banking markets. Convention uncertainty made it rational for agents to hoard liquid capital and withhold financing from shadow banking conduits given their perception of the Federal Reserve and US Treasury's ambivalence toward bailouts. ABCP and repo counterparties withdrew their funds from shadow banks and sold risky assets while also purchasing safe havens like short-term Treasury securities. The contraction of credit in the wholesale funding markets made it difficult for both bank and non-bank financial institutions to finance their operations, leading to further financial dislocation. Other indicators of convention uncertainty include rising stock market volatility, the flight to quality in foreign exchange markets, and the ceasing of trading in certain derivatives markets because of a lack of information symmetry. During the most acute phase of the global financial crisis, information asymmetry about collateral quality caused an *adverse selection* problem in some securities markets, in which the market sells securities of disparate quality at the same low price, so the market supplies too much of the low quality good and too little of the high-quality good (Pindyck and Rubinfeld 2013, 634). Chapter 6 proposes that convention uncertainty explains why some financial derivatives ceased trading after Lehman Brothers, just as George Akerlof and other scholars of asymmetric information would have predicted (Akerlof 1970).

Proposition 5 *Elite responses to financial instability are a function of their economic ideas used to diagnose crises and their intervention capacity.*

This proposition claims that regulators' response to financial instability is a function of their conventions about markets and the market's conventions about regulators. It applies the insights of economic constructivists such as Mark Blyth and Matthias Matthijs to understand how regulators respond to financial instability (Blyth 2002; Matthijs 2011). It also draws on the work of Jonathan Kirshner, who argued that open capital markets allow market participants to set the bounds of regulatory intervention by denouncing bad policies via capital flight and sanctioning good policies via capital inflows (Kirshner 2003). This proposition builds on the Post-Keynesian model by specifying the constraints on elite intervention in the economy during crises and outlines why the market deems identical policy responses legitimate in some contexts but not others.

After Lehman Brothers went bankrupt, regulators chose to bail out other systemically important financial institutions such as AIG, Bank of America, and Citigroup, among many others. Their response to the market's *convention uncertainty* encompassed a wide array of policies to stem the banking panic and restore confidence in America's wholesale funding markets, including granting investment banks access to the Federal

Reserve's discount window, asset purchases, the extension of Federal deposit insurance to bank and non-bank short-term market-based liabilities, the passage and adoption of the $700 billion Troubled Asset Relief Program, among other measures. Together, these interventions restored *convention certainty* that regulators stood as *liquidity providers of last resort* in wholesale funding markets, successfully reducing funding pressures facing financial institutions.

Social Finance argues that regulators' response to the crisis stemmed from two sets of economic conventions, including those held by regulators about appropriate crisis responses and the market's conventions about regulators and America's sovereign creditworthiness. Chapter 6 demonstrates that regulators' response to the crisis followed from their fears of repeating the Great Depression (i.e. ergodicity), which biased them toward bailing out the entire US financial system. Moreover, regulators' ability to extend de facto deposit insurance to the shadow banking system depended on the market's willingness to accept such invasive interventions and deem them credible over alternatives. This credibility stemmed from the United States' high degree of sovereign creditworthiness, which granted US regulators significant intervention capacity. This book defines intervention capacity as *the ability and willingness of regulators to deploy domestic, international, private, and public resources against the locus of crisis in a timely manner*. Since creditworthiness and precepts of credibility transfer are fundamentally ideational processes, conventions play a role in determining the efficacy of crisis response.

Operationalizing the Model

Having outlined the five theoretical propositions of *Social Finance*, this chapter now explains how the subsequent empirical chapters operationalize the book's framework via a case study of shadow banking during the global financial crisis. This section provides a summary of the study's causal standards, empirical methods, and justification for its case study method.

One of the primary difficulties of operationalizing a conventions-based model of continuity and change in financial markets is that it does not lend itself to telling a clean causal story with clearly delineated independent and dependent variables, linked by observable and non-recursive causal pathways. Reality, unfortunately, is far too complex. Constructivists like Mark Blyth, R. Ned Lebow, John Ruggie, and Alexander Wendt recognize that linear causal standards are inapplicable to matters of social construction (Blyth 2011; Lebow 2009; Ruggie 1998; Wendt 1998). They argue that financial markets are *emergent* systems, in which outcomes follow from the complex interplay and cross-cutting feedback loops of the system's overall dynamics. Matters are complicated further because ideas and material phenomena in markets are inseparable—agents' thoughts and perceptions are causally integrated into asset prices and market outcomes. For this reason, Mark Blyth believes that ideational scholarship occupies its own ontology because economic ideas and material fundamentals are often the same thing. Blyth finds that the interdependence of economic subjects and objects renders linear causal standards inapplicable because the very narratives and conventions divined about how markets operate has a two-way, reflexive relationship with the causal generators of markets themselves. Thus, the relationship between ideas and outcomes is endogenous and recursive, such that it is impossible to separate them when attempting to determine causality (Blyth 2011, 84–97).

So, if *Social Finance* rejects linear causality on ontological grounds, how can this book make an affirmative case that conventions matter to financial stability? R. Ned Lebow identifies a unique method of social inquiry related to the study of economic ideas known as *constitutive causality*. This causal standard does not attempt to form law-like views of human behavior. Rather it studies the deeper causes of cognition in agents that cannot be separated from actions and outcomes (Lebow 2009, 4). Markets are apt arenas for investigating outcomes via constitutive causal standards since ideas and market outcomes (e.g. prices) are often the same thing. For instance, scholars and market observers such as Robert Skidelsky and George Soros implicity support a constituitively causal view of markets—as Skideksly claims, conventions *are* fundamentals, while Soros has argued for decades that prices and material fundamentals are recursive (Skidelsky 2009; Soros 2003). As argued subsequently, conventions explain how agents elevate certain behavioral choices over alternatives and delineate the cognitive pathways by which economic ideas motivate agent behavior and translate into material outcomes in the economy.

Social Finance thus adopts strongly constitutive standards of causation and argues that economic conventions delimit the bounds of permissible and preferable actions for market participants. Cognitive frameworks like conventions influence how market participants formulate goals (e.g. optimizing between maximizing the potential of capital appreciation versus capital preservation) and choose the means of attaining these goals. To prove the causal role that conventions play in financial markets, the researcher must start with observed behavior and work backwards to study how economic ideas may have influenced agents' behavior, demonstrating how observed behavior would have been incompatible with other types of economic ideas (Lebow 2009, 6–7).

To illustrate the applicability of this book's theoretical framework to shadow banking during the global financial crisis based on the above ontology, this study marshals evidence from author interviews, discourse analysis of archival documents and speeches, descriptive economic statistics, and other secondary sources to show that economic conventions were causal drivers of stability and change in financial markets. The empirical techniques employed by *Social Finance* include counter-factual analysis, process-tracing, and quantitative methods.

According to sociologist Max Weber, counter-factual analysis involves "the mental construction of a course of events which is altered through modifications in one or more 'conditions'" (Weber [1905] 1949, 173). In evaluating the relationship between conventions and market outcomes, one must judge whether conventions and conventional change have independent causal weight in determining market outcomes or are epiphenomenal to other, material causal processes. One way of solving this puzzle is to envision how different conventions might have altered the decision-making calculi of agents and thus produce different outcomes (King et al. 1994, 10–11). Counter-factual analysis of economic conventions allows the researcher to speculate how variance in agents' conventions might have caused them to make different decisions, thus producing variance in market outcomes. *Social Finance* uses counter-factual analysis to consider situations in which *different* economic conventions would have produced *different* economic outcomes as intermediated by agents' cognition and subsequent choices.

While counter-factual analysis can give the researcher *prima facie* support for the notion that conventions shape agent behavior and thus outcomes in financial markets, it is necessary to employ other methods to show the causal links between *specific* conventions and outcomes. *Social Finance* uses process-tracing research techniques to observe underlying causal processes at play by understanding "…the decision process that makes use of these stimuli to arrive at decisions; the actual behavior that then occurs; the effect of various institutional arrangements [i.e. conventions] on attention, processing, and behavior; and the effect of other variables of interest on attention, processing, and behavior" (George and McKeown 1985). To find this evidence, King et al. believe that process-tracing often requires the researcher to conduct elite interviews and to review the written record to explain choices over plausible alternatives, as this book does when studying the decision-making processes of market participants, regulators, and policymakers (King et al. 1994, 226–227). As Matthias Matthijs claims, process-tracing is well-suited to ideational analysis because it allows the researcher to study actors' goals and rationales for making decisions that shape aggregate outcomes, in turn illuminating underlying causal processes at play (Matthijs 2011, 7). More information about the interviews conducted to test the above propositions is available in the interview appendix at the end of this book.

Social Finance also uses descriptive economic statistics to show how changes in conventions change financial markets. These statistics can identify correlations between market phenomena, in turn helping to identify causality (e.g. FOMC interest rates and mortgage rates) or timing (the flight to quality after the failure of Lehman Brothers) of conventional processes. Of course, the researcher can always cherry pick data to fit his preferred narrative. Therefore, this book tries to present quantitative evidence as transparently as possible. The reader can then judge how convincing and scientific they find this evidence.

Taken together, these three empirical methods—counter-factual analysis, process-tracing, and quantitative techniques—help the researcher paint a complete picture in understanding the role of economic conventions and financial market outcomes.

Social Finance employs the above empirical methods in the context of a "single-n," representative case study on the global financial crisis. Helen Simons defines a case study as "an in-depth exploration from multiple perspectives of the complexity and uniqueness of a particular project, policy, institution, program or system in a 'real life' context" (Simmons 2009, 20). *Social Finance* qualifies as a case study because it provides an exploration of the global financial crisis from a new perspective that follows from a close study on what occurred. In so doing, this examination provides evidence for the utility of *Social Finance*'s theoretical framework. John Odell characterizes this type of research as a "preliminary illustration of a theory" form of inquiry, since *Social Finance* "puts concrete flesh on the bare bones of an abstract idea…to help readers see its meaning more clearly, and to convince them that the idea is relevant to at least one significant real-world instance" (Odell 2001, 163). Likewise, John Gerring would characterize *Social Finance*'s empirical chapters as a "pathway case" since it provides an opportunity to conduct an "intensive analysis of an individual case" that in turn allows the researcher to understand the underlying "causal mechanisms" at play (Gerring 2007, 233). Regardless of the terminology used, the researcher should keep in mind Gary Thomas' caveat that a successful case study requires both a subject and object—i.e. the topic of study (in this case, the global financial crisis) and a frame of understanding this study (a conventions-based account of continuity and change in financial markets) (Thomas 2011, 515).

To conduct an effective case study, George and Bennett claim that "the investigator should clearly identify the universe—that is, the 'class' or 'subclass' of events—of which a single case or a group of cases to be studied are instances." In this case, the global financial crisis is part of the broader universe of systemic financial crises. The authors find several strengths associated with the case study approach. First, case studies allow for "conceptual validity," as social science concepts like power, legitimacy, democracy, among others are context dependent, so forming causal propositions that consider contextual idiosyncrasies that cloud our ability to elucidate specific concepts can lead to better theory building. Second, case studies allow the researcher to "derive new hypotheses" for deviant cases. Whereas traditional, large-n approaches to financial markets increase the number of data points and lose precision as the sample size grows, a targeted single-n study on the global financial crisis can identify the causal links that large-n theorizing ignores. Third, George and Bennett argue that case studies allow the researcher to "explore causal mechanisms" in detailed cases. Fourth, case studies lend themselves to "modeling and assessing complex causal relations," which is important when trying to understand why humanly-devised social systems like markets erupt into crisis, as these domains are rife with feedback loops and deeper, idiosyncratic complexity that large-n case studies can often overlook.

That said, the case study method is not without its faults. George and Bennett identify the following weaknesses of the case study method that the researcher must consider before committing to a case study research design. First, they argue that case studies are subject to case selection bias or picking cases because they share a desired outcome. Selection bias can lead to invalid results because the researcher might ignore negative cases that also share the same proposed causal variables, in turn leading to false confidence in results.[34] Second, George and Bennett argue that case studies do not allow the researcher to test for *variances in scope* of variables. In the parlance of statistics, case studies might not allow the researcher to gauge the magnitude of the variance coefficients of the factors studied. This challenge is stark when considering that this study advances the claim that convention uncertainty leads to financial market instability. More formally, this study argues that convention uncertainty is a *necessary* (if not sufficient—the critical complement being the existence of a fragile financing matrix) condition for initiating financial market instability. Yet a single-case study would make it difficult to conclude that convention uncertainty, coupled with a fragile financial system, generates financial instability *across all cases in all contexts*. Third, George and Bennett argue that case studies might exhibit a "lack of representativeness" that could result in concept stretching if the researcher mechanically jumps to conclusions based on a single case (George and Bennett 2004, 22–30). In other words, even if *Social Finance* explains the global financial crisis, there is a risk that readers could universalize its findings to disparate cases for which the theoretical framework does not apply.

Although it is impossible to address all these weaknesses of the case study method, one of the best defenses against these pitfalls is to be aware of them, so *Social Finance* makes every effort to eschew hyperbole, bias, and ideology when presenting the reader with an argument for taking economic conventions seriously as causal drivers within the case in question. This book does not claim to hold a monopoly of explanation over other interpretations of financial instability across all cases. Rather, it argues that a fuller consideration of economic conventions within pre-established and popular lenses of investigating asset market outcomes such as Post-Keynesian asset market theory lends itself to better theory and greater empirical validity. It is up to the reader to judge the merits of a conventions-based approach compared to alternatives.[35]

Conclusion

The purpose of this chapter was four-fold: first, it placed the present study in its academic context, summarizing the core weaknesses of Post-Keynesian asset market theory and the main theoretical contentions of Keynesian epistemology, Doran's power cycle theory, and economic constructivism. Second, this chapter presented *Social Finance*'s primary theoretical framework, which consists of five inductively derived causal propositions about economic conventions, continuity, and change in financial markets. This chapter linked these propositions to the Post-Keynesian model of financial instability while also discussing their operationalization in the subsequent case study. Third, this chapter discussed this book's ontology and methodological posture of "strong constitutive causality," which treats economic conventions and market outcomes as mutually constituted, endogenous, and recursive. Fourth, the chapter described the operationalization of the *Social Finance* theoretical framework in the context of a representative case study of the global financial crisis. It described the book's empirical methods of counter-factual analysis, process-tracing, and descriptive economic statistics, and the types of evidence marshaled via these techniques to illustrate the applicability of the study's causal propositions.

Having detailed this study's research design, the next four chapters make the empirical case for *Social Finance*. Chapters 3 and 4 operationalize the first two propositions of the study and describe how many of America's systemically important financial institutions adopted risky financing arrangements in tandem with the unsustainable increase in housing prices. Chapter 3 explains how the U.S. economy's upward sloping interest rate term structured followed form Fed monetary policy, which in turn depended on economic conventions. Chapter 4 argues that the emergence of financial fragility was due to several enabling economic conventions, including pro-cyclical conventional expectations in the wholesale funding markets; bank-determined capital charges based on ergodic risk models; and institutionalized, favorable bond ratings for risky asset-backed securities. These factors permitted financial institutions to proliferate risky financing arrangements prior to the global financial crisis, sowing systemic vulnerability when the housing market collapsed.

Notes

1. Jaromir Benes et al., provide an augmented DSGE model to take the financial sector into account. They claim that DSGE models prior to the global financial crisis ignored the critical role that lending markets play in determining macroeconomic equilibria. They also note that most DSGE models omitted the presence of financial frictions caused by financial intermediation, treating bank lending as direct and not intermediated by banks

(Haldane 2012). For a rejoinder to Bank of England Director Andrew Haldane, see Wren-Lewis (2012). For one of the most cited studies on the failure of the "systemic failure of academic economists," (especially those focused on asset markets), see Colander et al. (2009). Recent work to improve DSGE models has focused on incorporating financial frictions into the DSGE framework, but prior to the global financial crisis, there was a general underappreciation of financial factors in DSGE models.
2. As Perry Mehrling argued, DSGE models can be understood as "jazzed up version[s] of the Walrasian equilibrium model that was at the center of the thinking of a previous generation." In such models, "abstraction from monetary plumbing remains of the essence" (Mehrling 2011, 108). This approach contrasts against Post-Keynesian asset market accounts, which describe the monetary system as endogenous, see Lavoie (1984).
3. This book directly addresses this critique of DSGE models by focusing on the *sociological micro-foundations* of actors in understanding macro dynamics.
4. For additional critiques of neoclassical finance, see Bresser-Pereira (2010), Frydman and Goldberg (2011), Mandelbrot and Hudson (2004) (among many other works by Mandelbrot) and Skidelsky (2009). For the neoclassical response both pre- and post-crisis see, Malkiel (2003) and Stiglitz (2010).
5. See, for example Barbera (2009), Soros (2008), and N. Taleb (2007).
6. See, for example Akerlof and Shiller (2009), Dow (2012), and Lo (2017).
7. Displacements can occur for a variety of reasons, such as an unanticipated decline in the price of a valuable commodity, the commercialization of disruptive technology, or wars and other political transitions, to name a few examples. In the Post-Keynesian model, displacements are *exogenous*.
8. See, for example Barbera (2009), Geithner (2014, 68), McCulley (2009), Reuters (2017).
9. Minsky claimed hedge financing units funded themselves primarily via equity and not debt. For a foundational paper on the distinction between liquidity and solvency, see Morton (1939).
10. As subsequent chapters demonstrate, none of the above constraints were present prior to the global financial crisis: firms were risk tolerant; they had access to a wide pool of counterparties eager to purchase money-like liabilities (such as asset-backed commercial paper and repurchase agreements); and the economy had many borrowers willing to supply long-term, speculative debt. Absent the related constraints and coupled with an upward sloping interest rate term structure, Post-Keynesians believe the economy's shift to speculative and Ponzi finance brought about by prolonged stability explains the economy's endogenous tendency to fragility (Minsky 1992, 7–8).

11. Minsky's notion that stability is destabilizing stands in contrast to the neoclassical assumption that equilibria will be self-sustaining absent frictions.
12. Of critical importance to the Post-Keynesian framework its recognition that situations in which self-interested actors trade financial assets can lead to self-fulfilling disequilibrating asset price movements in which prices deviate from fundamental value over a sustained period. Therefore, the Post-Keynesian model affords for both individual (e.g. manias about price increases) and macro-level (e.g. sustained price deviations from fundamentals) irrationality in inflating and sustaining bubbles.
13. Neoclassical finance assumes that the probabilities of future states of the world are both time-invariant and ex ante correct—i.e. historical co-variances establish the range of future co-variances, while agents have a firm understanding of the drivers of future potential states of the world. According to rational expectations, agents' expectations about the future comport with realized future outcomes in a probabilistic sense. While some individual forecasts could be wrong, the expected value of the market's average individual forecast will not have any error (i.e. will be consistent with market prices) (Bossaerts 2002, 41–43).
14. See also Blyth (2009), Keynes (1937a), and Skidelsky (2009, 83–87) on Keynes.
15. Uncertainty as such features prominently in *Social Finance's* empirical and theoretical chapters. For instance, the study's foundational propositions view agents' response to overwhelming uncertainty, economic conventions, as key causal drivers of continuity and change in financial markets. Chapters 5 and 6 also show how market uncertainty about the willingness of banking regulators to serve as liquidity providers of last resort for shadow banking conduits was a key crisis driver—a concept overlooked by orthodox approaches to financial markets and macroeconomics.
16. For an apt discussion of uncertainty, risk, and the global financial crisis, see Nelson and Katzenstein (2014).
17. Minsky himself acknowledges the existence of epistemic blindness prior to crises and places much of this blame on neoclassical approaches themselves that lend themselves to *laissez-faire* approaches, see Minsky (2008), especially Chapter 5, "Perspectives on Theory." The global financial crisis had its own forms of epistemic blindness sowed by multiple actors, including by banks' risk management committees, rating agencies, and policymakers who believed sound policy vanquished macroeconomic volatility, among many others.
18. Still, such methods do not study the micro-foundations of blindness, which is a theoretical focus of this book.
19. Colander et al. argued that the positivist methodology of applied economics, including its formalistic method of logical deduction, leads to results

that are highly internally valid but lack external validity. The authors claim outcomes in the economy take place in a sociological and political context that are highly imprecise, thus muddling the applicability of methodologically-neat conclusions of orthodox models to the real world (Colander et al. 2009).
20. Although Post-Keynesians do not principally focus on the political economy dynamics on how market participants socially construct stable markets, several scholars have applied Post-Keynesian insights to studying financial market phenomena, particularly how market dynamics influence the money supply and broader financial stability. In a foundational article endogenous monetary theory, Marc Lavoie shows how Post-Keynesian theory provides a more realistic understanding of money and banking. Unlike neoclassical accounts of financial markets, endogenous money theory finds that preferences of banks and non-banks for deposits and loans causes the money supply to fluctuate endogenously (Lavoie 1984). In an extension of Lavoie's work, Paul Ramskogler argues that Post-Keynesian notions of endogenous money help researchers understand bank solvency and creditworthiness (Ramskogler 2011). Antonio Alves, et al. show convincingly that balance-sheet structures of individual banks are only partially under the control of bank management. Rather, balance sheet decisions of other banks influence bank management's decisions to expand credit (Alves et al. 2008). For additional foundational texts on Minsky-Kindleberger extensions, see Davidson (2011), Lavoie (2009), and Lavoie (2015).
21. To be sure, subsequent Post-Keynesian literature studied how bursting speculative bubbles trigger financial crashes (see, for example Aglietta 1996, 556). But these accounts do not study the central role that expectations formation and shocks to expectations catalyze financial instability.
22. This book remedies this under specification by providing a description of the causal triggers of financial panics as informed by the causal mechanism within Charles Doran's power cycle theory, a mechanism which he generalized to the problem of forecasting non-linearities and explaining how they can precipitate crisis, see Doran (1991, 1999).
23. For instance, Chapters 4–6 present evidence that the liquidity of shadow banking conduits critically depended on the stability of the market's conventional expectations. When investors feared that fellow investors would ration credit to shadow banking conduits, this dynamic created financial distress.
24. The concept of investors attempting to guess the intentions of fellow investors is colloquially known as a "Keynesian beauty contest." For more, see Allen et al. (2006).

25. Richard N. Cooper and Richard Layard encourage academics from a variety of fields to prioritize improving their forecasting through rigorous analysis and methods. They identify both the difficulty and necessity of forecasting in policy analysis. This account of the central role of forecasting and the need to forecast with more accuracy is consistent with Doran's depiction of the leaders of states in anarchy who constantly attempt to derive accurate forecasts of the future. See Cooper and Layard (2002, 1–16).
26. See also Doran (1989, 2003).
27. There is a rich tradition in international relations scholarship of investigating the role of uncertainty on statecraft. For instance, Peter Katzenstein and Lucia Seybert introduce the concept of "protean power" that focuses on the ability of actors to make sound decisions under uncertainty. By dichotomizing risk and uncertainty, these authors show how statecraft can play a decisive role during international crises. See Katzenstein and Seybert (2018).
28. When a majority of the market's central actors cope with the stress of dealing with this acute uncertainty and given the prevalence of a sufficient number of fragile financing structures (in the Minsky sense), the likelihood of systemic panic rises significantly.
29. Abdelal (2007), Abdelal et al. (2010), Best (2005), Blyth (2002), Matthijs (2011), and McNamara (1998).
30. Daniel Drezner finds that despite the considerable deepening of globalization, there is still significant scope for state agency in a globalized market. Drezner rejects the notion that globalization leads to a race to the bottom in international economic policy. Rather, domestic considerations still give states latitude to respond to globalization in unique ways. This argument is consistent with this book's contention that intervention capacity varies across national contexts even with globalized capital markets (Drezner 2001). Moreover, Jeffrey Frankel claims that despite the deepening of trade and financial globalization since 1950, states still have national autonomy in economic policy. Again, this concept and related argument are consistent with *Social Finance*'s concept of state intervention capacity (Frankel 2000).
31. George Soros identified this mutual dependence of economic ideas and market outcomes as *reflexivity*, see for example Soros (2003).
32. Banks' reliance on short-term funding made them vulnerable to creditor panics, however, and when conventional expectations became unstable, as they did after the failure of Lehman Brothers, financial instability ensued.
33. Keynes himself recognized that markets were plagued by situations in which individually rational behavior led to aggregately irrational outcomes. Keynes' paradox of thrift (if everyone practices austerity at the same time, the system will contract, thus obviating the individual logic

of austerity) and the paradox of liquidity (if everyone sells risky assets and gets liquid at the same time, aggregate systemic liquidity falls) are examples of the *fallacy of composition* (Keynes 1972).
34. This concern is mitigated by the fact that the present study investigates the global economy over a period of *both financial market stability and instability*, so there is adequate variance within the single case to mitigate selection bias.
35. Finally, this study does not endeavor to provide a mutually exclusive explanation for the global financial crisis, nor all financial crises for that matter. Instead, the goal of this book is to show how a theoretical synthesis of different strands of investigating outcomes in complex environments (economics, both neoclassical and Post-Keynesian, on one hand, and ideational studies, including economic constructivism and expectations within power cycle theory, on the other) can enable the researcher to get closer to the limit point of truth of understanding why crises occur. This book's conventions-based account of continuity and change in financial markets sits among other competing paradigms of understanding financial market instability.

WORKS CITED

Abdelal, Rawi. 2007. *Capital Rules: The Construction of Global Finance*. Cambridge: Harvard University Press.

Abdelal, Rawi, Mark Blyth, and Craig Parsons. 2010. *Constructing the International Economy*. Ithaca: Cornell University Press.

Aglietta, Michel. 1996. "Systemic Risk, Financial Innovations, and the Financial Safety Net." In *Money in Motion: The Post Keynesian and Circulation Approaches*, by Ghislain Deleplace and Edward J. Nell (eds.), 552–581. Basingstoke: Macmillan Press.

Akerlof, George A. 1970. "The Market for 'Lemons': Quality Uncertainty and the Market Mechanism." *Quarterly Journal of Economics* 84 (3): 488–500.

Akerlof, George A., and Robert J. Shiller. 2009. *Animal Spirits: How Human Psychology Drives the Economy, and Why It Matters for Global Capitalism*. Princeton: Princeton University Press.

Allen, Franklin, Stephen Morris, and Hyun Song Shin. 2006. "Beauty Contests and Iterated Expectations in Asset Markets." *The Review of Financial Studies* 19 (3): 719–752.

Alves, Jr., Antonio J., Gary A. Dymski, and Luiz-Fernando de Paula. 2008. "Banking Strategy and Credit Expansion: A Post-Keynesian Approach." *Cambridge Journal of Economics* 32 (3): 395–420.

Barbera, Robert J. 2009. *The Cost of Capitalism: Understanding Market Mayhem and Stabilizing Our Economic Future*. New York: McGraw-Hill.

Best, Jacqueline. 2005. *The Limits of Transparency: Ambiguity and the History of International Finance*. Ithaca: Cornell University Press.

Blyth, Mark. 2002. *Great Transformations: Economic Ideas and Institutional Change in the Twentieth Century.* Cambridge: Cambridge University Press.

———. 2009. "Coping with the Black Swan: The Unsettling World of Nassim Taleb." *Critical Review: A Journal of Politics and Society* 21 (4): 447–465.

———. 2011. "Ideas, Uncertainty and Evolution." In *Ideas and Politics in Social Science Research*, by Robert Cox and Daniel Beland (eds.), 83–101. Oxford: Oxford University Press.

———. 2013. "This Time It Really Is Different." In *The Third Globalization: Can Wealthy Nations Stay Rich in the Twenty-First Century?* by Dan Breznitz and John Zysman (eds.), 207–231. Oxford: Oxford University Press.

Blyth, Mark, and Matthias Matthijs. 2017. "Black Swans, Lame Ducks, and the Mystery of IPEs Missing Macroeconomy." *Review of International Political Economy* 203–231.

Bossaerts, Peter. 2002. *The Paradox of Asset Pricing.* Princeton: Princeton University Press.

Boyland, Thomas A., and Paschal F. O'Gorman. 2013. "Post-Keynesian Economics, Rationality, and Conventions." In *The Oxford Handbook of Post-Keynesian Economics: Volume 2*, by Geoffrey C. Harcourt and Peter Kriesler (eds.), 62–79. Oxford: Oxford University Press.

Bresser-Pereira, Luiz Carlos. 2010. "The Global Financial Crisis and a New Capitalism?" *Journal of Post Keynesian Economics* 32 (4): 499–534.

Chick, Victoria. 2013. "Endogenising Uncertainty." *Annual Plenary Conference of the Institute for New Economic Thinking (INET)*, 1–12 Hong Kong: Institute for New Economic Thinking.

Colander, David, Hans Follmer, Armin Haas, Michael Goldberg, Katarina Juselius, Alan Kirman, Thomas Lux, and Brigette Sloth. 2009. "The Financial Crisis and the Systemic Failure of Academic Economics." *Kiel Working Papers* (Kiel Institute for the World Economy) 17.

Colander, David, Peter Howitt, Alan Kirman, Axel Leijonhufvud, and Perry Mehrling. 2008. "Beyond DSGE Models: Toward an Empirically Based Macroeconomics." *Middlebury College Economics Discussion Paper* 1–12.

Cooper, Richard N., and Richard Layard. 2002. *What the Future Holds.* Cambridge: MIT Press.

Crotty, James. 1994. "Are Keynesian Uncertainty and Macrotheory Incompatible? Conventional Decision Making, Institutional Structures and Conditional Stability in Keynesian Macromodels." In *New Perspectives in Monetary Macroeconomics: Explorations in the Tradition of Hyman Minsky*, by G. Dymski and R. Pollin (eds.), 105–142. Ann Arbor: University of Michigan Press.

Davidson, Paul. 2011. *Post Keynesian Macroeconomic Theory: A Foundation for Successful Economic Policies for the Twenty-First Century.* Northampton: Edward Elgar.

Davidson, Paul. 1993. "The Elephant and the Butterfly: Or Hysteresis and Post Keynesian Economics." *Journal of Post Keynesian Economics* 15 (3): 309–322.

Doran, Charles F. 2003. "Economics, Philosophy of History, and the "Single Dynamic" of Power Cycle Theory: Expectations, Competition, and Statecraft." *International Political Science Review* 24 (1): 13–49.

Doran, Charles F. 1989. "Systemic Disequilibrium: Foreign Policy Role and the Power Cycle Challenge for Research Design." *Journal of Conflict Resolution* 33: 371–401.

———. 1991. *Systems in Crisis: New Imperatives of High Politics at Century's End*. Cambridge: Cambridge University Press.

———. 1971. *The Politics of Assimilation: Hegemony and Its Aftermath*. Baltimore: Johns Hopkins University Press.

Doran, Charles F. 1999. "Why Forecasts Fail: The Limits and Potential of Forecasting in International Relations and Economics." *International Studies Review* 1 (2): 11–41.

Doran, Charles F., and Wes Parsons. 1980. "War and the Cycle of Relative Power." *The American Political Science Review* 74 (4): 947–965.

Dow, Sheila C. 2012. *Foundations for New Economic Thinking*. New York: Palgrave Macmillan.

Dow, Sheila C. 2013. "Keynes on Knowledge, Expectations, and Rationality." In *Rethinking Expectations: The Way Forward for Macroeconomics*, by Roman Frydman and Edmund S. Phelps (eds.), 112–129. Princeton: Princeton University Press.

Drezner, Daniel W. 2001. "Globalization and Policy Convergence." *International Studies Review* 3 (1): 53–78.

Fenton-O'Creevy, Mark, Nigel Nicholson, Emma Soane, and Paul Willman. 2007. *Traders: Risks, Decisions, and Management in Financial Markets*. Oxford: Oxford University Press.

Frankel, Jeffrey A. 2000. "Globalization of the Economy." In *Governance in the Globalizing World*, by Joseph S. Nye and John D. Donahue (eds.), 45–71. Washington: Brookings.

Frydman, Roman, and Michael D. Goldberg. 2011. *Beyond Mechanical Markets: Asset Price Swings, Risk, and the Role of the State*. Princeton: Princeton University Press.

Geithner, Timothy F. 2014. *Stress Test: Reflections on Financial Crises*. New York: Crown Publishers.

George, Alexander L., and Andrew Bennett. 2004. *Case Studies and Theory Development in the Social Sciences*. Cambridge: MIT Press.

George, Alexander L., and Timothy J. McKeown. 1985. "Case Studies and Theories of Organizational Decision Making." *Advances in Information Processing in Organizations* 2: 21–58.

Gerring, John. 2007. "Is There a (Viable) Crucial-Case Method?" *Comparative Political Studies* 40 (3): 231–253.

Gorton, Gary B. 2010. *Slapped by the Invisible Hand: The Panic of 2007*. Oxford: Oxford University Press.

Gorton, Gary B., and Andrew Metrick. 2010b. "Haircuts." *Federal Reserve Bank of St. Louis Review* 92 (6): 507–519.

Haldane, Andrew. 2012. "VoxEU." *What Have the Economists Ever Done for Us?* October 1. Accessed December 3, 2017. http://voxeu.org/article/what-have-economists-ever-done-us.

Harcourt, Geoffrey Colin. 2008. "The Structure of Post-Keynesian Economics: The Core Contributions of the Pioneers." In *The Continuing Relevance of 'The General Theory'*, by Mathew Forstater and L. Randall Wray (eds.), 185–190. New York: Palgrave MacMillian.

Harcourt, Geoffrey Colin, and Peter Kriesler. 2013. *The Oxford Handbook of Post-keynesian Economics: Volumes 1 and 2*. Oxford: Oxford University Press.

Katzenstein, Peter J., and Lucia A. Seybert. 2018. *Protean Power: Exploring the Uncertain and Unexpected in World Politics*. Cambridge: Cambridge University Press.

Keen, Steve. 2017. *Can We Avoid Another Financila Crisis? (The Future of Capitalism)*. Cambridge: Polity Press.

Keynes, John M. 1972. "Francis Ysidro Edgeworth 1845–1926." In *Essays in Biography. Collecting Writings Volume X*, by Royal Economic Society. London: Macmillan.

Keynes, John M. 1936. *The General Theory of Employment, Interest and Money*. Cambridge: Cambridge University Press (1972).

———. 1937a. "The General Theory of Employment." *The Quarterly Journal of Economics* 51 (2): 209–223.

———. 1937b. "Some Economic Consequences of a Declining Population." *The Eugenics Review* 13–17.

Kindleberger, Charles P., and Robert Aliber. 2005. *Manias, Panics, and Crashes: A History of Financial Crises*. Hoboken: Wiley.

King, Gary, Robert O. Keohane, and Sidney Verba. 1994. *Designing Social Inquiry: Scientific Inference in Qualitative Research*. Princeton: Princeton University Press.

Kirshner, Jonathan. 2003. "Money Is Politics." *Review of International Political Economy* 10 (4): 645–660.

Knight, Frank H. 1921. *Risk, Uncertainty, and Profit*. Chicago: University of Chicago Press.

Krasner, Stephen D. 1982. "Structural Causes and Regime Consequences: Regimes as Intervening Variables." *International Organization* 36 (2): 185–205.

Krugman, Paul. 2009. "How Did Economists Get It So Wrong?" *The New York Times Magazine*, September 2.

Lavoie, Marc. 2009. *Introduction to Post-Keynesian Economics*. Basingstoke: Palgrave Macmillan.

———. 2015. *Post-Keynesian Economics: New Foundations*. Nothampton: Edward Elgar.

Lavoie, Marc. 1984. "The Endogenous Flow of Credit and the Post Keynesian Theory of Money." *Journal of Economic Issues* 18 (3): 771–797.
Lebow, R. Ned. 2009. "Constitutive Causality: Imagined Spaces and Political Practices." *Millenium: Journal of International Studies* 38 (2): 211–239.
Leijonhufvud, Axel. 2009. "Out of the Corridor: Keynes and the Crisis." *Cambridge Journal of Economics* 33 (4): 741–757.
Lo, Andrew. 2017. *Adaptive Markets: Financial Evolution at the Speed of Thought.* Princeton: Princeton University Press.
Malkiel, Burton G. 2003. "The Efficient Market Hypothesis and Its Critics." *Journal of Economic Perspectives* 17 (1): 59–82.
Mandelbrot, Benoit, and Richard L. Hudson. 2004. *The Misbehavior of Markets: A Fractal View of Financial Turbulence.* New York: Basic Books.
Matthijs, Matthias. 2011. *Ideas and Economic Crisis in Britain from Attlee to Blair (1945–2005).* London: Routledge.
McCulley, Paul A. 2009. *PIMCO.com.* May. Accessed December 3, 2017. https://www.pimco.com/en-us/insights/economic-and-market-commentary/global-central-bank-focus/the-shadow-banking-system-and-hyman-minskys-economic-journey/.
McNamara, Kathleen R. 1998. *The Currency of Ideas: Monetary Politics in the European Union.* Ithaca: Cornell University Press.
Mehrling, Perry. 2011. *The New Lombard Street: How the Fed Became the Dealer of Last Resort.* Princeton, NJ: Princeton University Press.
Minsky, Hyman. 1982. *Can "It" Happen Again? Essays on Instability and Finance.* Armonk, NY: M. E. Sharpe.
———. 2008. *Stabilizing an Unstable Economy.* New York: McGraw-Hill.
Minsky, Hyman. 1992. "The Financial Instability Hypothesis." *Levy Economics Institute of Bard College Working Papers* 1–9.
Morton, Walter A. 1939. "Liquidity and Solvency." *The American Economic Review* 29 (2): 272–285.
Nelson, Stephen C., and Peter J. Katzenstein. 2014. "Uncertainty, Risk, and the Financial Crisis of 2008." *International Organization* 68 (2): 361–392.
Odell, John S. 2001. "Case Study Methods in International Political Economy." *International Studies Perspectives* 2: 161–176.
Pierce, Andrew. 2008. "The Telegraph." *The Queen Asks Why No One Saw the Credit Crunch Coming.* November 5. Accessed December 3, 2017. http://www.telegraph.co.uk/news/uknews/theroyalfamily/3386353/The-Queen-asks-why-no-one-saw-the-credit-crunch-coming.html.
Pierson, Paul. 2000. "Increasing Returns, Path Dependence, and the Study of Politics." *American Political Science Review* 94 (2): 251–267.
Pindyck, Robert S., and Daniel L. Rubinfeld. 2013. *Microeconomics*, 8th ed. Upper Saddle River: Pearson.
Ramskogler, Paul. 2011. "Credit Money, Collateral and the Solvency of Banks: A Post Keynesian Analysis of Credit Market Failures." *Review of Political Economy* 23 (1): 69–79.

Reuters. 2017. *Reuters.com*. October 19. https://www.reuters.com/article/us-china-congress-debt-minskymoment/china-central-bank-warns-against-minsky-moment-due-to-excessive-optimism-idUSKBN1CO0D6.

Ruggie, John Gerard. 1998. "What Makes the World Hang Together? Neo-Utilitarianism and the Social Constructivist Challenge." *International Organization* 52 (4): 855–885.

Runde, Jochen, and Sohei Mizuhara. 2003. *The Philosophy of Keynes's Economics: Probability, Uncertainty and Convention*. London: Routledge.

Schinasi, Gary J. 2004. "Defining Financial Stability." *IMF Working Paper* 4 (187): 1–19.

Sent, Esther-Mirjam. 2004. "Behavioral Economics: How Psychology Made Its (Limited) Way Back into Economics." *History of Political Economy* 36 (4): 735–760.

Simmons, Helen. 2009. *Case Study Research in Practice*. London: Sage.

Skidelsky, Robert. 2009. *Keynes: Return of the Master*. New York: Public Affairs.

Soros, George. 2003. *The Alchemy of Finance*. Hoboken: Wiley.

———. 2008. *The New Paradigm for Financial Markets: The Credit Crash of 2008 and What It Means*. New York: Public Affairs.

Stiglitz, Joseph. 2010. *The Non-existent Hand*. April 22. Accessed January 2, 2017. https://www.lrb.co.uk/v32/n08/joseph-stiglitz/the-non-existent-hand.

Stiglitz, Joseph. 2018. "Where Modern Macroeconomics Went Wrong." *Oxford Review of Economic Policy* 34 (1–2): 70–106.

Taleb, Nassim. 2004. *Fooled by Randomness: The Hidden Role of Chance in the Markets and in Life*. New York: Texere.

Taleb, Nassim. 2007. *The Black Swan: The Impact of the Highly Improbable*. New York: Random House.

The Financial Crisis Inquiry Commission. 2011. *The Financial Crisis Inquiry Report: Final Report of the National Commission on the Causes of the Financial and Economic Crisis in the United States*. Washington, DC: U.S. Government Printing Office.

Thomas, Gary. 2011. "A Typology for the Case Study in Social Science Following a Review of Definition, Discourse, and Structure." *Qualitative Inquiry* 17 (6): 511–521.

Weber, Max. [1905] 1949. "Critical Studies in the Logic of the Cultural Sciences." In *The Methodology of the Social Sciences*, by Edward A. Shils and Henry A. Fluch (eds.). New York: Free Press.

Wendt, Alexander. 1998. "On Constitution and Causation in International Relations." In *International Relations, 1919–1999*, by Tim Dunne, Michael Cox and Ken Booth (eds.), 101–117. Cambridge: Cambridge University Press.

Wolf, Martin. 2018. "Economics Failed Us Before the Global Crisis." *Financial Times*. March 20. Accessed May 10, 2018. https://www.ft.com/content/28e2f9ac-2b66-11e8-9b4b-bc4b9f08f381.

CHAPTER 3

Monetary Policy and the Housing Bubble

Introduction

This is the first of four empirical chapters of *Social Finance*. This chapter and Chapter 4 study the conventional forces that enabled the US economy's shift from stability to fragility in the decade prior to the global financial crisis. These chapters demonstrate the utility of the first two theoretical propositions of *Social Finance*: first, that economic conventions stabilize markets while also facilitating the endogenous transition from stability to fragility, and second, economic conventions blind market participants to the possibility of nonroutine change in markets. Recall that Hyman Minsky argued that economic fragility followed from four factors: (1) an upward-sloping interest rate term structure that created incentives for financial institutions to issue short-term debt to fund their purchase of longer-term risky assets via credit, liquidity, and maturity transformation; (2) risk tolerance among financial institutions to engage in interest rate term structure arbitrage with low precautionary buffers; (3) the presence of counterparties willing to purchase financial institutions' short-term, money-like liabilities; and (4) borrowers willing to emit longer-dated, risky debt.

Figure 3.1 depicts a schematic of this chapter's argument. Briefly, this chapter studies the economic conventions behind the Federal Reserve's accommodative monetary policy prior to the global financial crisis. It argues that after the deflation of the technology stock bubble in 2001, the US Federal Reserve adopted an accommodative monetary policy

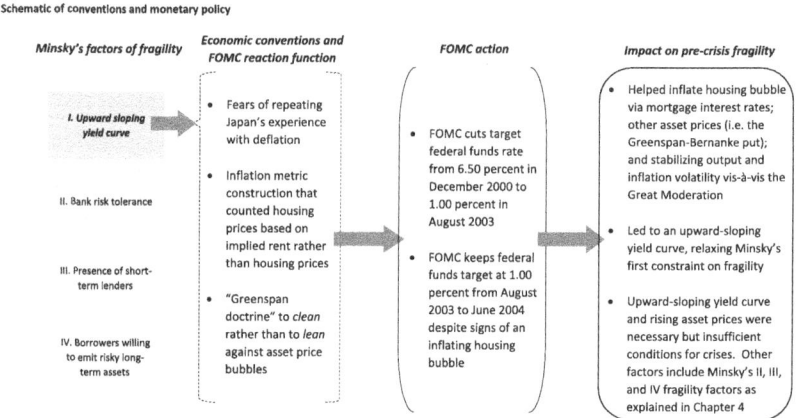

Fig. 3.1 Schematic of conventions and monetary policy (Author)

by decreasing the target federal funds rate to 1.00% from 6.50%, causing the benchmark United States yield curve to become upward sloping and providing opportunities for banks to engage in interest rate term structure arbitrage. Several economic conventions explain this monetary policy stance and yield curve steepening, including the Federal Reserve's Federal Open Market Committee's (FOMC) memory of Japan's experience with deflation; how the FOMC counted housing prices in their preferred inflation metrics; and FOMC members' philosophical approach to asset price bubbles. Accommodative monetary policy helped inflate the housing bubble by impacting other housing-related interest rates, inflating other asset prices, and stabilizing output and inflation volatility. Different economic conventions may have led to different monetary policy choices, potentially averting the relaxation of Minsky's first constraint on fragility.

Monetary Policy After the 2001 Recession

Like the 2000s, which bore witness to the housing bubble, the late 1990s had its own version of "irrational exuberance" in the public equity markets. The NASDAQ composite, a stock index of technology companies, increased over 200% from 1500 in August 1998 to nearly 4700 in February 2000, with many of its constituent companies having stock prices worth several hundred times annual earnings (Brunnermeier and Nagel 2004).[1] It did not take long for the stock market's momentum to succumb to fundamental economic realities, however, and from 2000 to 2002, the NASDAQ composite stock index lost 70% of its value (see Fig. 3.2).

The deflation of the technology stock bubble, along with the September 11 terrorist attacks, caused the US economy to fall into recession in 2001. GDP growth contracted 1.3% and 1.1% on a quarter-on-quarter annualized basis in the first and third quarters of that year, respectively, while the unemployment rate increased from 4% in 2000 to just above 6% in 2003 (see Figs. 3.3 and 3.4). In 2002, a wave of corporate scandals hit Wall Street, further compounding the dynamic of economic uncertainty.

In response to falling equity markets, contracting output, and rising unemployment, the Federal Reserve's interest rate-setting body, the FOMC, cut the target federal funds rate from 6.50% in January 2001 to 1.00% by June 2003.[2] Accommodative monetary policy succeeded in

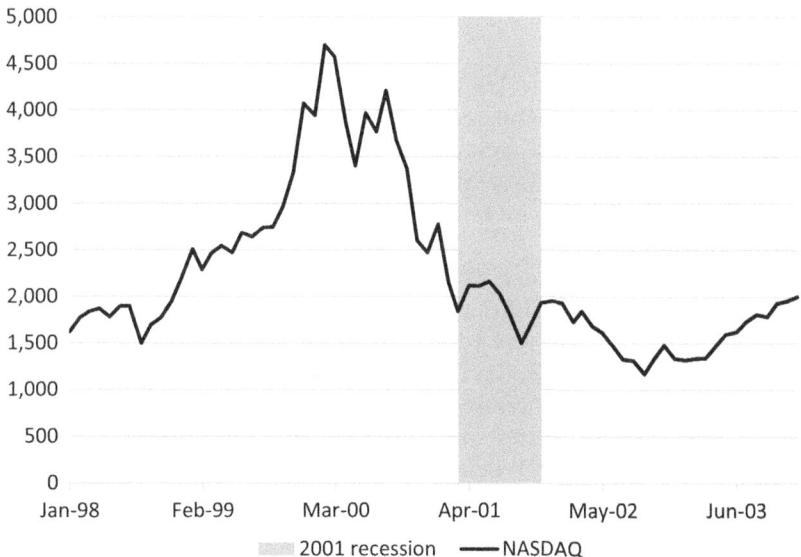

Fig. 3.2 The NASDAQ composite boom and bust: 1998–2003 (Federal Reserve Economic Data)

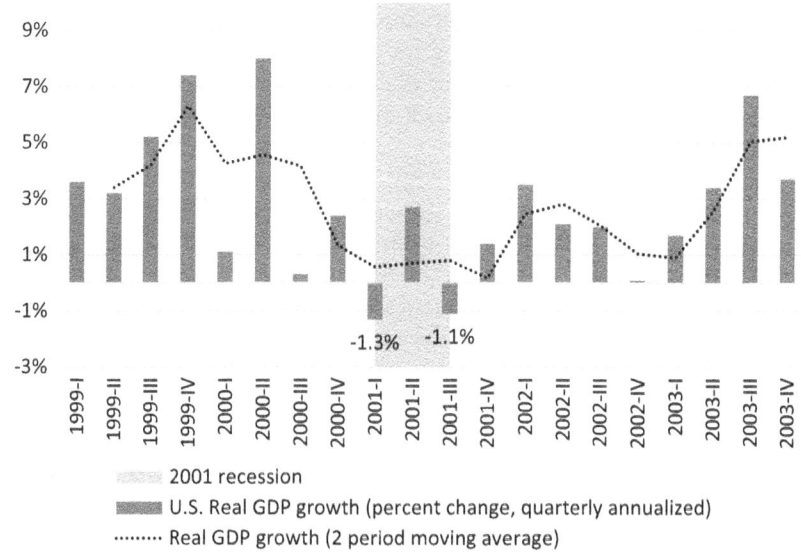

Fig. 3.3 US GDP growth: 1999–2003 (US Bureau of Economic Analysis)

cushioning growth in the US economy, as the 2000–2002 contraction was relatively shallow compared with other postwar recessions, though unemployment remained elevated throughout 2003 (Bernanke 2010).[3] The FOMC chose to keep interest rates at 1.00% from July 2003 through June 2004, despite evidence that the US economy, and housing prices, were heating up.

Indeed, there is evidence that lax monetary policy correlated with rising housing prices from 2001 to 2007. In 2002, the average annual federal funds effective rate was 1.7%, and home prices increased 15% over the same period. In 2003, the Fed's policy rate hovered near 1% on average, while home prices increased another 13%. When the Fed was debating whether to raise interest rates in 2004, housing inflation spiked to roughly 19% on the year. When the FOMC tightened monetary policy in 2006 and kept the federal funds rate at 5.00% on average, housing prices increased a scant 0.2% (see Table 3.1 and Fig. 3.5). Based on the below annual averages, the effective federal funds rate inversely correlated with housing prices approximately −0.85 from 2001 to 2007.

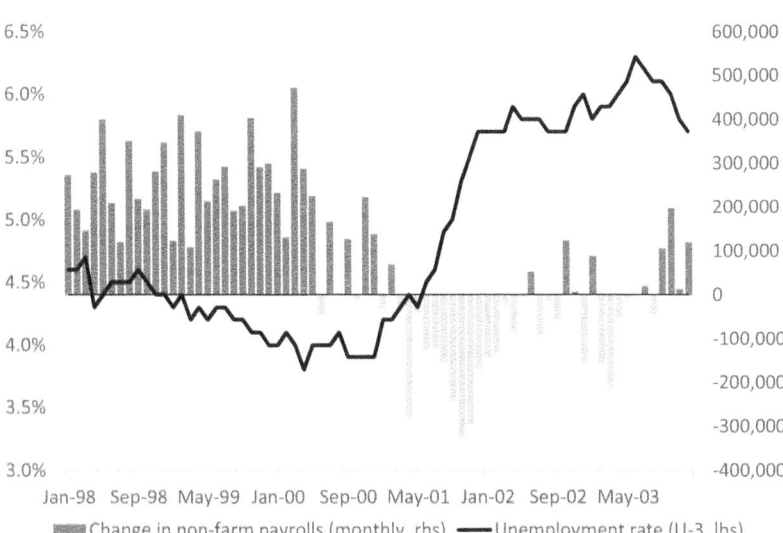

Fig. 3.4 US unemployment rate and job creation: 1998–2003 (US Bureau of Labor Statistics)

Table 3.1 Average annual federal funds rate and change in housing prices (Federal Reserve Bank of St. Louis 2018)

Year	Federal funds effective rate (average annual level %)	Change in national home prices (percent change y/y %)
2001	3.7	8.9
2002	1.7	15.0
2003	1.1	13.4
2004	1.3	18.7
2005	3.2	15.9
2006	5.0	0.2
2007	5.0	−9.8

Still, the existence of an inverse correlation between interest rates and rising housing prices does not necessarily mean there was a causal relationship between these variables. To see the link between monetary policy and housing prices, it is necessary to study how accommodative

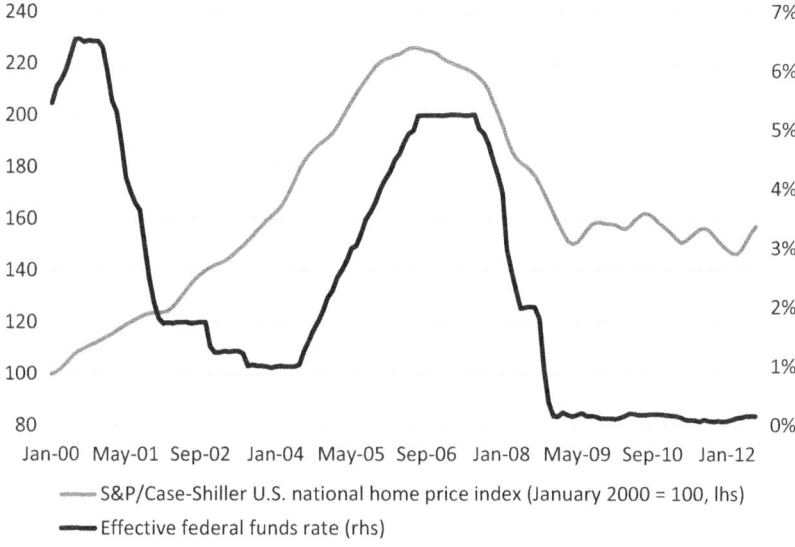

Fig. 3.5 Monetary policy and US housing prices: 2000–2012 (Federal Reserve Economic Data, Standard & Poor's)

monetary policy interacted with several other variables that impact the housing market. These intermediating factors between monetary policy and housing prices included mortgage-related interest rates; other asset prices; and output and unemployment volatility. These factors, coupled with bubble-permissive global macroeconomic conditions (discussed briefly at the end of this chapter), created an upward-sloping interest rate term structure in the US economy after the 2001 recession.

The first channel through which accommodative monetary policy affected housing prices was by reducing interest rates tied to real estate investment, in turn adding incremental demand to the housing market. The federal funds rate is the interest rate at which banks borrow from one another on an overnight basis to maintain their Fed-mandated required reserves. If banks can borrow cheaply in the federal funds market, so the theory goes, then they will be more inclined to lend at lower interest rates to other borrowers. Therefore, when the Fed wants to stimulate the economy, it will lower the federal funds target rate to loosen financial conditions and encourage economic activity. When the Fed wants to contain inflation and curtail economic activity (usually to combat demand-pull inflation pressures), the Fed will raise interest rates to reduce lending, consumption, investment, output, and prices.

There is a correlation between the federal funds rate and those interest rates tied to residential real estate investment, which could have contributed to the market's irrational exuberance in the housing market (Greenspan 2005). From early 2001 through mid-2004, when the FOMC cut the federal funds rate from above 6.00 to 1.00%, thirty-year fixed mortgage rates fell from above 8.00 to 5.00%. From January 2000 through December 2008, the thirty-year conventional mortgage rate had a 0.66 correlation to the federal funds effective rate based on monthly data (see Fig. 3.6). Lower policy interest rates also affected real interest rates, as measured by the yield on the 1997-issued 10-year Treasury Inflation Protected Security (TIPS). From 1997 to 2006, the TIPS yield correlated approximately 0.84 to the federal funds rate and appears to fall lock-step with the Fed's interest rate cutting cycle in 2001 to 2003, falling from just above 4.00% in 2000 to less than 0.00% by early 2004 (see Fig. 3.7).

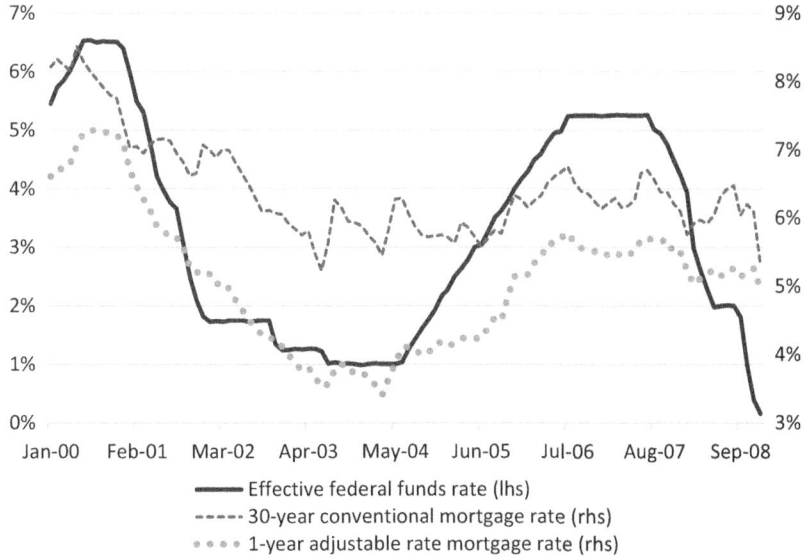

Fig. 3.6 Monetary policy and selected mortgage rates: 2000–2008 (Federal Reserve Economic Data)

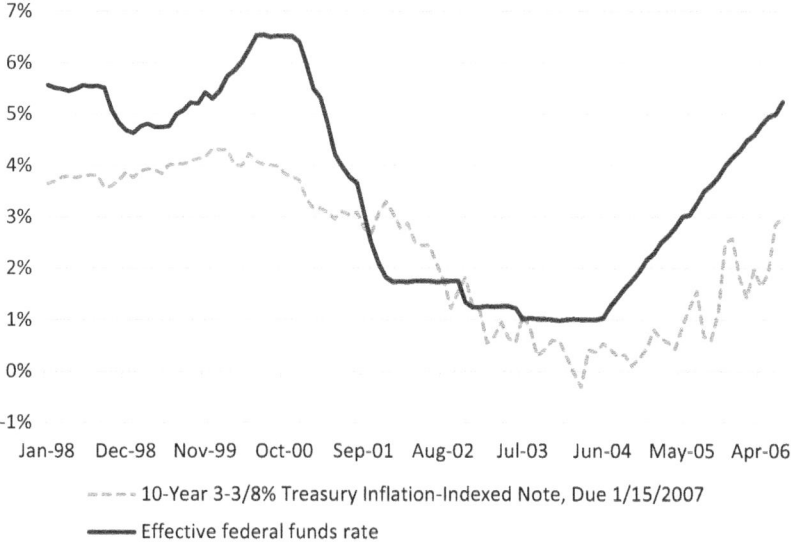

Fig. 3.7 Monetary policy and real interest rates: 1998–2006 (Federal Reserve Economic Data)

Low interest rates also allowed mortgage originators to offer adjustable-rate mortgages (ARM) to borrowers with poor credit histories, many of whom borrowed at low "teaser" rates tied to short-term interest rates. From 2000 through 2008, adjustable mortgage rates had a 0.86 correlation to the federal funds effective rate. When the FOMC raised interest rates, these teaser interest rates rose as well, increasing borrowers' monthly payments and their likelihood of default. Anthony Sanders argued that the Fed's rate tightening cycle was an important determinant in the timing of rising defaults after the housing bubble burst and claimed that the "payment shock" accompanied by higher interest rates in 2006 was "enormous" for ARM homeowners (Sanders 2008, 256). Using Bayesian vector autoregression techniques, Federal Reserve economists Marek Jarociński and Frank Smets found that monetary policy had a "significant effect on housing investment and house prices," concluding that "easy monetary policy… contributed to the boom in the housing market in 2004 and 2005" (Jarociński and Smets 2008, 362). Other factors such as the rise of global macroeconomic imbalances facilitated by low investment and high precautionary savings in current account surplus countries such as emerging Asia, China, and Germany, may have contributed to the decline in benchmark interest rates as well (Dunaway 2009; Schwartz 2009; Obstfeld and Rogoff 2009; Wolf 2008, 2014).

The second channel by which monetary policy affected housing demand was via other asset prices in the economy, including stock prices. According to Barry Eichengreen, lax monetary policy tended to increase equity valuations, which made banks more likely to lend across sectors. Higher share prices also made consumers feel wealthier and more willing to spend money on consumption and assets, including housing (Eichengreen 2011, 113). Andrew Smithers found that low short-term interest rates created "excessive liquidity" in the loanable funds market, which served as a "major transmission mechanism between monetary policy and aggregate demand" (Smithers 2009, 3–5). Harold Vogel argued that based on his empirical tests, accommodative monetary policy can have an appreciable effect on asset prices: past a certain point of the real economy's absorption capacity, excess capital caused by accommodative monetary policy can "spill over" into "leverageable financial assets," including housing assets (Vogel 2009, 224).

Moreover, some commentators believed that the FOMC implicitly targeted asset prices when formulating monetary policy. This notion, colloquially described as the "Greenspan-Bernanke Put," held that the Federal Reserve, led by Chairmen Alan Greenspan and later Ben Bernanke, cut interest rates to buoy market confidence whenever share valuations fell past a certain level. Expected lax monetary policy in the case of declining asset prices provided an insurance policy to markets, increasing the risk tolerance of market participants and further fueling to the mania in housing prices during the 2000s (Goodhart 2009). Anecdotal evidence supports the case for the existence of the Greenspan (and later Bernanke) put option for markets. After every recession in the United States since the 1980s, the FOMC responded with monetary accommodation (Federal Reserve Bank of St. Louis 2018). The real economy rebounded during these periods (with unemployment lagging), and the financial economy took off as well. The Greenspan Put helps explain a source of moral hazard among equity market investors, many of whom may have believed that the Fed would intervene and bail out equity investors when valuations fall beyond a certain point (Miller et al. 2001).

The third channel by which monetary policy contributed to the US housing bubble was by stabilizing output and unemployment volatility. Throughout the mid-2000s, the US economy exhibited signs of resilience and stability, leading some policymakers to hypothesize that the United States underwent a macroeconomic shift that conquered economic volatility. In 2004, Ben Bernanke gave a speech about the decline in macroeconomic volatility in the United States since the 1980s, noting that based on most macroeconomic aggregates, including the variability of quarterly GDP growth and quarterly inflation, US macroeconomic volatility was declining. He termed this development the "Great Moderation." Bernanke argued that sound macroeconomic management by the Federal Reserve had improved the resilience of the economy, since better monetary policy could lessen the sensitivity of wage and price functions to external shocks. Better managed monetary policy could dampen inflation expectations, making firms less likely to pass on the costs of commodity price shocks to customers, thus insulating the broader economy from macroeconomic volatility (Bernanke 2004).[4]

By calculating the coefficients of variation of GDP growth and inflation, this book found evidence that from 1970 to 2008, macroeconomic volatility in growth and inflation declined in the United States since 1970 (see Figs. 3.8 and 3.9). The coefficient of variation allows the researcher to normalize and control for scalar changes in underlying series. In this case, the coefficients of variation are found by using the three-year rolling standard deviations of the variables in question and normalizing them across the three-year rolling sample mean. Reduced macroeconomic volatility, as evidenced in this book's GDP and inflation volatility series, may have lulled financial market participants into taking more risk, per a Minsky process of stability begetting fragility over time (Keen 2011; Kohn 2008).[5]

Furthermore, this rapid decline in short-term interest rates caused the US Treasury yield curve to become upward sloping during the FOMC's rate cutting cycle from December 2000 through August 2003, during which the FOMC cut the target federal funds rate 550 basis points to stimulate the economy in the wake of the 2001 recession. Over the course of the rate cutting cycle, the difference in yield between three-month Treasury bills and ten-year Treasury bonds rose from about −82 basis points (i.e. an inverted yield curve) to 350 basis points (see Fig. 3.10). This rise in term structure yield spreads created an opportunity for financial institutions to engage in interest rate term structure

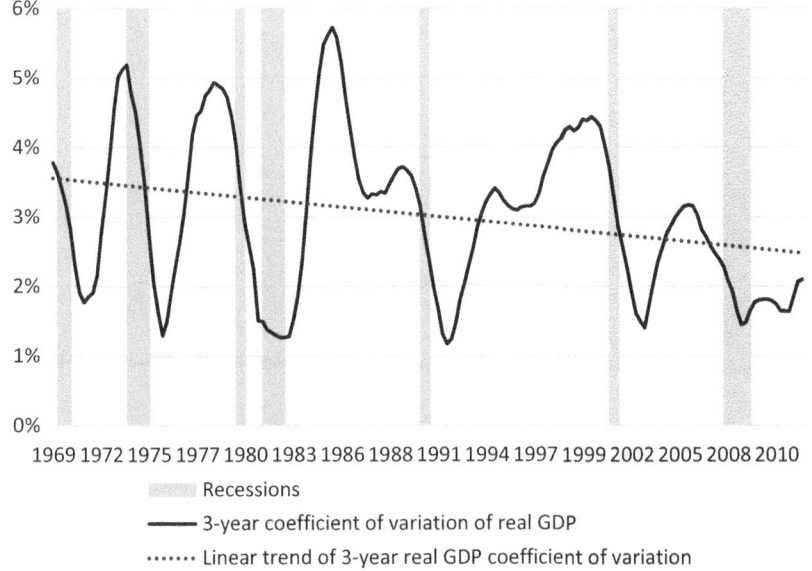

Fig. 3.8 GDP volatility: 1969–2012 (US Bureau of Economic Analysis, author calculations)

arbitrage by issuing short-term debt to accumulate long-term assets. During the period following the FOMC's rate cutting cycle, short-term debt issuance in the form of asset-backed commercial paper (ABCP) and repurchase agreements ("repo") took off, as argued in the subsequent chapter. As Minsky argued, an upward-sloping interest rate term structure is a necessary precondition for an economy's shift from stability to fragility over time.

Economic Conventions and Monetary Policy

Given the potential causal importance of US monetary policy to US housing market outcomes, this chapter now explains the economic conventions that motivated the Fed's precrisis monetary policy. These conventions include the Fed's fears of repeating Japan's historical experience with deflation, how Fed technocrats measured inflation in the US economy, and the FOMC's widespread belief in the "Greenspan Doctrine" regarding central bank posture toward asset price bubbles. This chapter

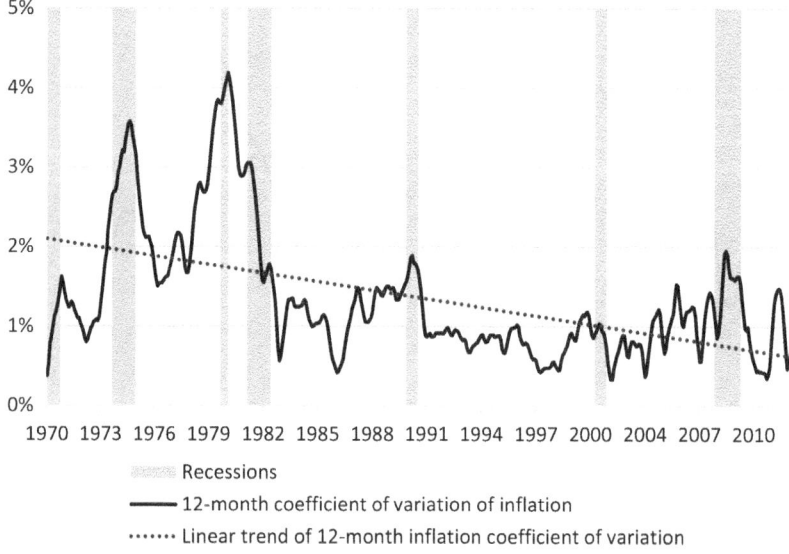

Fig. 3.9 Inflation volatility: 1969–2012 (US Bureau of Labor Statistics, author calculations)

proposes that these economic conventions motivated the FOMC to cut short-term interest rates from 6.50% in November 2000 to 1.00% by August 2003 and to keep them at 1.00% through June 2004, despite evidence of a growing housing bubble.

The first economic convention that motivated the Federal Reserve's monetary policy was the Fed's fears of the US economy falling into a deflationary spiral, much like Japan did in the 1990s. From 2002 to 2004, fears of deflation loomed large in the minds of the Federal Reserve's central bankers. As a result, FOMC members believed that accommodative monetary policy might have been necessary to stave off deflation in the US economy.

To see why the FOMC was so concerned about deflation, it is worth discussing some macroeconomic theory. While the Federal Reserve sets nominal short-term interest rates, real interest rates are the primary transmission mechanism between monetary policy and the real economy. Economist Irving Fisher points out that the real interest rate is equal to nominal interest rates less the inflation rate. Central banks can lower

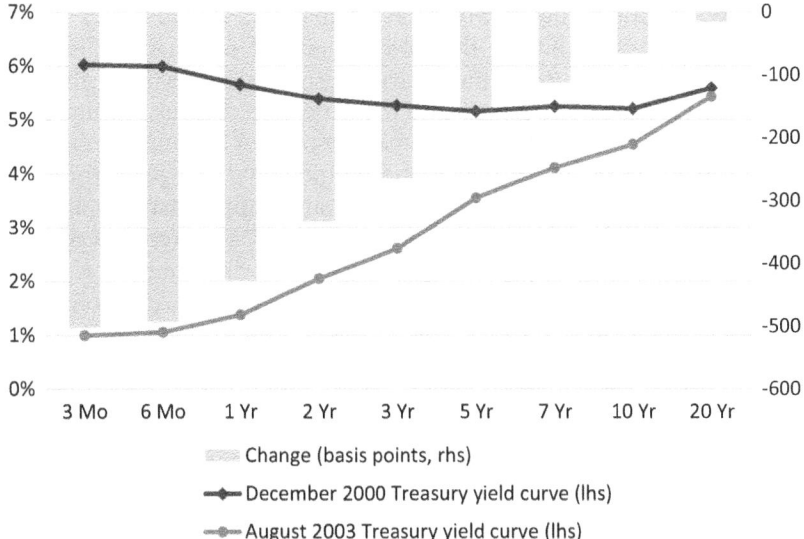

Fig. 3.10 US Treasury yield curve: December 2000 vs. August 2003 (U.S. Department of the Treasury 2018, author calculations)

nominal interest rates to 0%, though the lowest real interest rate possible (i.e. the most accommodative potential monetary policy rate) is the negative inflation rate. For example, if inflation were 3% annually and nominal interest rates were zero, then the lower bound of monetary policy would be real interest rates of negative 3% (Levi and Makin 1978).

The Fisher relationship highlights the circumstances under which monetary policy might not be effective at spurring growth: with deflation (or more formally, negative inflation), real interest rates rise as the price level falls. Left unchecked, the momentum of falling prices can lead to a deflationary spiral wherein rising real interest rates depress consumption and investment, leading to lower aggregate demand, falling prices and further increasing real interest rates, leading to a phenomenon that Keynes identified as a "liquidity trap." Under these conditions, the momentum of falling prices might render traditional monetary policy ineffective (Krugman et al. 1998; Sutch 2014).

Fears of repeating Japan's experience with deflation contributed to the Fed's precrisis accommodative monetary policy. According to Ben

Bernanke, in 2002, the FOMC worried that the United States might experience deflation, hitting the lower bound of monetary policy and rendering monetary policy ineffective to spurring growth in the US economy. Bernanke claimed that at the time, the consensus opinion of the FOMC was that when facing the prospect of deflation, monetary policy should become preemptively accommodative to avoid hitting the lower bound of policy interest rates. Bernanke noted that the FOMC "[took] note of the painful experience of Japan" and recognized that the Fed may hit the zero bound of policy, in turn "limiting the scope of further monetary accommodation." Therefore, "FOMC decisions during [2002–2004] were informed by a *strong consensus* among researchers that, when faced with the risk of hitting the zero lower bound, policymakers should lower interest rates preemptively, thereby reducing the probability of ultimately being constrained by the lower bound on the policy interest rate" (Bernanke 2010).[6] In this way, the FOMC viewed the potential for above-target inflation as a cost worth bearing to avoid deflation, even if it meant the economy could overheat for some period.

In a 2002 study, Federal Reserve economists Alan Ahearne, Joseph Gagnon, Jane Haltmaier, and Steve Kamin argued that when on the verge of a deflationary spiral, both fiscal and monetary stimulus "should go beyond the levels conventionally implied by baseline forecasts of future inflation and economic activity" (Ahearne et al. 2002, 1). As Frederic Mishkin argues, Ahearne et al.'s findings might have influenced the thinking of FOMC members in the early 2000s (Mishkin 2011, 20). FOMC minutes from 2003 reveal that the Fed fixated on the prospect of a Japan-style deflationary trap, which cemented the FOMC's consensus to cut interest rates and keep them low. At the June and December 2003 FOMC meetings, Fed officials repeatedly mentioned the prospect "pernicious" deflation as a reason to keep monetary policy accommodative (Federal Open Market Committee 2003a, c). Based on this evidence, Japan proved a cautionary tale that justified the FOMC's decision to keep short-term interest rates low, despite the increase in housing prices over the same period.

The second convention that motivated the Fed's accommodative monetary policy was how Fed technocrats chose to measure inflation. The Federal Reserve Act of 1913 states that the Federal Reserve is responsible for ensuring three goals: maximum employment, stable prices, and moderate long-term interest rates. Since the great inflation of the 1970s, the Fed has focused on price stability as its main monetary policy target, based on the rationale that stable prices lead to both sustainable growth and low unemployment overall. While the "price level" is a straightforward concept, coming up with an appropriate measure of the actual price level in the economy is subject to policymakers' discretion (Mehra and Sawhney 2010, 123–124).[7] Had the FOMC included housing prices in their preferred inflation metric, they may have been more inclined to raise interest rates as the housing bubble inflated.

Consider the case of the Consumer Price Index (CPI), which is an inflation metric compiled by the Bureau of Labor Statistics (BLS) that measures the prices of a "representative basket" of goods and services across twenty-three thousand retail stores in eighty-seven municipalities in the United States (Tainer 2006, 160–188). This representative consumption basket includes food and beverages, housing, water and utilities, clothing, transportation, and medical care, among other categories. The BLS weights the different components of the market basket to come up with an index of prices for the entire economy. Housing is the biggest component of the CPI, comprising nearly 42% of the consumption basket (see Fig. 3.11).

The BLS calculates housing inflation based on "owners' equivalent rent," which the BLS finds by asking survey respondents the following two questions: for those who own their own homes, the survey asks, "if someone were to rent your home today, how much do you think it would rent for monthly, unfurnished and without utilities?" And for those respondents who rent their primary residences, the BLS CPI survey asks, "What is the rental charge to your [household] for this unit including any extra charges for garage and parking facilities? Do not include direct payments by local, state or federal agencies. What period of time does this cover?" Based on these questions, it is evident that the BLS does not measure housing inflation based on actual housing prices but on changes in actual and imputed housing rent paid by consumers (Bureau of Labor Statistics 2009). The effect of using owners' equivalent rent rather than housing prices in the CPI is as follows.

During periods of rising housing prices relative to owners' rent, overall inflation rates as measured by the CPI might understate the prevailing inflation rate facing consumers, particularly those who might be seeking to purchase a home rather than to rent one. For instance, owners' equivalent rent increased 3.3% in 2002, while housing prices increased 15% over the same period. In 2004, a banner year for homeowners in which prices increased nearly 19%, owners' equivalent rent increased only

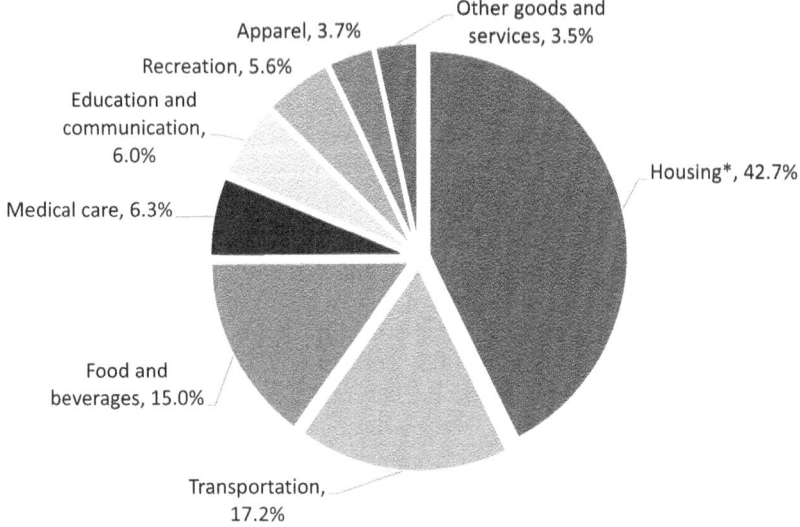

*Housing computed by using owners' equivalent rent

Fig. 3.11 CPI weights by category: 2006 (US Bureau of Labor Statistics)

2.3%. Based on original CPI data, the Case-Shiller home price index, and homeownership rates, it is possible to construct counterfactual CPI measure that better accounts for the cost of living facing consumers in the US economy. Doing so shows that if the BLS were to have weighted housing based on the relative proportion of homeowners to renters (and otherwise holding all other components of the CPI constant in both their weightings and values), then the average annual inflation rate between 2001 and 2005 would have been 7.5%. The original value of the CPI, using only owners' equivalent rent, showed an average annual CPI increase of 2.6% during the same period (see Table 3.2 and Fig. 3.12).

In August 2003, just as the housing bubble took off, meeting minutes reveal that FOMC members believed that "further disinflation was probable over the year ahead," during which this book's modified CPI measure increased roughly 7% (Federal Open Market Committee 2003b). Minutes from the FOMC's January 2004 meeting show that a majority of FOMC members believed that "disinflation appeared to be the most

Table 3.2 Counterfactual inflation measurement (US Bureau of Labor Statistics, US Census Bureau, Federal Reserve Economic Data, author calculations)

	OER	Case-Shiller index	Home-ownership rates	Weighted average housing index^	CPI	Modified CPI
	(% Δ)	(% Δ)	Level (%)	(% Δ)	(% Δ)	(% Δ)
1996	2.80	1.90	65.3	2.20	3.00	2.70
1997	2.60	5.40	65.5	4.40	2.30	3.20
1998	2.20	9.10	66.0	6.80	1.60	3.70
1999	2.10	10.80	66.7	8.10	2.20	5.10
2000	3.40	14.10	67.1	11.10	3.40	7.00
2001	3.90	8.90	67.6	7.70	2.80	4.90
2002	2.20	15.00	67.9	11.80	1.60	6.60
2003	2.40	13.40	68.1	10.90	2.30	6.80
2004	2.50	18.70	68.7	15.60	2.70	9.80%
2005	3.20	15.90	69.2	13.90	3.40	9.50
2006	3.70	0.20	68.6	0.40	3.20	1.50
2007	3.00	−9.80	68.5	−7.50	2.80	−3.10
2008	3.10	−19.20	67.9	−14.90	3.80	−6.30
2009	0.40	−2.40	67.4	−1.90	−0.40	−1.10
2010	−0.40	−1.30	67.2	−1.20	1.60	1.10
2011	1.30	−4.10	66.5	−2.90	3.20	0.90

Source US Bureau of Labor Statistics, US Census Bureau, Federal Reserve Economic Data, author calculations
^The weighted average is calculated by the following equation: a*(1 − c) + b*c, where a=owners' equivalent rent, b=Case-Shiller home price index, and c=homeownership rates

likely prospect" for the US economy following from their forecasts of inflation based on the CPI. Over the course of 2004, the modified CPI measure increased nearly 10% (Federal Open Market Committee 2004). Throughout the inflation of the housing bubble, Fed officials affirmed that inflation threats remained subdued based on their inflation metrics, while ignoring evidence of home price inflation.

Rent was also used to represent housing prices in the Fed's other preferred measures of inflation, including the Personal Consumption Expenditures (PCE) deflator. In the 2000s, Chairman Alan Greenspan claimed that the PCE deflator was a better approximation of the "real" inflation rate of the economy because it measures the price change of a

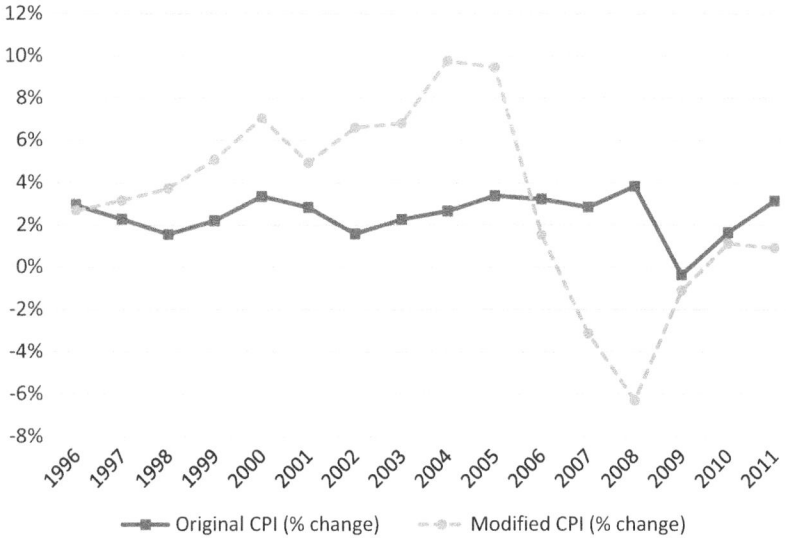

Fig. 3.12 CPI vs. Modified CPI: 1996–2011 (US Bureau of Labor Statistics, Standard & Poor's, author calculations)

variable basket of goods, rather than the CPI, which uses a fixed basket of goods. The PCE deflator is based on the CPI though it measures housing prices based on "rent of nonfarm owner-occupied homes," which is like owners' equivalent rent since it measures inflation based on rent paid and not housing prices. Owners' equivalent rent is computed based on the unobserved opportunity cost of foregone rent in an owner-occupied home in the CPI, while the PCE deflator measures rent based on actual rent paid. In both cases, rent represents housing in the respective inflation basket. Therefore, the methodological deficiencies that existed with the CPI are also present in the construction of the PCE deflator (Bureau of Economic Analysis 2014, Chapter 5.17). Many Fed officials also expressed their preference for so-called "core" CPI, which is the CPI subtracting food and energy prices. According to economists at the Federal Reserve Bank of Cleveland, core CPI is a better measure of the price level because food and energy prices can cause transitory changes in inflation that are not reflective of long-term trends. However, core CPI also measures housing inflation based on owners' equivalent rent, so it too is subject to the same blindness as the regular CPI measure (Meyer and Pasaogullari 2011).

This counterfactual analysis shows that metric construction could have affected the FOMC's monetary policy. The choice of a specific inflation measure (e.g. between one that includes housing prices and one that uses owners' rent) may have caused the FOMC to make different monetary policy choices, depending on which economic metric they employed, in turn influencing prices not included in preferred inflation metrics. Monetary policy decisions made because of a specific inflation basket impact the inflation rates of *all* commodities in an economy, not just those in the representative basket. Based on the above exercise, it follows that if the Fed used an inflation metric that better captured the underlying realities of homeownership in America, the likelihood that the FOMC would have raised interest rates given appreciating home prices would have increased.[8] By choosing to measure inflation based on owners' equivalent rent as opposed to actual home prices, the Fed might have underestimated the cost of living facing consumers and kept interest rates too accommodative given prevailing macroeconomic conditions as a result. This exercise shows the essence of the two-way relationship between metric construction and market outcomes. In this case, the first-order decision about what to include in an inflation basket has secondary effects on market outcomes, as intermediated by the cognition of central bankers and their short-term interest rate decisions.

A third convention that motivated the FOMC's interest rate policy was the belief, professed by Chairman Alan Greenspan and shared by fellow members of the FOMC, that it was better for central banks to allow asset price bubbles to run their course and deflate on their own momentum rather than to use monetary policy to pop bubbles preemptively. This view, known as the "Greenspan Doctrine" explains why the FOMC was reluctant to raise interest rates when faced with evidence of a housing bubble.

In general, there are two schools of thought regarding central bank posture toward potential bubbles: the first view holds that monetary policy should *lean* against an inflating asset price bubble by raising interest rates and popping the bubble before it grows too large.[9] The second view, as articulated by Fed Chairman Alan Greenspan, states that it is easier to *clean* up after a bubble bursts rather than to lean against its inflation. This view rests on the assumption that the costs for leaning against a bubble with monetary policy are high, whereas the costs of cleaning up a bubble are low (Mishkin 2011, 17–21).[10] The Greenspan Doctrine traces its roots to a speech given by Fed Chairman Alan Greenspan at the Federal Reserve Bank of Kansas City's 2002 Jackson Hole Economic Policy Symposium of central bankers in which he claimed that "it was very difficult to identify a bubble until after the fact—that is, when bursting confirmed its existence" and that "it was far from obvious that bubbles, even if identified early, could be pre-empted short of the central bank inducing a substantial contraction in economic activity – the very outcome [monetary authorities] would be seeking to avoid" (Greenspan 2002).

The Greenspan Doctrine rested on four pillars. First, central bankers faced an "identification problem" of discerning the difference between a bubble and a secular shift in equilibrium market prices. Deflating a bubble using monetary policy would imply that the Fed had an information advantage over private markets. According to the rational expectations and efficient markets hypothesis, if there were a bubble, financial market participants would make trades to restore equilibrium to the market. Why should the Fed's economists, many of whom were strong adherents to neoclassical financial economics, believe that they had a unique advantage in identifying bubbles when compared with private actors? Second, proponents of the Greenspan Doctrine did not believe that raising interest rates can pop bubbles, since market participants already expected high returns from buying bubble-inflated securities, such that different monetary policy would do little to alter agents' bubble-level optimism. If an investor expects double-digit returns from the bubble asset class, why should marginally higher borrowing costs deter speculation? Third, the Greenspan Doctrine held that monetary policy was too blunt of a tool to target asset prices and that the spillover effects of trying to target a narrow asset class using broad-based monetary aggregates diminished the net benefit of popping a bubble in the first place. After all, monetary aggregates affect all prices, not just the bubble asset class. Fourth, Fed officials believed that attempting to pop a bubble could cause the bubble to burst more severely and undershoot equilibrium prices than had it just run its own course, thus violating the central bankers' Hippocratic Oath to the economy. If private markets are prepared for a looming bubble deflation, then fickle monetary policy could make things worse (Mishkin 2011, 18–20).

Discussion

What does all this evidence imply for this book's conventions-based theoretical framework put forth in the prior chapter?

The first issue is identifying whether the fears of deflation, inflation metrics, and the Greenspan Doctrine qualify as economic conventions. Recall that according to J.M. Keynes, economic conventions can take three forms: the past as a guide to the future (i.e. ergodicity), expert opinion, and conventional expectations (Keynes 1937a, 214). The FOMC's fears of repeating Japan's historical experience with deflation qualifies as an economic convention, since the recency and poignancy of Japan's monetary policy history loomed large in the minds of FOMC members. As Keynes argued, the chief tendency of agents when faced with uncertainty is to assume that the "future will resemble the past" (Keynes 1937b, 13). Much as Keynes would have argued, FOMC members considered information in idiosyncratic and historically contingent ways. Had the FOMC adopted a broader appraisal of Japan and other advanced-industrial states' monetary policy, they might have viewed accommodative monetary policy as a precursor to financial fragility and economic stagnation, rather than a tool to fight deflation. With hindsight, the FOMC may have "extrapolated too mechanically" from the Japanese case, as Barry Eichengreen put it, and their decision to keep short-term interest rates low to stave off deflation might have sowed the seeds for "an even greater boom and bust down the road" (Eichengreen 2011, 111). Indeed, 'mechanical extrapolation' is a tell-tale sign of conventional judgment, as argued by Keynes and Doran. The tendency of FOMC officials to extrapolate linearly from Japan's historical case illustrates how Federal Reserve technocrats are subject to the same types of conventional biases as market participants. The FOMC's fixation on avoiding Japan's past errors caused the Fed to adopt a monetary policy posture that may have paradoxically produced the economic malaise their policies intended to avoid.

The second explanatory variable of the Fed's policy studied in this chapter, inflation metrics, qualify as economic conventions, as it would be impossible for the Fed to make interest rate decisions without first rendering an *expert opinion* or judgment on how best to measure the price level. There is nothing materially preordained about using rent instead of housing prices in a preferred inflation metric. Rather, central bankers must make an authoritative judgment about what constitutes the price level and what does not, which in turn serves as a basis of knowledge for their decisions when faced with uncertainty about how to operationalize abstract notions like the "price level."

The third monetary policy rationale studied, the Greenspan Doctrine, also qualifies as a convention of *expert opinion*, since Chairman Greenspan occupied a privileged position within the FOMC and could thus set the discursive boundaries of appropriate policy among other voting FOMC members. The Greenspan Doctrine also reflected Chairman Greenspan's tendency to adopt conventions of expert opinion, since one of the pillars of the Greenspan Doctrine was that the Fed did not maintain an informational advantage over private markets in identifying bubbles before their deflation. When defending the Greenspan Doctrine, Greenspan argued that it was difficult for central banks to identify nascent bubbles, invoking information uncertainty as a key reason for his Doctrine. He claimed that if central banks could access information about the existence of a bubble, then "so would private agents, rendering the development of bubbles highly unlikely" (Greenspan 2002). Implicit in Greenspan's defense of the Greenspan Doctrine is his tendency to defer to the collective judgment of informationally efficient private markets, exhibiting the natural tendency of economic agents to "assume that the *existing* state of opinion as expressed in prices…is based on a *correct* summing up of future prospects," as Keynes put it (Keynes 1937a, 214).[11] So not only was the Greenspan Doctrine a convention of expert opinion that guided the FOMC's behavior, but it was also based on the conventional premise of expert opinion regarding the information efficiency of the market.

Based on the above discussion, is it possible to conclude that the Fed's economic conventions motivated FOMC decision-making in the early 2000s? There is no way to know for sure. The evidence marshaled by this chapter includes speeches by senior central bankers, FOMC meeting minutes, and secondary accounts of the Fed's governing ideas in the mid-2000s. This chapter also presented the results of a counter-factual analysis that showed how metric construction could influence the market's perceived "prevailing" inflation rate. Underpinning this chapter's evidentiary standard was an assumption that the FOMC practiced good faith in preparing their meeting minutes and that secondary source material accurately depicted the prevailing views of key FOMC decision-makers prior to the global financial crisis. While it is hard to say that conventions *caused* the FOMC's monetary policy, it is equally difficult to account for the fact that had it not been for economic conventions, something else had to have driven the FOMC's decisions. Was it caprice, randomness, or some underreported cause for which their stated conventions served as public justifications? Researchers cannot know for sure. What does follow from the above analysis, however, is that that conventions suffice as the most probable explanation for the Fed's interest rate decisions, and that different economic conventions would have raised the probability of the Fed making different monetary policy choices. Had Japan not experienced deflation; if headline inflation were 7%, as opposed to more benign level of 2–3%; and if the Greenspan Doctrine advocated for central bank hawkishness in the face of potential asset market imbalances rather than ambivalence, the Fed would have been more likely to raise short-term interest rates when faced with rapidly appreciating housing prices, possibly preventing the yield curve from becoming steeply upward sloping and dampening the rapid increase in housing prices and incentives for fragility (Mehra and Sawhney 2010; Mishkin 2011; White 2009).

Conclusion

The Federal Reserve does not deserve mono-causal blame for inflating the housing bubble and causing the global financial crisis. After all, the Fed only controls short-run interest rates, so even if the FOMC wanted to raise interest rates to pop the housing bubble, it is unclear whether their actions could have influenced long-term interest rates more closely tied to mortgage rates (Wu 2008).[12] Also, it would be a stretch to hold the Fed responsible for the systematic dismantling of America's Depression and Bretton Woods-era regulatory apparatus, most of which stemmed from legislation by the US Congress and other bodies over which the Federal Reserve had no regulatory jurisdiction (Kohn 2008).[13] The FOMC did not control the lending activity of America's government-sponsored enterprises (GSEs), Fannie Mae and Freddie Mac—Chairman Greenspan himself testified to Congress about the potential consequences of the GSEs' populist credit expansion (Greenspan 2005). The Fed did not render unrealistically favorable credit ratings on risky asset-backed securities, nor does America's central bank control foreign savings and investment decisions, which might have also contributed to lower long-term interest rates. And the Fed was not responsible for global savings and investment conditions that may have led to a surge in global liquidity from emerging Asia, surplus savers in

Europe, and petro states (Wolf 2008, 2014). Therefore, even if monetary policy did influence the housing market, it would be a significant stretch to pin all the blame for the bubble and global financial crisis on the Fed.

From the viewpoint of the Minsky approach to financial instability, however, FOMC actions helped contribute to Treasury yield curve becoming upward sloping during the rate-cutting cycle, which, despite whatever impact the Fed's actions may have had on housing prices, created an incentive for financial institutions to engage in interest rate term structure arbitrage sponsoring fragile financing structures. The existence of an upward-sloping interest rate term structure is a necessary and insufficient condition for a financial crisis. Therefore, the creation of fragile financing structures that emerged in tandem with accommodative FOMC policy is the subject of the next chapter.

NOTES

1. As Silicon Valley entrepreneur Peter Thiel recalled, during this period, "there were billionaires from Idaho…giving money to anyone with an idea and a polished pitch" and that "fairly broke entrepreneurs racked up thousand-dollar dinner bills and tried to pay in shares of their companies…" (Masters 2012).
2. Minutes from the FOMC's November meeting in 2002 reveal the Fed's rationale for their 2001–2003 rate cutting cycle: "While the current stance of monetary policy was still accommodative and was providing important support to economic activity, [FOMC] members were concerned that the generally disappointing data since the previous meeting, reinforcing the general thrust of the anecdotal evidence in recent months, pointed to a longer-lasting spell of subpar economic performance than they had anticipated earlier. In the circumstances, *a relatively aggressive easing action could help to ensure that the current soft spot in the economy would prove to be temporary and enhance the odds of a robust rebound in economic activity next year*" (Federal Open Market Committee 2002). Emphasis added.
3. Even though GDP growth remained positive, the broader economic recovery was "jobless" throughout 2003, which might have contributed to the Fed's decision to keep interest rates low despite rebounding output. The Fed has a dual mandate to support stable employment and stable prices, and with inflation low, the Fed may have believed it was within

its purview to maintain accommodative monetary policy to spur employment growth in the early 2000s. For more, see Rajan (2010).
4. Bernanke hypothesized three explanations of diminished macroeconomic volatility: 'structural change', better macroeconomic management, and luck. Bernanke's first explanation, structural change, held that changing economic institutions, smarter inventory management by firms, and the sophistication of financial markets made the United States economy more resilient to cyclical fluctuations. Bernanke's second explanation for the Great Moderation, monetary policy, claimed that sound macroeconomic management by the Fed improved the resilience of the economy, since better monetary policy could lessen the sensitivity of wage and price functions to external shocks. Chairman Ben Bernanke, a proponent of this view, also believed that better monetary policy could dampen inflation expectations, which made firms less likely to pass on the costs of commodity price shocks to customers, thus insulating the broader economy from these forms of macroeconomic volatility. The third explanation, luck, views lower volatility as the result of randomness: while reduced macroeconomic volatility might have correlated with certain monetary policy choices, there was no causal link between the two.
5. The Federal Reserve Vice Chairman Donald Kohn suggested that stability was the proximate cause for fragility in a speech given during the height of the global financial crisis: "In a broader sense, perhaps the underlying cause of the current crisis was complacency. With the onset of the 'Great Moderation' back in the mid-1980s, households and firms in the United States and elsewhere have enjoyed a long period of reduced output volatility and low and stable inflation."
6. Emphasis added.
7. According to Yash Mehra and Bansi Sawhney, the FOMC's preferred inflation measure has evolved over time, with the Fed originally opting for the GDP deflator measure of inflation through 1988, followed by the Consumer Price Index (CPI) through 2000, and thereafter choosing for the Personal Consumption Expenditures (PCE) deflator (with an emphasis on so-called "core" PCE inflation) from 2004 onwards. See Mehra and Sawhney (2010).
8. At least, the probability of the FOMC raising short-term interest rates would have risen, given the overwhelming evidence of housing prices affecting the overall inflation rate. The point of this exercise was not to indict the Fed with hindsight bias and claim that Fed officials *ought* to have used a consumption basket based on home prices instead of rents. On the contrary, there is considerable debate about where to draw the line with expanded price indices. Should the Fed include stock and bond prices, in addition to housing? Should they target commodity prices too?

Moreover, if the Fed were to use monetary policy to target one specific sector (e.g. residential real estate), they would run the risk of cooling sectors that might have been growing at sustainable rates. This chapter simply argues that *how* the Fed chooses to construct its economic metrics has a causal, intervening effect on macroeconomic outcomes in the US economy as intermediated by economic conventions.

9. See, for example, Roubini (2006).
10. For an example of a piece that staunchly urges central banks to *refrain* from popping bubbles, see Posen (2006). Postcrisis, William White argued that it is better for central banks only to lean against bubbles backed by unsustainable credit expansions (White 2009).
11. Emphasis in the original.
12. Federal Reserve economist Tao Wu identified that long-term interest rates might have decoupled from short-term rates in the years preceding the global financial crisis, so if the Fed had raised the federal funds target to cool the housing bubble, this action might not have achieved its intended result. Worse, pre-emptively raising interest rates prior to the housing bubble bursting runs the risk of causing the rest of the economy, which might be operating at or below potential, to contract as well, essentially causing an "elective" economic recession. Wu identified four factors that might have accounted for this conundrum: higher foreign official purchases of long-term U.S. Treasury debt, higher demand from pension funds, decreases in macroeconomic uncertainty, and lower asset market volatility.
13. In a speech during the crisis, Federal Reserve Vice Chairman Donald Kohn openly questioned whether the Fed could have reversed the "complacency" of excessive risk taking in the housing market and among financial institutions, thus averting the crisis. He answered his rhetorical question thusly: "Would a somewhat tighter stance of policy in recent years have reversed this complacency? It seems doubtful. Central banks would likely have needed to produce recessions of some consequence in order to force agents to reevaluate the costs of taking on risk--an outcome unlikely to improve societal welfare. Rather than using the blunt tool of monetary policy to induce prudence, we should examine more closely the possibility of using regulation and prudential supervision to address concerns about overleveraging and other risk-taking behavior." That said, many top Fed officials, including Greenspan himself, were proponents of financial sector deregulation, to the point where Greenspan felt it necessary to recant his prior support for deregulation after the global financial crisis. For more, see Andrews (2008).

WORKS CITED

Ahearne, Alan, Joseph Gagnon, Jane Haltmaeir, and Steve Kamin. 2002. "Preventing Deflation: Lessons form Japan's Experience in the 1990s." *International Finance Discussion Papers* (729): 1–62.

Andrews, Edmund L. 2008. "Greenspan Concedes Error on Regulation." *The New York Times.* October 23. Accessed March 11, 2018. http://www.nytimes.com/2008/10/24/business/economy/24panel.html?_r+1&.

Bernanke, Ben S. 2004. "Speech: The Great Moderation." *Federal Reserve Board of Governors.* February 20. Accessed March 3, 2019. https://www.federalreserve.gov/boarddocs/speeches/2004/20040220/.

———. 2010. "Speech: Monetary Policy and the Housing Bubble." *Federal Reserve Board of Governors.* January 3. Accessed March 4, 2018. https://www.federalreserve.gov/newsevents/speech/bernanke20100103a.htm.

Brunnermeier, Marcus K., and Stefan Nagel. 2004. "Hedge Funds and the Technology Bubble." *The Journal of Finance* 54 (5): 2013–2040.

Bureau of Economic Analysis. 2014. *Concepts and Methods of the U.S. National Income and Product Accounts.* Washington, DC: U.S. Department of Commerce.

Bureau of Labor Statistics. 2009. "How the CPI Measures Price Changes of Owners' Equivalent Rent of Primary Residence (OER) and Rent of Primary Residence (Rent)." *The Bureau of Labor Statistics.* April. Accessed March 11, 2018. http://www.bls.gov/cpi/cpifacnewrent.pdf.

Dunaway, Steven. 2009. "Global Imbalances and the Financial Crisis." *Council on Foreign Relations—Council Special Report* (44): 1–56.

Eichengreen, Barry. 2011. *Exorbitant Privilege: The Rise and Fall of the Dollar and the Future of the International Monetary System.* Oxford: Oxford University Press.

Federal Open Market Committee. 2002. "Minutes of the Federal Open Market Committee." *The Federal Reserve Board.* November 6. Accessed March 3, 2018. https://www.federalreserve.gov/fomc/minutes/20021106.htm.

———. 2003a. "Minutes of the Federal Open Market Committee." *The Federal Reserve Board.* June 24–25. Accessed March 11, 2018. http://www.federalreserve.gov/fomc/minutes/20030625.htm.

———. 2003b. "Minutes of the Federal Open Market Committee." *The Federal Reserve Board.* August 12. Accessed March 31, 2018. http://www.federalreserve.gov/fomc/minutes/20030812.htm.

———. 2003c. "Minutes of the Federal Open Market Committee." *The Federal Reserve Board.* December 9. Accessed March 11, 2018. http://www.federalreserve.gov/fomc/minutes/20031209.htm.

———. 2004. "Minutes of the Federal Open Market Committee." *The Federal Reserve Board*. January 27–28. http://www.federalreserve.gov/fomc/minutes/20040128.htm.

Federal Reserve Bank of St. Louis. 2018. *Federal Reserve Economic Data Database*. St. Louis, Missouri, 15 March.

Goodhart, Charles. 2009. "Financial Crisis and the Future of the Financial System." *100th BRE Bank—CASE Seminar*, 1–13. Warsaw: Center for Social and Economic Research.

Greenspan, Alan. 2002. "Remarks by Chairman Alan Greenspan: Economic Volatility." *The Federal Reserve Board*. August 30. http://www.federalresreve.gov/boarddocs/speeches/2002/20020830.

———. 2005. "Testimony of Chairman Alan Greenspan." *The Federal Reserve Board*. April 6. http://www.federalreserve.gov/boarddocs/testimony/2005/20050406/default.htm.

Jarociński, Marek, and Frank Smets. 2008. "House Prices and the Stance of Monetary Policy." *Federal Reserve Bank of St. Louis Review* 90 (4): 339–366.

Keen, Steve. 2011. "A Monetary Minsky Model of the Great Moderation and the Great Recession." *Journal of Economic Behavior & Organization* (2672): 1–15.

Keynes, John M. 1937a. "The General Theory of Employment." *The Quarterly Journal of Economics* 51 (2): 209–223.

———. 1937b. "Some Economic Consequences of a Declining Population." *The Eugenics Review* 13–17.

Kohn, Donald L. 2008. "Speech: Monetary Policy and Asset Prices Revisited." *The Federal Reserve Board*. November 19. https://www.federalreserve.gov/newsevents/speech/kohn20081119a.htm.

Krugman, Paul R., Kathryn M. Dominquez, and Kenneth Rogoff. 1998. "It's Baack: Japan's Slump and the Return of the Liquidity Trap." *Brookings Papers on Economic Activity* 1998 (2): 137–205.

Levi, Maurice D., and John H. Makin. 1978. "Anticipated Inflation and Interest Rates: Further Interpretation of Findings of the Fisher Equation." *The American Economic Review* 68 (5): 801–813.

Masters, Blake. 2012. "Peter Thiel's CS183: Startup—Class 2 Notes Essay." *Blake Masters*. April 6. Accessed March 30, 2018. http://blakemasters.com/post/20582845717/peter-thiels-cs183-startup-class-2-notes-essay.

Mehra, Yash P., and Basni Sawhney. 2010. "Inflation Measure, Taylor Rules, and the Greenspan-Bernanke Years." *Economic Quarterly* 96 (2): 123–151.

Meyer, Brent, and Mehmet Pasaogullari. 2011. *How Can Inflation Be Considered Low When Food and Gas Prices Are so High?* Cleveland: Federal Reserve Bank of Cleveland.

Miller, Marcus, Paul Weller, and Lei Zhang. 2001. "Moral Hazard and the U.S. Stock Market: Analysing the 'Greenspan Put'." *Center for the Study of Globalization and Regionalisation Working Paper* 83 (1): 1–26.

Mishkin, Frederic. 2011. "Monetary Policy Strategy: Lessons from the Crisis." *NBER Working Paper Series* (16755): 1–63.
Obstfeld, Maurice, and Kenneth Rogoff. 2009. "Global Imbalances and the Financial Crisis: Products of Common Causes." *Federal Reserve Bank of San Francisco Asia Economic Policy Conference*, 1–64. Santa Barbara: Federal Reserve Bank of San Francisco.
Posen, Adam S. 2006. "Why Central Banks Should Not Burst Bubbles." *Institute for International Economics Working Paper Series* 1–15.
Rajan, Raghuram. 2010. *Fault Lines: How Hidden Fractures Still Threaten the World Economy*. Princeton: Princeton University Press.
Roubini, Nouriel. 2006. "Why Central Banks Should Burst Bubbles." *International Finance* 9 (1): 87–107.
Sanders, Anthony. 2008. "The Subprime Crisis and Its Role in the Financial Crisis." *Journal of Housing Economics* 17: 254–261.
Schwartz, Herman. 2009. *Subprime Nation: American Power, Global Capital, and the Housing Bubble*. Ithaca: Cornell University Press.
Smithers, Andrew. 2009. *Wall Street Revalued: Imperfect Markets and Inept Central Bankers*. West Sussex: Wiley.
Sutch, Richard. 2014. "The Liquidity Trap, the Great Depression, and Unconventional Policy: Reading Keynes and the Zero Lower Bound." *Berkeley Economic History Laboratory Working Paper Series* 2014 (5): 1–80.
Tainer, Evelina M. 2006. *Using Economic Indicators to Improve Investment Analysis*. Hoboken: Wiley.
U.S. Department of the Treasury. 2018. "Daily Treasury Yield Curve Rates." *Treasury.gov*. March 30. Accessed March 30, 2018. https://www.treasury.gov/resource-center/data-chart-center/interest-rates/Pages/TextView.aspx?data=yield.
Vogel, Harold L. 2009. *Financial Market Bubbles and Crashes*. Cambridge: Cambridge University Press.
White, William R. 2009. "Should Monetary Policy 'Lean or Clean'?" *Federal Reserve Bank of Dallas Globalization and Monetary Policy Institute* 1–24.
Wolf, Martin. 2008. *Fixing Global Finance*. Baltimore: Johns Hopkins University Press.
———. 2014. *The Shifts and the Shocks: What We've Learned—And Have Still to Learn—From the Financial Crisis*. New York: Penguin.
Wu, Tao. 2008. "Accounting for the Bond-Yield Conundrum." *Insights from the Federal Reserve Bank of Dallas* 3 (2): 1–8.

CHAPTER 4

The Rise of Fragile Finance

INTRODUCTION

This chapter describes the economic conventions behind the relaxation of Minsky's second, third, and fourth constraints on fragility, which include bank risk tolerance; the presence of short-term lenders to finance fragile financial structures; and borrowers willing to emit risky long-term assets. This chapter explains how many systemically important financial institutions sat at the crossroads of trillions of dollars in risky bets on financial assets funded by short-term borrowing, making them vulnerable to bank runs once asset prices fell. It builds on the work of Viral Acharya, Tobias Adrian, Gary Gorton, Eric Helleiner, Paul McCulley, Perry Mehrling, Zoltan Pozsar, Andrew Metrick, Matthew Richardson, and Hyun Song Shin, among others, to argue that shadow banking is analogous to traditional banking.[1]

On the eve of the global financial crisis, America and Europe's financial institutions stood at the crossroads of a global banking system that fell largely outside of the purview of banking regulators but still allocated credit across the global economy. In the early 2000s, financial institutions took advantage of favorable financing conditions to engage in credit, liquidity, and maturity transformation to borrow in the wholesale funding markets via asset-backed commercial paper (ABCP) and repurchase agreements ("repo") to purchase longer-dated (and higher yielding) asset-backed securities (ABS) (Kodres 2013). Heading into the crisis, America's banks were overreliant on short-term funding and undercapitalized relative to the risk in their loan portfolios, such that rising credit delinquencies and the failure of Lehman Brothers caused credit and counterparty risks to surge, in turn tipping the fragile financial system into a full-blown bank run on all wholesale funding markets and shadow banking conduits.

Economic conventions fundamentally drove this process of shadow banking fragility prior to the global financial crisis. These conventions include: (1) pro-cyclical *conventional expectations* about the liquidity and solvency of shadow banking conduits by ABCP and repo counterparties, which created a steady pool of investors in short-term liabilities emitted by banks; (2) banks' risk management technologies based on *ergodicity* that fed their risk tolerance to take advantage of term structure arbitrage opportunities while also making them vulnerable to so-called "left tail" risks in their loan portfolios; and (3) institutionalized expert opinions via bond ratings for measuring the credit risk of ABS, which enabled the creation of higher-yielding but risky shadow banking assets. Bond ratings also convinced shadow banking counterparties that their deposits were *information-insensitive* and could be redeemed at par value.

Figure 4.1 depicts a schematic of this chapter's argument by presenting a consolidated balance sheet of a parent bank and its sponsored shadow bank. Its core features are as follows:

- The shadow bank's assets are regulatory capital and ABS.
- Its liabilities are traditional deposits, ABCP, and repo. Pro-cyclical conventional expectations and expert opinion via bond ratings facilitate shadow banks' ability to roll over their maturing ABCP and repo. These conventions explain the relaxation of Minsky's second constraint on fragility, namely the availability of short-term financing for speculative and Ponzi financing structures.
- Banks reserve regulatory capital using internal risk-weightings based on value-at-risk underpinned by conventions of ergodicity. Banks' ability to write their own capital rules based on ergodic conventions explains the relaxation of Minsky's third constraint on fragility, sufficient bank risk tolerance.
- The shadow bank uses the proceeds raised from ABCP and repo to engage in credit, liquidity, and maturity transformation by purchasing ABS and other collateral, taking advantage of the upward-sloping interest rate term structure (Minsky's first constraint, see Chapter 3).
- ABS is comprised of pools of underlying securities such as mortgages, credit card receivables, student loans, and other ABS.

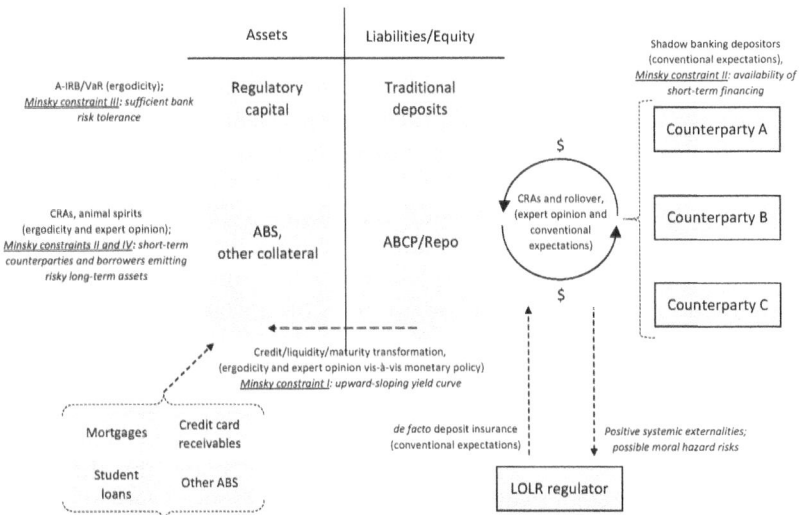

Fig. 4.1 Stylized shadow bank consolidated balance sheet with parent bank (Author)

- Favorable credit ratings (conventions of expert opinion) based on ergodicity assumptions enable the supply and demand side of the securitization chain, relaxing Minsky's second and fourth constraints on fragility, enabling short-term counterparties and borrowers willing to emit risky long-term assets.
- The availability of de facto deposit insurance from the lender of last resort (LOLR) regulator determines the stability of these shadow banking conduits when asset losses trigger rollover risks. The provision of this quasi-deposit insurance insures positive systemic externalities but may also exacerbate moral hazard.

Conventional Expectations and Short-Term Funding Markets

Why was the global financial system vulnerable to disruptions in the supply of wholesale funding when housing prices fell in 2007? After all, asset price bubbles occur regularly in market economies but do not always cause systemic crises.

As Hyman Minsky argues, bubbles are necessary but insufficient conditions for systemic crises. The presence of financial fragility, coupled with a deflating asset price bubble, explains why some bubbles produce systemic crises while others deflate benignly. So, to understand the US economy's proneness to systemic crisis in 2007, it is necessary to investigate the sources of financial fragility that emerged in tandem with the inflating housing bubble from 2001 to 2007. Two developments in particular, including securitization and banks' reliance on wholesale funding, explain the US economy's vulnerability to systemic financial collapse on the eve of the global financial crisis (Adrian and Shin 2009; Gorton 2010; Mehrling 2011; McCulley 2007; Pozsar 2008).

Securitization is the process by which financial intermediaries pool loans to resell them as a tradable security to a third party. The buyer of a securitized asset receives the cash flows generated by the loans constituting the underlying pool of assets and also bears the risks associated with the underlying collateral (Helleiner 2011, 70–72).[2] Although securitization was invented in the late 1960s, it took off in the mid-2000s, with financial institutions pooling and securitizing a wide array of different loans into tradable securities, including automobile leases, credit card receivables, health club membership fees, mortgages, movie ticket receipts, and student loans, among other asset classes. There are several reasons why securitization volumes rose in the 2000s. Zoltan Pozsar claimed that accommodative monetary policy created liquidity for short-term borrowing and boosted investor demand for risky assets. Therefore, Fed policy made short-term funding attractive while also bidding up prices of securitized assets (Pozsar 2008, 13–14, see chapter 3). Gary Gorton speculated that securitization reflected demand pressures among short-term lenders such as money market mutual funds and cash-rich corporations. Bankers issued ABCP and repo to meet this demand for short-term, money-like liabilities. These funding sources required high-quality collateral, so banks began securitizing assets to increase the supply of assets available to risk-averse pools of collateral through financial engineering of collateralized debt obligations (CDOs) and other derivatives (Gorton 2010, 40–41). One hedge fund manager who invested in securitized assets interviewed for this book tied the rise of securitization to China's currency peg. The subject claimed that China's demand for dollars to support its fixed exchange rate during the early 2000s bid up the price of risk-free assets such as US Treasury securities. Fund managers seeking extra yield demanded more securities from banks, which met this demand to earn origination fees for ABS (Hedge fund manager 2018). Regardless of the underlying causes, from 2002 to 2007, the total market of securitized loans rose from roughly $2 trillion to over $6 trillion (Gorton 2010, 39).

While in theory securitization lowered the barriers to "Pareto optimal" financial transactions by distributing risks to lenders with commensurate risk appetites, in practice financial institutions ended up becoming the primary investors in risky ABS prior to the global financial crisis (Helleiner 2011, 70–72). Why did banks end up becoming the biggest investors in securitized assets, especially if securitization allowed banks to move loans off their balance sheets? Viral Acharya and Matthew Richardson found that from 2002 to 2007, banks opted to keep securitized assets on their balance sheets to increase their leverage and exposure to risky assets while skirting capital requirements. Banks would often sell the riskiest portions, or *tranches*, of their securitized assets and keep the highest rated tranches. These highly rated ABS tranches proved risky when realized default rates surpassed the risk represented by high ratings. Therefore, securitization ended up concentrating the risk associated with ABS on banks' balance sheets, rather than dispersing this risk completely among investors (Acharya and Richardson 2011). Gorton and Metrick find that the potential profit opportunities offered between the cost of borrowing in short-term markets and lending via long-term ABS created an incentive for banks to engage in *term structure arbitrage*, capturing rents from the upward-sloping yield curve (Gorton and Metrick 2010b).[3] Banks financed these ABS purchases with funds borrowed via ABCP and repo.

ABCP is senior, secured, collateralized debt issued for short durations (usually between ninety and two hundred and seventy days). Banks would pledge ABS as collateral backing ABCP, such that if banks did not repay ABCP loans on time, borrowers could seize the underlying collateral to get their money back. Issuing ABCP with credit guarantees also helped banks avoid regulatory capital requirements, further boosting banks' profits (Acharya et al. 2013).

Repo is a form of collateralized borrowing in which a bank sells an asset that it agrees to repurchase at a future date at a predetermined price. The percentage difference between the future price paid and present price received is the functional equivalent of an interest rate on a bank deposit.[4] The discount to face value of collateral backing repo is known as a 'haircut', and the greater the repo haircut facing a bank (i.e. the deeper the discount of the present value relative to the repurchase price of a repo transaction), the more expensive it is for banks to borrow in repo markets (Gorton and Metrick 2010a; The Financial Crisis Inquiry Commission 2011, 29–34). Because ABCP and repo transactions were short-term and collateralized, such that in the case of default, a repo counterparty could seize the underlying collateral and sell it in the open market, repo interest rates tended to be several percentage points lower than the yields on ABS. Thus, ABCP and repo were attractive funding sources for financial institutions provided they could post high-quality collateral. Money market mutual funds and other ABCP and repo investors found these assets attractive because of their deposit-like qualities (i.e. depositors could redeem these liabilities at par value at any time) and higher yields compared to cash deposits.

By 2007, US and European commercial banks sponsored some $1.2 trillion worth of asset-backed commercial paper with full or partial credit and liquidity guarantees, up from about $600 billion in 2002 (Pozsar 2008, 19, see Fig. 4.2).[5] On the eve of the global financial crisis, broker-dealers' net repo liabilities were over 30% of their total, and in 2008, the total repo market was about $4.5 trillion, of which about $2 trillion was collateralized by mortgage securities (Baklanova et al. 2015, 37; Toomey et al. 2017, 2).

Many analysts contend that shadow banking *was* banking and, for this reason, can be conceptualized similarly to traditional banking (Blyth 2013, 23–24; Gorton 2010; Mehrling 2011; Pozsar et al. 2010; The Financial Crisis Inquiry Commission 2011, 29–34). In shadow banking, many money market mutual funds, institutional investors, corporations with extra cash, and other counterparties deposit funds at financial institutions via ABCP and repo, which in turn make loans to borrowers via ABS. Unlike in traditional banking, however, where banks kept minimum reserves and depositors had deposit insurance to protect their assets, shadow banking had repo haircuts and collateral to protect counterparties from losses. The ultimate bank sponsor provides credit guarantees to the SIV and earns profits from the SIV's term structure arbitrage,

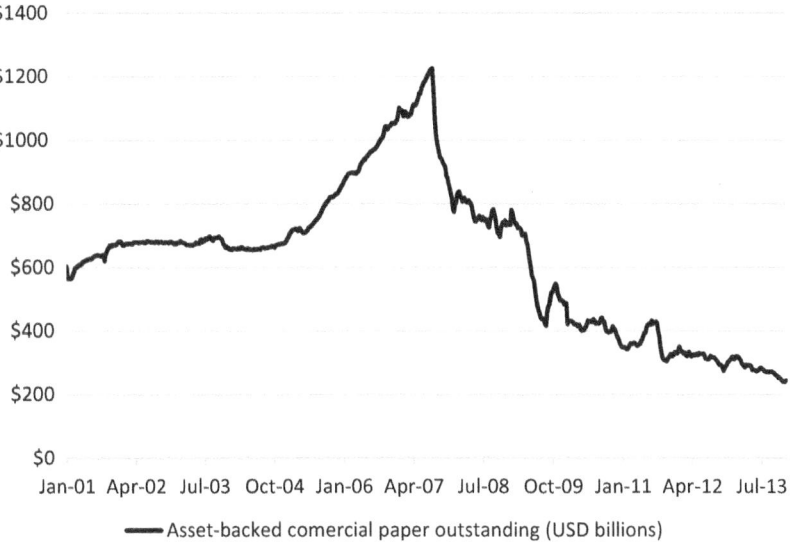

Fig. 4.2 The rise and fall of ABCP: 2001–2013 (Federal Reserve Economic Data)

via credit, liquidity, and maturity transformation (Gorton and Metrick 2010a, b); see Figs. 1.2 and 4.1.

In the years prior to the global financial crisis, financial institutions sponsored structured investment vehicles that borrowed in wholesale funding markets to purchase ABS (Brunnermeier 2009, 79–80). By issuing debt via ABCP and repo, financial institutions could borrow at near-LIBOR interest rates and then invest their proceeds into higher yielding (but riskier) assets (Gorton and Metrick 2010b, 278–280). Furthermore, ABCP and repo enabled financial institutions to hypothecate and re-hypothecate their risky collateral and increase their leverage to maximize returns. Repo allowed broker-dealers to run leverage ratios thirty to forty times their equity, making them vulnerable to minor declines in the value of their collateral (Blyth 2013, 25–26). Prior to the crisis, shadow banking structures did not count against banks' regulatory capital ratios, and thus provided banks with an opportunity to engage in *regulatory arbitrage* by avoiding regulatory capital requirements on ABS exposure.

There was nothing inherently fragile about using short-term debt to purchase longer-dated, risky assets. Indeed, borrowing short and lending long is what banks do. If ABCP and repo counterparties believe that banks' ABS collateral was information-insensitive, such that no actor could gain an advantage based on private information about the quality of ABCP and repo collateral and their deposits can thus be redeemed at par value, then investors would continue to roll over maturing ABCP and repo, rendering shadow banking structures liquid. Even if banks faced a creditor strike in the wholesale funding market or credit losses in their ABS portfolios, as long as they had reserves sufficient to absorb losses, then shadow banking would not carry substantial risk. However, it was banks' susceptibility to roll over risk, on the one hand, along with their undercapitalization, on the other (see next section), that made financial institutions vulnerable to creditor panics when housing prices fell, exposing shadow banks to both liquidity and credit risks.[6]

It is here where economic conventions, specifically *conventional expectations*, play a decisive role in determining the stability of shadow banks. Recall that according to Keynes, conventional expectations described the tendency of agents to "conform with the behavior of the majority or the average" when faced with uncertainty about the future (Keynes 1937a, 214). Furthermore, Keynes analogized investment decisions to a beauty contest in which investors attempt to guess what other investors think before acting. Under such conditions, investors will look to each other for signals regarding the creditworthiness of a borrower (Allen et al. 2006). Such is the case of counterparty confidence in the shadow banking system. Provided a majority of ABCP and repo counterparties believe that *fellow* counterparties will extend credit to ABCP or repo conduits, then the market will continue to roll over maturing SIV obligations. If, however, ABCP and repo counterparties believed that other counterparties would no longer deem SIVs and their sponsors creditworthy, then creditors might refuse to roll over SIVs' maturing obligations, in turn disrupting the supply of credit available to financial institutions and triggering financial instability (Gorton and Metrick 2010b).[7] In the absence of deposit insurance, favorable conventional expectations were necessary to provide liquidity to shadow banking conduits and their sponsors. Pro-cyclical conventional expectations explain the relaxation of Minsky's second constraint on financial instability: the presence of buyers willing to purchase shadow banks' liabilities.

Bank Risk Tolerance and Capital Rules

If financial institutions had adequate capital buffers when housing prices fell, then buyer strikes by ABCP and repo counterparties would not have necessarily led to financial instability during the global financial crisis. With sufficient precautionary reserves, banks would have had the liquidity necessary to withstand a creditor boycott and absorb write-downs when asset prices fell. As is now clear, banks were undercapitalized heading into the global financial crisis, leading some to seek government support to make up for their capital shortfalls. Bank capital inadequacy was thus a key source of fragility prior to the global financial crisis distinct from the liquidity risk associated with rolling over maturing shadow banking liabilities. This chapter now explains how banks' risk management techniques assumed that future asset price returns would adhere to historical returns (i.e. conventions of ergodicity), which simultaneously made banks appear well capitalized during the bubble years while increasing their vulnerability to declining prices.

While there is broad agreement among both banks and regulators that financial institutions should hold capital reserves in case of losses (and indeed, it is in society's interest that they do), there is far less consensus about the "right" amount of regulatory capital banks should hold. Banks could be perfectly capitalized, with a 100% capital ratio (i.e. zero non-cash assets), though this condition would make it impossible for banks to earn revenue to pay their depositors. Conversely, banks could carry a thin capital cushion as a percentage of their loans outstanding but doing so could leave them exposed to falling collateral prices should default rates rise (Tarullo 2008, 1–9). Regulators thus face two challenges when determining banks' regulatory capital. First, there is a natural tension between banks' desire to hold capital while also maximizing profits. When growth is strong and default rates are low, banks prefer to hold the minimum capital required under the law so they can increase their profits by making more loans (or, in the case of shadow banking, buy more securities). Therefore, banks' preference for regulatory capital varies pro-cyclically with changing market conditions. Regulators, on the other hand, prefer that banks reserve capital countercyclically to serve as a buffer against losses during downturns (Gordy and Howells 2006).[8] So banks and regulators have divergent interests about optimal amounts of regulatory capital banks should hold. Second, the market faces a quantification problem regarding how best to determine capital charges commensurate with the risk associated with a given asset. In theory, regulatory capital charges should reflect the probability of default of a loan. In practice, it is difficult to estimate default rates on securities prior to stressful periods during the business cycle.

Regulators' solution to this capital quantification problem prior to the global financial crisis was to let banks determine their own regulatory capital charges via their internal ratings methodology. Regulators' choice to let banks "risk-weight" capital charges meant that banks' capitalization became predicated on their ability to predict the default risk in their loan portfolios. Since banks' risk management techniques assumed market ergodicity, banks were systemically vulnerable to non-ergodic changes asset prices.

Risk-weighting ties the capital charge of an asset to its perceived risk of default, such that banks reserve less capital for less risky investments and vice versa. Under risk-weighting, a loan to a start-up company carries a greater risk-weighted capital charge than a loan to a triple A-rated government. While intuitively sensible, risk-weighting presents banks and regulators with a practical challenge of how best to identify the appropriate level of regulatory capital given imperfect knowledge about borrowers. New financial products that lack a trading history to guide estimates of future default probabilities such as exotic ABS exacerbate this issue. And even for products with long trading histories, historical default rates might not provide a meaningful guide to future default rates, especially if the market's historical data generating process evolves in non-ergodic ways. As Keynes would argue, risk-weighting is uncertain because "there is no scientific basis on which to form any calculable probability whatsoever" about the appropriate capital charges associated with opaque financial instruments (Keynes 1937a, 214). Of course, agents nevertheless try to divine calculable probabilities of future default risk and often rely on ergodic measures to do so. But these methods are mere approximations of knowledge because no amount of past sampling can give the practitioner certainty about the future (Blyth 2010, 457).

Notwithstanding these caveats, national regulators and financial institutions alike began favoring risk-weighted capital requirements by the 1980s. Banks preferred risk-weighting because it allowed them to make more loans ostensibly to less risky borrowers. Regulators also preferred risk-weighting because it leveled the playing field among different national regulations, thus reducing cross-national regulatory requirements and the incentives for regulatory arbitrage. This convergence of preferences between bankers and regulators among the G10 countries culminated in the 1988 Basel Accord (i.e. Basel I) by the Basel Committee on Banking Supervision, which issued international standards for risk-weighting by classifying five risk profiles of bank assets (and thus reduced cross-national idiosyncrasies of risk-weighted capital adequacy regimes). Basel I's risk tranches ranged from assets that carried no capital charge, such as cash and loans made to highly rated sovereign governments, to assets that carried 100% capital charges (e.g. claims on non-OECD governments). Basel I also mandated that banks with international operations hold an 8% capital buffer of the total value of their risk-weighted assets at any given time. Risk weighting involves multiplying an asset's capital charge by the notional amount of assets held by the minimum capital standard. For instance, under Basel I, a $1000 loan to a non-OECD government would carry a $1000 capital charge, such that a bank that holds this loan would need to keep $80 in tier one capital on their balance sheet to act as a buffer against potential losses (100% times $1000 notional value times 8% minimum capital) (Tarullo 2008, 45–60).[9]

Despite some initial success at synchronizing national capital adequacy regimes, regulators realized that Basel I fell short in several respects. Risk-weighting created incentives for banks to lend more to borrowers that required less regulatory capital. Securitization complicated matters further, since retained ABS were riskier than their capital charges would suggest. Other limitations of Basel I included limited risk buckets, a lack of an explicit recognition of counterparty risk, and understatement of portfolio diversification benefits of loans to diverse borrowers. By the late 1990s, regulators agreed that something had to be done (Crotty 2009, 570; Tarullo 2008, 90–95).[10] The 2004 Basel II agreement was signed in response to these concerns and amended Basel I by changing the weighting system used by banks to determine capital charges, creating more latitude for national regulators to demand higher capital requirements in excess of international standards, and encouraging banks to disclose their risks more transparently.

Basel II also constituted a clear break from Basel I by permitting banks to use their own internal ratings to determine the credit risk of loan portfolios, as opposed to Basel I's centrally directed risk weights. This "advanced internal ratings-based approach" (A-IRB) allowed banks to gauge portfolio risk to determine regulatory capital charges using internal risk models (*The Economist* 2004; Basel Committee on Banking Supervision 2005). Banks preferred A-IRB because it allowed them to hold lower levels of regulatory capital and thus make more loans (and earn more profit), provided that they could justify their actions based on internal ratings (Tarullo 2008, 65). From regulators' perspective, financial institutions seemed like the ideal arbiters of the risks that they faced. Regulators supported A-IRB because they deemed that the alternative, ratings from external agencies, were not rigorous and subject to abuse via "ratings shopping." Knowing that member states' financial institutions could abuse A-IRB, the Basel Committee placed several eligibility requirements on banks before they could use their own internal ratings for assessing capital charges, based on the rationale that banks that met the Basel Committee's stringent A-IRB prerequisites had a stake in disclosing their risks to national regulators.

The Basel Committee suggested that banks use the value-at-risk (VaR) approach to calculate market risk and determine capital charges for different assets under Basel II. VaR is a weighted risk measure that looks at historical asset price returns to estimate the likelihood of loss in a loan portfolio over a given period (Risk.net 2012). Even though the Basel Committee advocated for VaR in the late 1990s and throughout the 2000s, VaR's flaws were well known by regulators and banks alike, particularly after the 1998 failure of hedge fund Long-Term Capital Management (LTCM, see the next chapter). VaR faced the following limitations:

VaR relies on historical price data to project future market prices, which is not a realistic assumption because future asset price distributions might not conform to their historical range. Said another way, the world is not ergodic, so VaR may understate the risk of losses if prices defy their historical bounds. Moreover, back testing VaR models was difficult because credit events (e.g. defaults and downgrades) rarely occurred in financial markets. This issue was compounded because financial cycles are longer than regular business cycles, so finding accurate historical data can be difficult even when there exists data from prior recessions. Additionally, VaR underestimated correlation risk, or the likelihood of spillover risks across portfolios. Correlation risk drove the contagion in the global banking system during the global financial crisis. Finally, VaR underestimated the likelihood of "tail risk" because it assumed a normal distribution of historical asset price returns. Asset prices might take on so-called fat tails, for which the normal distribution is ill-equipped to describe (usually classifying low probability, high impact events as "ten standard deviation" occurrences) (Tarullo 2008, 63–65). For these reasons, VaR did not capture the full range of possible futures in financial markets and drove banks' underestimation of portfolio risk prior to the global financial crisis (Colander et al. 2009, 571–572). While the inadequacy of VaR is well documented by after-the-fact accounts of the crisis, VaR's flaws reveal a lot how misplaced faith in economic metrics based on ergodicity can sow financial fragility. There are three conclusions one can draw about VaR for this book's conventions-based theoretical framework.

First, it turns out that the methodologies used by financial institutions to gauge portfolio risk were *endogenous drivers* of adding cumulatively more risk into America's financial system prior to the global financial crisis. As more banks used VaR, the credit available to ostensibly riskless asset classes increased, leading to lower bond yields, greater risk appetites, and broader fragility. VaR also allowed broker-dealers to carry thinner capital cushions than a simple approach would suggest, and thus helped broker-dealers lower average capital charges by 40% on average (The Financial Crisis Inquiry Commission 2011, 152). To the extent that VaR provided banks with an adequate gauge of risk, the trading prescriptions suggested by VaR's computer models often caused banks to purchase derivatives that would lower their VaR numbers but also presented a risk to banks if derivatives proved inadequate risk mitigations during crises. Banks' derivatives exposed them to counterparty risk if their counterparties failed to meet their obligations, which often occurred when many banks purchased the same types of hedges from the same company. Concentration risk of a single over-levered firm providing a majority of the market's insurance describes what happened to insurance giant American International Group (AIG), which ended up becoming Wall Street's de facto insurance provider of last resort for risky ABS (see Mehrling 2011, 132–134, Chapter 6). This example shows that VaR (and the policy prescriptions suggested by VaR, such as purchasing credit default swap insurance on risky ABS) might sow the very fragility that it was meant to avoid by crowding the market into specific hedges originated by an undiversified pool of counterparties.

Second, VaR *blinded* market participants to tail risks in banks' portfolios. Because VaR assumed that asset prices followed a normal distribution, individual banks' VaR levels underestimated the expected value of loss in banks' portfolio. Normal distributions based on historical asset price returns were proven inapplicable to all market states since, as Mark Blyth surmised, "ten-sigma events actually happen nine years apart" (Blyth 2013, 35). The point is not to impugn the intellectual progenitors of VaR, nor to fault bank risk managers for their incompetence and moral failings like so many other accounts of the crisis. Rather, VaR illustrates an important point about the risks of *institutionalizing* economic metrics based on ergodicity (via assumptions of normally distributed asset prices based on historical returns) in a non-ergodic world, since misplaced faith in ergodic measures of market risk blind market participants to non-ergodic shifts in financial markets. The more widely market participants share an ergodic risk metric, the more vulnerable the market is to sudden shifts in sentiment when these risk metrics no longer prove to be a reliable guide to future market outcomes.

Third, the use of VaR prior to the global financial crisis meant that VaR was a causal driver of financial market outcomes, such as instability in VaR could create instability in financial markets. When outcomes revealed to banks that VaR underestimated portfolio risk, asset managers logically liquidated risky assets and purchased safe assets. This individually rational behavior proved collectively disastrous, as the correlation risk among disparate markets spiked as multiple asset managers attempted to "get liquid" at the same time. VaR deserves some of the blame for this phenomenon, as far as VaR caused multiple systemically linked financial institutions to adopt the same risk hedges, thus increasing the serial correlation of the entire global banking system. As more firms adopted VaR, the stability of the financial system became increasingly predicated on the reliability of VaR methodology. During the Asian financial crisis, when the price of short-dated options rose with volatility as the Asian financial crisis spread, many financial institutions sought to reduce their overall VaR numbers and liquidate large portions of their portfolios, leading to widening bond spreads across asset classes unrelated to the Asian financial crisis. Mark Blyth notes that no material change in the underlying riskiness of banks occurred: it was simply the increase in the cost of insurance via equity derivatives that caused banks to sell risky assets. In this case, a convention adopted to measure the risk of losses led to real effects on market outcomes (Blyth 2003).

These three insights show what happens when the stability of the financial system depends on an ergodic risk measure based on the assumption of normally distributed asset price returns. VaR stands out as an institutionalized metric based on key economic conventions that, once adopted, sowed epistemic blindness to the risks in banks' loan portfolios while also making banks seem well capitalized headed into the crisis. Daniel Tarullo finds that the ten largest US banks had risk-weighted capital ratios more than 10% in 2006, well above the 8% Basel II minimum. Therefore, from the standpoint of regulators, banks were well capitalized heading into the global financial crisis.[11] VaR made it easier for banks to extend credit to risky asset classes that, for a time, supported rising prices and seemingly justified the favorable risk ratings generated by VaR. On the downside, VaR contributed to adverse feedback loops wherein risks were magnified by the fact that since many banks used VaR, they all sought to sell the same assets simultaneously, thus exacerbating already tumultuous market conditions (Tarullo 2008, 155). From the viewpoint of the Minsky model and constraints on fragility, banks' techniques for measuring capital charges that were based on ergodic risk measures provided a justification for banks to sponsor risky financial structures and explain banks' risk tolerance prior to the global financial crisis.

Bond Ratings and the Creation of Information Insensitive Debt

In January 2011, the Financial Crisis Inquiry Commission (FCIC) issued a report summarizing the results into their investigation of the primary causes of the global financial crisis. While there was some dissent among the Commission about the crisis' primary causes, the Commission agreed that the credit rating agencies (CRAs) were "essential cogs in the wheel of financial destruction" prior to the crisis. The report found that investors would rely on ratings "often blindly" and concluded that the global financial crisis "could not have happened without the rating agencies" (The Financial Crisis Inquiry Commission 2011, xxv).

Why did investors "blindly" rely on credit ratings? How did the three independent CRAs—Moody's, Standard and Poor's, and Fitch—become "key enablers" of America's real estate bubble and credit boom? What led the bipartisan FCIC to conclude the CRAs were *decisive* factors that enabled the unsustainable increase in real estate prices and related credit boom, such that ratings were necessary preconditions for the global financial crisis? Why did CRAs face incentives to grant high ratings to in hindsight risky ABS? And what do ratings tell us about the role of economic conventions in financial markets?

All credit markets suffer from information asymmetries—in general, borrowers know more about their ability to repay than lenders. In extreme cases, this information asymmetry can cause adverse selection problems in financial markets, wherein the least creditworthy borrowers crowd out the most creditworthy, leading to foregone Pareto-optimal transactions and market failure (Akerlof 1970). One way to solve this market failure is for borrowers to enlist third parties to render independent judgments on their creditworthiness, based on the rationale that dispassionate observers lack a financial interest in a transaction and can thus be trusted to provide an objective appraisal of a borrower's ability to repay their loans. The big three CRAs, including Moody's, Standard and Poor's, and their European counterpart, Fitch, provided authoritative opinions on the creditworthiness of different borrowers, including sovereign governments, corporations, and ABS, to name a few examples. Ratings satisfied a mutual need in capital markets: creditors valued having third party opinions on the creditworthiness of their borrowers, while debtors found that ratings from the CRAs enhanced their ability to borrow.

Are credit ratings conventions? Moody's Investors Service defines credit ratings as "credible and independent assessments of credit risk" that "contribute to efficiencies in fixed-income markets and other obligations" (Moody's Investors Service 2018). Standard & Poor's (S&P) states that credit ratings are "opinions about credit risk" that describe "the ability and willingness of an issuer…to meet its financial obligations." They also caution that "credit ratings [are] not an exact science" and just one factor investors ought to consider while making investment decisions (Standard & Poor's Ratings Services 2014, 2–3).

Based on the rating agencies' own descriptions, credit ratings qualify as economic conventions of *expert opinion*. The widespread use of bond ratings shows that market participants and regulators believe that the CRAs have an information advantage that allowed them to render authoritative judgments about borrowers *that would otherwise be unattainable by the investor public absent significant due diligence costs*. In this sense, ratings represent agents' tendency to "fall back on the judgment of the rest of the world which is perhaps better informed," as Keynes argued about conventions of expert opinion (Keynes 1937a, 214). As the FCIC found, "many investors, such as some pension funds and university endowments, relied on credit ratings because they had neither access to the same data as the rating agencies nor the capacity or analytical ability to assess the securities they were purchasing" (The Financial Crisis Inquiry Commission 2011, 119). The FCIC's findings comport with Keynes' depiction of conventions, specifically that time, resource, and information constraints compel agents to employ economic conventions to mitigate uncertainty in financial markets, allowing agents to "save [their] faces as rational, economic men" by providing anchors upon which they can base their decisions (Keynes 1937a, 214).

In 1975, the Securities and Exchange Commission (SEC) mandated that bond issuers have their securities rated by one of the "nationally recognized statistical rating organizations" (or NRSROs, such as S&P, Moody's and Fitch) when issuing bonds to investors (Abdelal and Blyth 2015, 44). Around the same time, the rating agencies switched their fee structure from an "investor pay" to an "issuer pay" business model. This fee structure change created incentives for potential conflicts of interest, since competition among the rating agencies for issuer business may have induced CRAs to shade upwardly their ratings to stay in their clients' good graces (White 2010, 215). This conflict of interest, coupled with the law requiring the CRAs to rate ABS, created a toxic mix of incentives for CRAs and ABS originators alike. As the FCIC found, these competitive pressures incentivized the CRAs to issue unrealistically favorable ratings to ABS issuers. CRAs faced pressure from both issuers, who wanted high ratings on their originated instruments less they take their business to other rating agencies, and internally from managers who urged front-line rating officials to maintain market share at all costs (The Financial Crisis Inquiry Commission 2011, 210).

Since the SEC required that CRAs rate ABS, the rating agencies became important enablers of mortgage origination and securitization prior to the global financial crisis. The SEC also set legal limits on the kind of collateralized debt ABCP and repo counterparties could purchase, limiting their holdings to top-rated collateral and raising demand for highly rated assets. Throughout the 2000s, financial institutions engineered risky financial products designed to game the CRAs' ratings methodology to garner the highest ratings possible for risky tranches of debt (White 2010, 214). Because ABS received high ratings from the

CRAs, many risk-averse investors such as money market mutual funds, pension funds, and university endowments could invest in ABCP and repo of conduits, based on the logic that sound collateral backed these loans (Kacperczyk and Schnabl 2010, 34–35).[12]

Shadow banking depositors depended on credit ratings to justify their belief that the collateral backing ABCP and repo was *information-insensitive*, or free from adverse selection issues because of information symmetry. Gorton et al. argue that information insensitivity is critical for depositor confidence in both traditional and shadow banking structures. Information symmetry implies the face value of a deposit will always be worth, at a minimum, the initial deposit value. Furthermore, information symmetry also suggests that there is no market premium for doing additional due diligence to produce private information on assets (Gorton 2009, 18). The ability to mint information-insensitive debt was "socially valuable" because it obviated depositor fears of information asymmetry in banking markets (Gorton et al. 2012, 1). Gorton finds that banking panics (in both traditional and shadow banking markets) occur when information-insensitive debt becomes information-sensitive, which shakes investors' faith in bank collateral (Gorton 2009, 5). Zoltan Pozsar adds that banking confidence depends on investors' continued belief in the moneyness of their shadow banking deposits that can be redeemed any time at par value, much like retail deposits (Pozsar 2014). This phenomenon explains why governments, which have a vested interest in financial stability, sponsor deposit insurance schemes for retail deposits, in turn preventing bank runs by ensuring depositors that their deposits will remain information-insensitive regardless of the idiosyncratic credit risks among depository institutions.

The CRAs played a critical role in enabling the rise of shadow banking by allowing financial institutions to mint ABS collateral that, for a time, was viewed as information-insensitive debt by ABCP and repo counterparties. For debt to qualify as information-insensitive, agents must have faith that it is immune from adverse selection problems that emerge due to information asymmetries about the underlying collateral quality of the bonds themselves. Further, Gorton claimed that favorable ratings signaled to investors that there was "no real point to doing due diligence because nothing will be found out (Gorton 2010, 181)" so investors ended up blindly relying on credit ratings (The Financial Crisis Inquiry Commission 2011, 206). Bond ratings filled a valuable market niche by rendering independent and credible opinions on the information-insensitivity of ABCP and repo ABS collateral as institutionalized economic conventions.

In this way, shadow banking was a socially contingent process enabled by economic conventions, which permitted financial institutions and ABCP and repo counterparties to create and invest in information-insensitive, high-grade assets to take advantage of the interest rate differential between short-term liabilities and long-term assets. Banks liked ratings because they allowed them to earn hefty ABS origination fees and profit form term structure arbitrage opportunities. ABCP and repo counterparties valued ratings because they gave them confidence in their shadow banking deposits that allowed them to earn higher returns than cash instruments. The creation of information-insensitive debt is a social process, which follows from financial market participants placing faith in certain key economic conventions about what qualifies as information-insensitive debt.

So why did the CRAs underestimate the probability of default of the assets underlying ABS prior to the global financial crisis? Rawi Abdelal and Mark Blyth find that the CRAs' ratings methodology was based on historical mortgage default rates from the worst post-Depression default episode, Texas in the 1980s (Abdelal and Blyth 2015, 47).[13] Furthermore, the FCIC found that the "M3 prime" model used by Moody's to automate ABS rating decisions assumed that home prices would increase roughly 4% per year in perpetuity, with a low probability of housing prices ever falling nationally (The Financial Crisis Inquiry Commission 2011, 120–121).

The CRAs needed some basis of projecting future default rates of residential mortgages and chose an ergodic measure that underestimated the *correlation risk* of multiple regional housing markets collapsing simultaneously. This underestimation should not come as a surprise, since Keynes notes that asset market participants have a tendency "to substitute for knowledge which is unattainable certain conventions, the chief of which is to assume, contrary to all likelihood, that the future will resemble the past (Keynes 1937b, 13)." When the CRAs rendered their credit opinions, they assumed that the future would resemble the past, with disastrous consequences when housing prices declined beginning in 2006.

There are five implications of bond ratings for this book's theoretical framework:

First, ratings sowed *epistemic blindness* in markets prior to the global financial crisis. Because the CRAs' opinions were codified into regulations governing allocation decisions of entire investor classes, market participants assumed that ratings provided an accurate assessment of the probability of default of ABS. After all, the CRAs employed the experts who could access proprietary data, had close relationships with ABS originators, and boasted sophisticated risk management techniques with the best human resources. Hence, market participants deferred to the judgment of the CRAs, especially when their record seemed impeccable during the boom years. One interview subject who served as the chief global market strategist for one of the world's premier alternative investment funds argued that the entire securitization chain was "corrupted" by the ratings process. The subject said that major investors believed that the major CRAs had close relationships with issuers were thus privy to information unavailable to outside investors. Therefore, private investors presumed the rating agencies had an information advantage, making them blind to the prospect that the CRAs could systematically underestimate default risk (Global Market Strategist 2019). Another prominent example of the relationship between bond ratings and epistemic blindness is the synthetic CDO, or an asset-backed security comprised of a pool of credit default swaps, created by Goldman Sachs known as Abacus 2007-AC1. The Securities and Exchange Commission (SEC) fined Goldman Sachs $500 million for withholding material information about the securities underlying the Abacus, specifically that the hedge fund Paulson & Company, a known short-seller of real estate, had selected the underlying securities (Securities and Exchange Commission 2010). An investigation by the United States Senate Permanent Subcommittee on Investigations found that although most of the securities underlying Abacus were rated BBB, Moody's and Standard and Poor's rated nearly eighty percent of the overall Abacus structure AAA. A Moody's representative told Senate investigators that the rating agency would have changed their methodology had they known that John Paulson was on the other side of the Abacus trade. However, because Moody's did not know this material information, they rated the Abacus deal according to their conventional models, thus lulling the end-buyers of the synthetic CDO into a false sense of security about the creditworthiness of the underlying collateral. By January 2008, nearly 99% of the reference securities for Abacus had been downgraded, with the primary investors losing about $1 billion on the transaction (and Paulson & Company earning the same amount) (Levin and Coburn 2010).

Second, the institutionalization of bond ratings into regulations about the types of collateral ABCP and repo investors could hold predicated market stability on the continued perceived truth-value of bond ratings. In other words, market stability depended on bond rating convention stability. If market outcomes comported with agents' convention-given expectations vis-à-vis ratings, markets would remain "tranquil" and "calm." If, however, default rates diverged from expectations expressed by bond ratings, then market participants would reappraise their governing conventions, thus precipitating change in financial markets. If the "shock" associated with a ratings downgrade were pervasive, this process could cause market participants to shun the commercial paper and repo issued by a specific shadow banking entity, leading to an idiosyncratic bank run. Hence, credit downgrades in 2007 and 2008 were closely watched by market participants. When the CRAs downgraded assets, markets had to reappraise their convention-given expectations, altering their decision-making calculi and leading to different market outcomes. As Keynes argued, downgrades (i.e. a change in conventions) can cause "the practice of calmness and immobility, of certainty and security," to "suddenly" break down. Market participants eventually realized that the assumptions underlying ratings were based on a "flimsy foundation" that housing prices would never decline nationally (Keynes 1937a, 214–215) When housing prices did decline, bond ratings changed too, thus precipitating change in financial markets.

Third, credit ratings might have changed the very material fundamentals of financial markets that they were meant to reflect. As Donald MacKenzie argues, bond ratings were not cameras that passively record events but were engines of financial change (MacKenzie 2008).[14] High ratings for ABS provided an *allocative* decision-making anchor for both financial institutions and ABCP and repo counterparties: all else being equal, highly rated assets were in greater demand than lower rated ones. Favorable ratings permitted large pools of risk-averse capital to invest in highly rated ABS (via ABCP and repo conduits), thus driving down credit spreads in highly rated asset classes. Lower risk spreads incentivized *greater credit extension* to the highly rated asset class in the short run, reifying the material creditworthiness that favorable ratings were meant to reflect. As Hyun Song Shin found, permissive credit conditions in the shadow banking market, via ABCP and repo conduits sponsored by American and European financial institutions, added fuel to the fire of the unsustainable increase in real estate prices in the US economy from 2001 to 2007 (Shin 2012). While it is difficult to dis-embed rising housing prices from the credit extension underpinning them, there is good reason to believe that credit expansion that financed the boom contributed to the unsustainable increase in housing prices in the 2000s. The empirical challenge facing analysts, who cannot run a controlled experiment holding the rest of the global economy constant, is showing that high ratings *caused* the credit boom that accompanied the housing bubble. A less ambitious (but more plausible) claim is that ratings contributed to the *amplitude* and *periodicity* of the housing bubble. During the bubble years, high ratings endogenously contributed to pro-cyclical capital flows into ABS, but when housing prices fell, downgrades sent the pro-cyclical process into reverse, lowering collateral prices and exposing banks' fragility. Without high ratings, it is hard to imagine a scenario in which so many risk-averse investors like money market mutual funds would have been legally permitted to invest in the risky collateral sold by America and Europe's shadow banking conduits.

Fourth, bond ratings' short-run success as economic conventions might have been responsible for sowing long-term structural changes in the economy that undermined their usefulness as value anchors. Because bond ratings were popular prior to the global financial crisis, more capital flowed into highly rated but risky asset classes, compounding the momentum of rising prices in the short term but reifying the inexorable downturn in prices in the long term. Such is the case of *data hysteresis*, which Post-Keynesians describe as the tendency of the macroeconomy to evolve, such that historical outcome generators shift in non-ergodic ways over time (Palley 2011, 42). Paradoxically, perhaps the rise in popularity of ratings in the short term sowed the seeds of their own irrelevance in the long term. Ratings may have thus exemplified "Goodhart's law," which states that observed historical relationships will begin to collapse once regulatory control is placed on them. In this case, ratings' short-term success led to credit allocation decisions that undermined their long-term applicability (Chrystal and Mizen 2001).

Fifth, bond ratings were a key driver of the US economy's fragility prior to the global financial crisis. Two of Minsky's conditions of fragility were the existence of lenders willing to purchase short-term, money-like liabilities and borrowers to emit higher-yielding, risky assets. Ratings facilitated both aspects of the shadow banking value chain by permitting financial institutions to bundle and divide risky ABS into salable securities. Legal restrictions placed on shadow banking counterparties such as money market mutual funds permitted them to purchase ABCP and repo liabilities backed by risky collateral. In hindsight, it is tempting to blame money managers for blindly relying on ratings to make investment decisions, but prior to the crisis, ratings seemed like good indications of the credit quality for financial derivatives. And, since triple-A rated credit derivatives yielded more than Treasury bonds, competitive pressures often induced money managers to purchase highly rated risky assets to maintain their edge among fellow fund managers. While institutional investors did have the option to ignore ratings, they did so at their own bureaucratic peril, since underperforming money managers were replaced with those willing to take on more risk during the boom years.

Conclusion

The purpose of this chapter was to identify the drivers of fragility in the US economy prior to the global financial crisis. It described the emergence of off-balance-sheet financial intermediation in which systemically important financial institutions sponsored asset-backed commercial paper and repurchase agreement conduits to borrow in wholesale funding markets to invest in asset-backed securities. This chapter argued that this parallel, or "shadow" banking system fell outside of the regulatory purview of banking authorities, and its lack of deposit insurance made shadow banking conduits vulnerable to bank runs in the wholesale funding markets. In the context of Minsky's financial instability hypothesis, shadow banking structures that emerged in the US economy prior to the global financial crisis were speculative in nature, in the Minsky sense, since ABCP and repo conduits relied on *fresh infusions* of capital to remain liquid.

The chapter then argued that the rise of shadow banking was best understood as a function of banks' accumulation of risky ABS and their capital inadequacy, both of which were convention-driven phenomena. Banks' undercapitalization stemmed from the regulatory practice of allowing banks to determine their own capital charges based on their internal risk models that assumed market ergodicity when reserving regulatory capital. Bond ratings issued by the credit rating agencies served as institutionalized conventions of expert opinion that permitted theretofore risk-averse investors like money market mutual funds to invest in the risky commercial paper and repo of banks. These developments created a toxic mix of incentives for financial institutions, allowing them to adopt speculative financing arrangements to capture rents from the inflating housing bubble and credit boom.

Once adopted, these conventions were responsible for two interrelated outcomes in financial markets: first, conventions made it easier for banks to extend credit to high-risk borrowers in the mortgage market and created ever-permissive credit conditions that in turn justified the rosy convention-given views of banks' risk. As a result, conventions became *self-stabilizing*, at least in the short run, but also contributed to the amplitude and periodicity of the unsustainable increase in housing prices in the US economy from 2001 to 2006 overall. Second, economic conventions blinded agents to non-routine (i.e. non-convention-given) risks in the shadow banking system.

By early 2007, the stage was set for a crisis. The following two chapters describe the market dynamic that ensued during these tumultuous years in the US and global economy. They explain how regulators' repeated interventions in financial markets created a *conventional expectation* that regulators would act as liquidity providers of last resort in shadow banking markets. This conventional expectation prevented funding pressures in wholesale funding markets from metastasizing into a full-blown banking panic, which is what happened after the failure of investment bank Lehman Brothers. Lehman's failure created *convention uncertainty* regarding regulators' intentions, thus catalyzing a generalized banking panic in wholesale funding markets. Regulators' unconditional bailouts can be understood as a by-product of the economic conventions held by senior economic technocrats in the US Federal Reserve and US Department of the Treasury. It is proposed that the bank bailouts were successful because they re-established convention equilibrium regarding regulators' willingness to serve as a liquidity provider of last resort to shadow banking conduits.

Notes

1. Acharya and Richardson (2011), Adrian and Shin (2009), Gorton and Metrick (2010a), Helleiner (2011), McCulley (2009), Mehrling et al. (2013), Pozsar (2008, 2014), and Shin (2012). A key difference between shadow banking and traditional banking, however, was that shadow banking lacked government-sponsored deposit insurance and was thus susceptible to bank runs and contagion effects once collateral prices fell.

Shadow banking structures depended on continued access to fresh capital to maintain their liquidity and solvency, and thus qualified as speculative finance per Minsky's taxonomy of finance. See Minsky (1992, 7–8, 2008, 230–235). It is worth noting that this book greatly simplifies the various iterations of shadow banking globally prior to the global financial crisis. Not every shadow bank borrowed in ABCP and repo markets to fund ABS purchases, and not all shadow banks were connected to traditional banks and broker-dealers. Readers interested in a more granular view of the shadow banking system would particularly benefit from reading (Mehrling 2011; Pozsar et al. 2010). For the purposes of clarity and illustration, this book describes a stylized shadow bank in Fig. 4.1 to show how economic conventions related to fragility in an abstracted shadow banking system. For an excellent and recent summary of the evolution of shadow banking after the global financial crisis, including on the role of official and synthetic substitutes for ABCP and repo after the crisis, see Pozsar (2018).
2. Not all investors in securitized assets bear idiosyncratic credit risk. For instance, securitized debt sponsored by the United States' government-sponsored enterprises, Fannie Mae and Freddie Mac, carried full credit guarantees (which themselves were implicitly and, after the financial crisis, explicitly backed by the US government). Holders of so-called agency-backed MBS were exposed to prepayment risk associated with changing mortgage interest rates.
3. See also Acharya and Richardson (2011), Gorton and Metrick (2010a), and Gorton (2010).
4. ([FP−PP]/PP), or the difference between the price the repo counterparty *receives in the future* (FP) for purchasing an asset at its *present price* (PP).
5. In addition to issuing ABCP, many financial institutions ended up insuring ABCP and repo conduits via liquidity puts. For instance, the Financial Crisis Inquiry Commission finds that commercial banks like Citigroup issued liquidity puts, or liquidity insurance contracts, that provided guarantees to mitigate the liquidity risk facing ABCP investors, which subsequently caused the credit rating agencies to issue favorable ratings on the ABCP backing risky ABS. As the FCIC found, banks like Citigroup "did not have to hold any capital against such contingencies. Rather, [they were] permitted to use [their] own risk models to determine the appropriate capital charge." The report goes on to discuss how Citigroup vastly underestimated the possibility that their liquidity puts would be triggered, thus leading to their undercapitalization when the ABCP market seized after Lehman Brothers. For more, see The Financial Crisis Inquiry Commission (2011, 137–138) and Kacperczyk and Schnabl (2010, 33).

6. Tobias Adrian and Hyun Song Shin estimate that by March 2008, Wall Street's five biggest commercial and investment banks rolled over roughly 25% of their balance sheets on an overnight basis (Adrian and Shin 2009).
7. The causal importance of conventional expectations of counterparty solvency in shadow banking is discussed in the following empirical chapters.
8. In other words, banks have a natural desire to maintain pro-cyclical capital reserves, wherein banks, facing competitive pressures, seek to hold fewer reserves during boom times and more reserves when they face economic headwinds.
9. The original Basel agreement received praise for its simplicity in that it enshrined a set of international principles on capital adequacy, which served an institutional function among signatory governments: namely how to ensure that national banking systems had robust capital cushions that adhered to a shared set of risk-weighted capital standards. Also, it is worth noting that originally, though the banks had a clear preference to risk-weight their capital charges, regulators still had a choice between accommodating banks and maintaining a simple approach that would require banks to make a fixed capital reserve for every asset on their books regardless of quality. The simple method lent itself to easy cross-bank and transnational comparisons of capital adequacy but did not cover off-balance-sheet risks nor account for risk heterogeneities across asset classes, so regulators opted for risk-weighting as well, despite its drawbacks.
10. The practice of regulatory arbitrage after Basel I shows how bank capital requirements had the capability of producing undercapitalized financial institutions while exacerbating internal imbalances in the economy.
11. Of course, much of this undercapitalization follows from the fact that banks housed many of these risky assets in off-balance-sheet vehicles such as SIVs, which, before the 2010 Dodd-Frank financial reform bill, were treated as separate entities rather than as one consolidated whole.
12. For instance, many financial institutions took pools of high-risk assets, such as bonds backed by subprime mortgages, and turned them into highly rated assets by slicing them into securities based on first losses in the underlying portfolio of assets. The riskiest slice, or *tranche*, of the newly created instrument (known as the equity portion of the asset pool's capital structure) absorbed first losses in the underlying portfolio of assets and as such, commanded the lowest ratings from the CRAs and thus offered the highest yields. The most senior part of the capital structure earned the highest ratings from rating agencies and offered the lowest yield, based on the logic that barring catastrophe (or an environment of 100% asset price correlation), total losses on the underlying mortgage

pool would never exceed the cushion of loss below the senior tranche of the asset pool, usually capped between 15 and 30%.
13. Another reason the CRAs might have been marginally more willing to grant favorable ratings to ABS is because of their fee-for-rating billing structure, which meant that the profitability of the CRAs depended on whether they could keep banks "happy" for repeat business. In 2005, over 40% of Moody's revenue came from rating ABS. And from 2003 to 2006, Moody's revenue tied to rating ABS rose from $12 million to $91 million.
14. MacKenzie dubs this phenomenon "performativity," or how economic theories influence the material constitution of financial markets.

Works Cited

Abdelal, Rawi, and Mark Blyth. 2015. "Just Who Put You in Charge? We Did: Credit Rating Agencies and the Politics of Ratings." In *Ranking the World: Grading States as a Tool of Global Governance*, by Alexander Cooley and Jack Snyder (eds.), 39–59. Cambridge: Cambridge University Press.

Acharya, Viral, and Matthew Richardson. 2011. "How Securitization Concentrated Risk." In *What Caused the Financial Crisis*, by Jeffrey Friedman (eds.), 183–199. Philadelphia: University of Pennsylvania Press.

Acharya, Viral, Philipp Schnabl, and Gustavo Suarez. 2013. "Securitization Without Risk Transfer." *Journal of Financial Economics* 107 (3): 515–536.

Adrian, Tobias, and Hyun Song Shin. 2009. "The Shadow Banking System: Implications for Financial Regulation." *Federal Reserve Bank of New York Staff Reports* 1–16.

Akerlof, George A. 1970. "The Market for 'Lemons': Quality Uncertainty and the Market Mechanism." *Quarterly Journal of Economics* 84 (3): 488–500.

Allen, Franklin, Stephen Morris, and Hyun Song Shin. 2006. "Beauty Contests and Iterated Expectations in Asset Markets." *The Review of Financial Studies* 19 (3): 719–752.

Baklanova, Viktoria, Adam Copeland, and Rebecca McCaughrin. 2015. "Reference Guide to U.S. Repo and Securities Lending Markets." *Federal Reserve Bank of New York Staff Reports* (740): 1–68.

Basel Committee on Banking Supervision. 2005. "An Explanatory Note on the Basel II IRB Risk Weight Functions." *Bank for International Settlements*, July: 1–19.

Blyth, Mark. 2003. "The Political Power of Financial Ideas: Transparency, Risk and Distribution in Global Finance." In *Monetary Orders*, by Jonathan Kirshner (eds.), 239–259. Ithaca: Cornell University Press.

Blyth, Mark. 2010. "Coping with the Black Swan: The Unsettling World of Nassim Taleb." *Critical Review: A Journal of Politics and Society* 24 (1): 447–465.

Blyth, Mark. 2013. *Austerity: The History of a Dangerous Idea.* Oxford: Oxford University Press.

Brunnermeier, Markus K. 2009. "Deciphering the Liquidity and Credit Crunch 2007–2008." *Journal of Economic Perspectives* 32 (1): 77–100.

Chrystal, K. Alec, and Paul D. Mizen. 2001. "Goodhart's Law: Its Origins, Meaning and Implications for Monetary Policy." *Festschrift in Honour of Charles Goodhart* 1–26.

Colander, David, Hans Follmer, Armin Haas, Michael Goldberg, Katarina Juselius, Alan Kirman, Thomas Lux, and Brigette Sloth. 2009. "The Financial Crisis and the Systemic Failure of Academic Economics." *Kiel Working Papers* (Kiel Institute for the World Economy) 17.

Crotty, James. 2009. "Structural Causes of the Global Financial Crisis: A Critical Assessment of the 'New Financial Architecture'." *Cambridge Journal of Economics* 33 (4): 563–580.

Federal Reserve Bank of St. Louis. 2018. "Federal Reserve Economic Data Database." *Federal Reserve Bank of St. Louis: Economic Research.* 15 March. Accessed March 31, 2018. https://fred.stlouisfed.org/.

Global Market Strategist, interview by Neil Shenai. 2019. *Author Interview* (May 6).

Gordy, Michael B., and Bradley Howells. 2006. "Procyclicality in Basel II: Can We Treat the Disease Without Killing the Patient?" *Journal of Financial Intermediation* 15 (3): 395–417.

Gorton, Gary B. 2009. "Slapped in the Face by the Invisible Hand: Banking and the Panic of 2007." *Federal Reserve Bank of Atlanta's 2009 Financial Markets Conference: Financial Innovation and Crisis*, 1–52. Atlanta: Federal Reserve Bank of Atlanta.

Gorton, Gary B. 2010. *Slapped by the Invisible Hand: The Panic of 2007.* Oxford: Oxford University Press.

Gorton, Gary B., and Andrew Metrick. 2010a. "Haircuts." *Federal Reserve Bank of St. Louis Review* 92 (6): 507–519.

Gorton, Gary B., and Andrew Metrick. 2010b. "Regulating the Shadow Banking System." *Brookings Papers on Economic Activity* 261–312.

Gorton, Gary B., Stefan Lewellen, and Andrew Metrick. 2012. "The Safe-Asset Share." *AER Papers & Proceedings, 2012* 1–16.

Hedge fund manager, interview by Neil Shenai. 2018. *Author Interview* (May 2).

Helleiner, Eric. 2011. "Understanding the 2007–2008 Global Financial Crisis: Lessons for Scholars of International Political Economy." *Annual Review of Political Science* 14 (2): 67–87.

Kacperczyk, Marcin, and Philipp Schnabl. 2010. "When Safe Proved Risky: Commerical Paper During the Financial Crisis of 2007–2009." *Journal of Economic Perspectives* 24 (1): 29–50.

Keynes, John M. 1937a. "The General Theory of Employment." *The Quarterly Journal of Economics* 51 (2): 209–223.

Keynes, John M. 1937b. "Some Economic Consequences of a Declining Population." *The Eugenics Review* 13–17.

Kodres, Laura E. 2013. "What Is Shadow Banking?" *Finance & Development* 42–43.

Levin, Carl, and Tom Coburn. 2010. *Wall Street and the Financial Crisis: The Role of Investment Banks*. Washington, DC, April 26. http://graphics8.nytimes.com/packages/pdf/business/2010April26_MemorandumonWallStreetCrisis.PDF.

MacKenzie, Donald. 2008. *An Engine, Not a Camera: How Financial Models Shape Markets*. Cambridge: The MIT Press.

McCulley, Paul. 2007. "Global Central Bank Focus: Teton Reflections." *Pimco*. September. Accessed April 14, 2018. http://www.pimco.com/en-us/insights/economic-and-market-commentary/global-central-bank-focus/teton-reflections.

McCulley, Paul. 2009. "The Shadow Banking System and Hyman Minsky's Economic Journey." *Pimco*. May. Accessed April 1, 2018. https://www.pimco.com/en-us/insights/economic-and-market-commentary/global-central-bank-focus/the-shadow-banking-system-and-hyman-minskys-economic-journey.

Mehrling, Perry. 2011. *The New Lombard Street: How the Fed Became the Dealer of Last Resort*. Princeton and Oxford: Princeton University Press.

Mehrling, Perry, Zoltan Pozsar, James Sweeney, and Daniel H. Neilson. 2013. "Bagehot Was a Shadow Banker: Shadow Banking, Central Banking, and the Future of Global Finance." *Institute for New Economic Thinking Shadow Banking Colloquium* 1–20.

Minsky, Hyman. 1992. "The Financial Instability Hypothesis." *Levy Economics Institute of Bard College Working Papers* 1–9.

Minsky, Hyman. 2008. *Stabilizing an Unstable Economy*. New York: McGraw-Hill.

Moody's Investors Service. 2018. *Moody's Role in the Capital Markets*. March 17. https://www.moodys.com/Pages/atc002.aspx.

Palley, Thomas. 2011. "A Theory of Minsky Super-Cycles and Financial Crises." *Contributions to Political Economy* 32 (1): 31–46.

Pozsar, Zoltan. 2008. "The Rise and Fall of the Shadow Banking System." *Moody's Economy.com: Regional Financial Review* 1–14.

Pozsar, Zoltan. 2014. "Shadow Banking: The Money View." *Office of Financial Research Working Paper Series* 14 (4): 1–71.

Pozsar, Zoltan. 2018. *The Safe Asset Glut*. Investment Research. New York: Credit Suisse.

Pozsar, Zoltan, Tobias Adrian, Adam Ashcraft, and Hayley Boesky. 2010. "Shadow Banking." *Federal Reserve Bank of New York Staff Report* (458): 1–82.

Risk.net. 2012. *Goodbye VAR? Basel to Consider Other Risk Metrics.* February 28. Accessed March 15, 2018. https://www.risk.net/risk-management/market-risk/2154611/goodbye-var-basel-consider-other-risk-metrics.

Securities and Exchange Commission. 2010. "Goldman Sachs to Pay Record $550 Million to Settle SEC Charges Related to Subprime Mortgage CDO." *U.S. Securities and Exchange Commission.* July 15. Accessed April 15, 2018. https://www.sec.gov/news/press/2010/2010-123.htm.

Shin, Hyun Song. 2012. "Global Banking Glut and Loan Risk Premium." *Mundell-Fleming Lecture, 2011 IMF Annual Research Conference*, 1–46. Washington, DC: International Monetary Fund.

Standard & Poor's Ratings Services. 2014. *Standard & Poor's*. https://www.spratings.com/documents/20184/760102/SPRS_Understanding-Ratings_GRE.pdf/298e606f-ce5b-4ece-9076-66810cd9b6aa.

Tarullo, Daniel. 2008. *Banking on Basel: The Future of International Financial Regulation*. Washington, DC: Peterson Institute for International Economics.

The Economist. 2004. *Bothersome Basel: The New Capital-Adequacy Rules Have Proved Tricky to Draw Up*. April 15. Accessed March 15, 2018. https://www.economist.com/node/2570061.

The Financial Crisis Inquiry Commission. 2011. *The Financial Crisis Inquiry Report: Final Report of the National Commission on the Causes of the Financial and Economic Crisis in the United States*. Washington, DC: U.S. Government Printing Office.

Toomey, Robert, Robert Rogerson, Justyna Podziemska, and Emily Losi. 2017. "U.S. Repo Market Fact Sheet, 2017." *Securities Industry and Financial Markets Association.* Accessed April 1, 2018. https://www.sifma.org/wp-content/uploads/2017/08/US-Repo-Factsheet-2017-07-25.pdf.

White, Lawrence J. 2010. "Markets: The Credit Rating Agencies." *Economic Perspectives* 24 (2): 211–226.

CHAPTER 5

Regulators as Liquidity Providers of Last Resort

INTRODUCTION

This chapter and Chapter 6 of this book explore the relationship between the market's conventional expectations of counterparty liquidity and solvency and the stability of shadow banking conduits prior to, during, and after the global financial crisis. These chapters demonstrate the utility of *Social Finance*'s third, fourth, and fifth propositions: specifically, that shocks to convention-given expectations catalyze convention uncertainty; given sufficient fragility, uncertainty disrupts the market's price discovery mechanism and triggers a flight to quality; and elite responses to financial instability are a function of their economic ideas used to diagnose the crisis and their intervention capacity.

This chapter begins by describing the counterparty bailout of hedge fund Long-Term Capital Management (LTCM) in 1998, arguing that this episode presaged the stresses experienced by the global economy during the global financial crisis. The chapter posits that LTCM's near bankruptcy situated regulators as central agents of preserving financial stability during periods of systemic stress, opening the door for greater interventions down the road. The chapter then examines the first stage of the crisis, encompassing early stress beginning in 2007 through the bailout and sale of investment bank Bear Stearns in March 2008 and nationalization of housing Agencies Fannie Mae and Freddie Mac in September 2008. This section marshals evidence from elite interviews with market participants and secondary sources to argue that regulators'

© The Author(s) 2018
N. Shenai, *Social Finance*,
https://doi.org/10.1007/978-3-319-91346-9_5

repeated interventions in markets created a *conventional expectation* that regulators would serve as liquidity providers of last resort for shadow banking conduits. As a result, bank runs were idiosyncratic and not generalized across all financial institutions during this period.

THE SCENE SETTER: LTCM AND THE ORIGINS OF THE WEEKEND BAILOUT

The global financial crisis was not without recent historical precedent. One episode in particular—the rise and fall of hedge fund LTCM in the 1990s—presaged the regular weekend meetings held at the Federal Reserve Bank of New York that took place throughout the global financial crisis. Many of the key players in the LTCM episode, including bank chief executives and senior Federal Reserve officials, were central players during the global financial crisis ten years later. And the problems that brought down LTCM, including exposure to tail risks amplified by leverage and exacerbated by insufficient capital buffers backed by runnable capital, foreshadowed the problems facing financial institutions during the crisis.

In addition to being a bellwether of the stresses to come, LTCM was a turning point in regulators' posture toward systemically important financial institutions, opening the door to more invasive interventions during the global financial crisis. Although the Federal Reserve did not risk its own capital to bail out LTCM, it arranged the market's private response to LTCM's insolvency, revealing its willingness to use its privileged market position to cajole private actors to bail out out a troubled counterparty in the name of financial stability. LTCM's bailout, deemed successful because it did not put taxpayer dollars at risk and avoided the disorderly bankruptcy of the fund, also had a subtle but ultimately more important consequence for the market's conventional expectations about the Fed's posture toward failing financial institutions. As Kevin Dowd contended, LTCM's bailout signaled "a major open-ended extension of Federal Reserve responsibilities," which established the market's belief that "the Fed should prevent the failure of large financial firms" (Dowd 1999, 1). Nobel Prize winning economist Myron Scholes, a board member of LTCM, also found that regulators' actions helped convince LTCM's creditors to post collateral to keep the fund afloat and to facilitate an orderly unwinding of the firm's liabilities. As Scholes concluded, "without the [Fed] acting quickly to mitigate these holdup activities, LTCM would have had to file for bankruptcy" (Scholes

2000, 17). Federal Reserve and US Treasury officials would repeatedly revisit the question of balancing moral hazard concerns and systemic stability goals when deciding how best to respond to the global financial crisis.

In 1993, a former bond arbitrageur from the investment bank Salomon Brothers named John Meriwether founded LTCM with $2.5 billion of funds raised from investors worldwide. Meriwether tapped into his network of Wall Street veterans and leading financial economists to recruit LTCM's investment professionals, which included numerous Nobel Prize laureates (such as Myron Scholes) and his former Salomon Brothers colleagues. LTCM's primary investment strategy was "fixed income arbitrage," or the simultaneous buying and selling of assets to take advantage of momentary price differences across different markets. LTCM's strategy was not pure arbitrage per se; rather, its trades involved assets that were nearly identical (such as an off-the-run twenty-nine-and-a-half-year vintage Treasury bond and its on-the-run thirty-year equivalent). LTCM based its trading strategy on ergodicity, or the assumption that historical price relationships determined long-run equilibrium asset prices. When prices deviated from their historical trends, LTCM's traders piled into the market and made big wagers with borrowed money betting that asset prices would self-correct back to their equilibrium value. When prices reverted, LTCM's leverage allowed it to earn many times its initial investment. At one point, LTCM had a leverage ratio of approximately one hundred-to-one.

LTCM was highly successful for its first years in operation. By 1996, LTCM had more assets than two investment banks, Lehman Brothers and Morgan Stanley, and was four-times bigger than the world's next-largest hedge fund. At the end of 1997, LTCM's traders brimmed with confidence in their ability to make above-market returns in what they viewed as relatively efficient markets, and the firm's phenomenal growth led Meriwether and his partners to engage in riskier strategies in under-traded asset classes, such as merger arbitrage in public equity markets.

By summer 1998, however, LTCM's fortunes began to turn. In August that year, the Russian Federation defaulted on its debt, which led to a flight to quality in bond markets. Risky bond prices fell and Treasury bond prices rose. LTCM was caught on the wrong side of this market stampede: having made levered bets against Treasuries to accumulate large holdings of risky bonds, LTCM's losses ballooned. Because of LTCM's high leverage ratio, estimated at nearly sixteen-to-one by the end of 1997, almost every bank on Wall Street had exposure to the fund. LTCM's counterparties began making collateral calls out of fears of counterparty insolvency. Bear Stearns, which served as LTCM's clearing bank, demanded additional $500 million to continue to clear LTCM's trades. LTCM also had an overlapping web of complex derivatives transactions, making it difficult for counterparties to have confidence in knowing the trades on LTCM's books. Facing simultaneous collateral calls and with market prices moving against the firm, LTCM scrambled for cash. Regulators feared that if LTCM went bankrupt, it would lead to cascading losses and bank runs against LTCM's counterparties. By September 1998, LTCM was a systemic risk to the global economy. Fearful of what a disorderly bankruptcy of LTCM might mean for the stability of the global financial system, the Federal Reserve Bank of New York (FRBNY) organized a consortium of banks to recapitalize LTCM by employing "moral suasion" to convince LTCM's main creditors that a private-sector bailout of LTCM would be preferable to a disorderly bankruptcy of the fund. The bailout consortium infused roughly $3.5 billion into LTCM and bought out the fund's remaining assets.[1] When markets stabilized, most of LTCM's counterparties sold their positions for small profits. Since then, the episode has been seen as a success for taxpayers, since the Fed did not risk its own capital and nevertheless succeeded in avoiding a chaotic unwinding of LTCM (Lowenstein 2000).

In defense of the Fed's involvement in LTCM, Fed Chairman Alan Greenspan previewed the language that his successor, Ben Bernanke, would often use to defend the Fed's bank bailouts during the global financial crisis. Greenspan testified to Congress that the Fed judged that it was far better for all parties, including LTCM's creditors and the broader economy, to "engender...an orderly resolution rather than let the firm go into disorderly fire-sale liquidation following a set of cascading cross defaults" (Greenspan 1998).[2] Federal Reserve Bank of New York President William McDonough affirmed Greenspan's view and claimed that "the American people would suffer in a way that is not appropriate for them to suffer if LTCM [had] failed." McDonough conjectured that LTCM would have failed had it not been for the Fed's involvement in its bailout (Haubrich 2007, 3).

LTCM's problems—its excessive leverage, its over-reliance on risk-management techniques like value-at-risk (VaR), its susceptibility to creditor panics and runs, and its traders' belief in the ergodicity of market prices—were universal pathologies exhibited by America's financial institutions throughout the 2000s. The Fed's ad hoc approach to LTCM's resolution also foreshadowed the regular weekend meetings at the Federal Reserve Bank of New York that took place throughout fall 2008. By organizing LTCM's creditor-led bailout, the Fed showed that it was willing to use its influence among financial institutions to narrate, cajole, and persuade private companies to aid its goals of financial market stability. Implicit in their involvement in LTCM was the Fed's belief that the economic costs of inaction (e.g. the uncertainty of defaults and financial contagion if LTCM were to have failed) exceed the benefits of exercising forbearance and allowing markets to clear on their own devices (in a "disorderly" fashion, as Greenspan described it). Although the Fed did not use its own capital to facilitate LTCM's bailout, the episode nevertheless marked the beginning of the market's conventional expectation that the Fed would serve as a liquidity provider of last resort in financial markets when systemically important financial institutions were on the brink of failure.

Early Tremors: Bear Stearns' Sale to J.P. Morgan and Nationalizing Fannie and Freddie

Despite the exigency and suspense of LTCM's bailout in 1998, the episode had faded to the recesses of the market's collective memory eight years later. 2006 was a banner year for financial institutions, and again, Wall Street's risk takers received the same praise that the media gave to John Meriwether and his traders a decade prior. Financiers only a few years removed from university earned seven-figure bonuses, while the real economy enjoyed the fruits of a widespread economic expansion (Anderson 2006). One former investment banker interviewed for *Social Finance* recalled that during this period, "people got fixated…on making a lot of personal wealth quickly," which in turn "drove the culture of risk taking." The investment banker noted that there the "fear of missing out" drove a lot of speculative investment. Incentives rewarded short-term trading strategies and increased risk tolerance among bankers and traders "to get to yes." The relaxation of bond covenants and investor protections were examples of this bubble mentality (Former investment banker 2 2018).

Beneath this placid surface, however, several developments were underway that would threaten the solvency of the entire US financial system. By 2006, signs emerged that the housing market was cooling. Rising interest rates caused adjustable-rate mortgage (ARM) monthly payments to rise, increasing default rates among the riskiest mortgage holders. By 2007, home prices in the most buoyant real estate markets fell, especially in the so called "sand states" of Arizona, California, Florida, and Nevada. With housing prices falling and mortgage default rates rising, the big three credit rating agencies (CRAs) downgraded swaths of high grade mortgage-backed securities (MBS) and collateralized debt obligations (CDOs). In July 2007, Moody's downgraded nearly four hundred subprime MBS. Banks booked losses in their mortgage portfolios, causing interest rates to rise in wholesale funding markets as counterparty risk rose. In August 2007, Countrywide Financial, a mortgage broker, experienced a buyers' strike in the commercial paper market and sold itself to Bank of America. Throughout fall 2007, America's largest financial institutions booked billions of dollars of losses in their mortgage portfolios: Citigroup and Merrill Lynch each lost roughly $24 billion, while Bank of America and Morgan Stanley lost about $10 billion each. Credit default swap insurance prices rose for the most exposed financial institutions, such as Bear Stearns and Lehman Brothers. At the end of 2007, it cost an investor $176,000 to insure $10 million of Bear Stearns' debt, compared to just $68,000 for the ostensibly less risky Goldman Sachs. Risk among financial institutions remained high for the rest of the year. The one-month dollar LIBOR-Overnight indexed swap (OIS) spread, a common measure of bank counterparty risk, shot up from about 8 basis points in summer 2007 to over 100 basis points by December 2007 and stayed elevated, as fears about collateral quality and counterparty solvency caused funding stress in interbank lending markets (The Financial Crisis Inquiry Commission 2011, 256).

According to a global macroeconomic hedge fund analyst whose firm managed roughly $3 billion in assets, the French bank BNP Paribas' suspension of redemptions on mortgage-related hedge funds in August 2007 was a turning point in his firm's thinking about housing markets. This analyst argued that this episode "disproved [his/her firm's] previously-held notion that globally systemically important banks were indestructible." From this point onward, the hedge fund analyst recalled markets being "choppy" (Global macro hedge fund analyst 2018). Another G7 sell-side foreign exchange trader said that during this period, "everyone knew there would be problems, but they were not sure to what extent the problems would pose a risk to the banks."

His firm started to adopt "defensive market positioning," including betting on volatility to rise and against bank stocks based on the premise that many banks had problems "under the hood" due to mortgage-related exposures (Sell-side foreign exchange trader 2018). One structured credit sell-side market maker, whose trading desk handled about $600 billion in annual notional order flows, said the market at this point did not have enough participants who remembered market volatility during the early pre-crisis period. This trader believed "most investors only looked four years back," and clients were lucky if members of their firm remembered LTCM, let alone historical lessons of other systemic crises. Prior to 2007, this trader never considered counterparty risk, but beginning in summer 2007, their firm started to price counterparty risk and considered the probability that their major counterparties could fail (Sell-side structured credit trader 2018). Another hedge fund macroeconomic strategist during the crisis and G7 finance ministry official recalled that during the summer of 2007, it was clear that there would be winners and losers from emerging losses, but that most of their firm's sell-side counterparties, which included the big banks, knew "they had to keep dancing" as long as there were profits to be made (Hedge fund macro analyst and G7 official 2018).

Despite these early signs of financial distress, most regulators seemed to believe that the fallout of the deflating housing bubble did not threaten financial stability nor the real economy. Federal Reserve Chairman Ben Bernanke said that "the impact on the broader economy and financial markets of the problems in the subprime market seems likely to be contained" (Bernanke 2007). US Treasury Secretary Henry Paulson echoed Bernanke's rosy view, arguing that "from the standpoint of the overall economy… [The crisis] appears to be contained" (Gross 2007).

Events soon belied Bernanke and Paulson's sanguine view when investment bank Bear Stearns experienced a shadow banking bank run in March 2008. Bear Stearns' issues paralleled LTCM's ten years earlier: hedge funds sponsored by Bear made highly levered bets on the US housing market via ABS funded by asset-backed commercial paper (ABCP) and repurchase agreements ("repo"). When housing prices fell and collateral prices collapsed, Bear Stearns' creditors feared for a total loss of their investment. Because of ambiguity about the relationship between Bear Stearns' parent company and its internal hedge funds, counterparties boycotted the entire firm, demanding greater repo haircuts and higher interest rates to continue to roll over Bear's maturing liabilities. These pressures led to a bank run that culminated in Bear Stearns' sale to J.P. Morgan for $2 a share (later revised upward to $10 per share after shareholder protests). The main difference between the LTCM episode and Bear Stearns was that for Bear, the Federal Reserve risked its own capital to backstop a private deal to save a troubled financial institution.

Like many investment banks during the 2000s, Bear Stearns geared its business toward profiting from the booming housing market. Mortgage securitization accounted for nearly fifty percent of Bear Stearns' pre-crisis revenue, and Bear had the second-largest prime brokerage business on Wall Street, which involves lending and brokering trades with hedge funds, as well as serving as a custodian of hedge fund assets. Bear's prime brokerage business may have also made it vulnerable to bank runs, as hedge fund clients were inclined to withdraw assets from Bear when they worried about Bear's solvency. Even though it was the smallest of the five biggest investment banks, Bear Stearns was a top three underwriter of private label MBS (i.e. MBS not sponsored by the federal housing giants Fannie Mae and Freddie Mac) from 2000 to 2007. It was a big end-buyer of ABS as well, sponsoring several in-house hedge funds to invest in real estate assets financed with short-term borrowing in the ABCP and repo markets. During the boom, Bear's strategy paid off—from 2001 to 2006, Bear Stearns' stock price tripled on the back of rising earnings from securitization fees and capital gains in the real estate market.

However, by June 2007, with mortgage ABS prices falling, Bear Stearns had to refuse redemptions from its High-Grade Structured Credit Strategies Enhanced Leverage Fund, which was an internal hedge fund that invested in highly-rated ABS financed by short-term borrowing. In July 2007, Bear Stearns liquidated two of its largest internal hedge funds. Despite these evasive maneuvers, by November 2007, Bear Stearns still had a leverage ratio of thirty-eight to one, with a bulk of its loan portfolio tied up in risky and illiquid ABS. As the crisis spread, Bear Stearns booked losses on its mortgage holdings, which hit the firm's earnings and further depressed its stock price. Facing mounting losses and downgrades from the rating agencies, Bear scrambled for capital but could not keep up with its deteriorating collateral quality and growing ABCP and repo redemptions from its counterparties (The Financial Crisis Inquiry Commission 2011, 280–281).

When Moody's downgraded fifteen Bear Stearns-issued MBS, this news sent Bear into a death spiral: market headlines read "Moody's downgrades Bear Stearns,"—technically untrue, but enough to ignite a full-blown creditor panic against the firm. Bear's reliance on short-term borrowing and its large prime brokerage business—businesses that boosted Bear's profitability during the boom years—turned into points of vulnerability that destroyed the company. Hedge funds stopped trading through Bear Stearns, closing their prime brokerage accounts and withdrawing their funds, further exacerbating Bear's dire cash position. ABCP and repo counterparties refused to roll over Bear's maturing obligations, demanding higher repo haircuts and more collateral to continue doing business with the firm (Fleming et al. 2009). From March 6, 2008 through March 13, 2008, Bear Stearns' daily liquidity fell from $21 billion to $2 billion.

With Bear Stearns entering terminal decline and recognizing that Bear Stearns' disorderly bankruptcy would be a considerable blow to investor confidence in global capital markets, the Federal Reserve and US Treasury organized a weekend meeting at the Federal Reserve Bank of New York to discuss Bear's fate on March 15, 2008. Negotiating with rival J.P. Morgan, Bear Stearns agreed to sell itself for $2 a share (a figure later raised to $10 a share at the behest of Bear Stearns' board of directors). J.P. Morgan financed its purchase with $1.15 billion of its own capital and a $28.82 billion loan from the New York Fed in a structure called "Maiden Lane," designed to get the bad assets off Bear's balance sheet before being sold to J.P. Morgan. Roughly half of Maiden Lane's thirty billion dollars in capital was used to purchase mortgage assets directly from Bear Stearns (The Financial Crisis Inquiry Commission 2011, 289–290, see Fig. 5.1).

Although some of the names had changed, Bear Stearns elicited the same reaction as LTCM a decade earlier: again, the Federal Reserve intervened in financial markets to avoid the disorderly bankruptcy of a key financial institution whose failure would have systemic consequences. This time, however, the Fed used its own funds to finance a private transaction to save a bank. When defending Bear Stearns' bailout to Congress, Federal Reserve Chairman Ben Bernanke echoed William McDonough's defense of the LTCM bailout ten years prior, arguing that the negative consequences of Bear Stearns' bankruptcy "would not have been confined to the financial system but would have been felt broadly in the real economy through its effects on asset values and credit

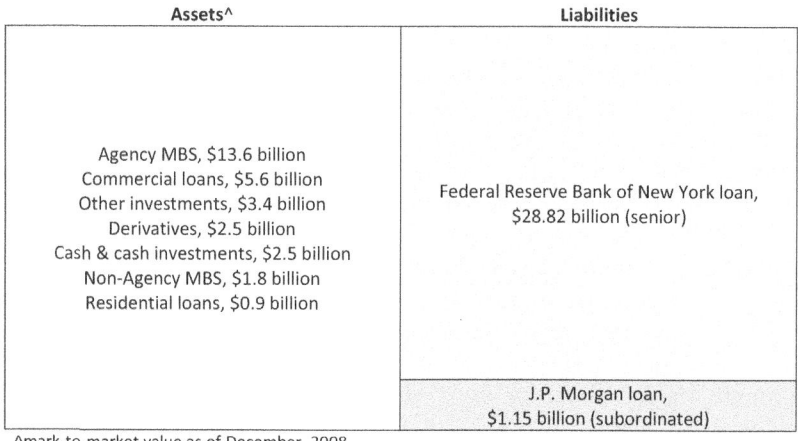

Fig. 5.1 Maiden Lane's capital structure (Federal Reserve Bank of New York n.d.)

availability" (Bernanke 2008). In other words, allowing Bear Stearns to fail would have had significant negative externalities across the financial system and in the real economy.[3]

Bear's bailout stabilized interbank lending, at least for a while. A popular metric of interbank credit risk, the TED spread, which measures the difference between three-month dollar LIBOR and the three-month Treasury bill rates, rose to two hundred basis points during the Bear Stearns episode, and immediately fell seventy basis points after the announcement of Bear's sale to J.P. Morgan (see Fig. 5.2). Investment bank CDS spreads also fell after Bear's bailout, demonstrating the palliative effect of Fed involvement on counterparty fears about the solvency of financial institutions. On the Friday before Bear Stearns' bailout, it cost an investor $300,000 and $240,000 to insure $10 million worth of Morgan Stanley and Goldman Sachs' senior debt. By the end of May 2008, these insurance prices fell to $150,000 and $86,000, respectively (Bernanke 2012).

What is the significance of the Bear Stearns sale to J.P. Morgan for this book's conventions-based theoretical framework on financial instability? There are three takeaways.

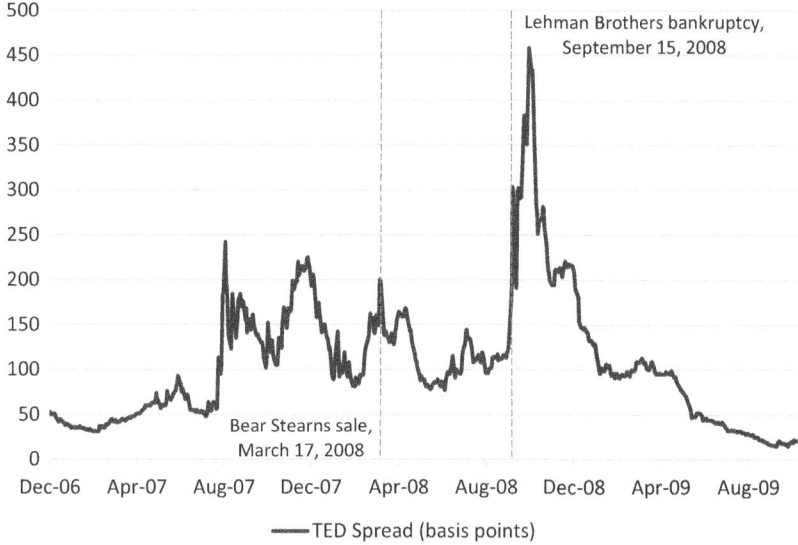

Fig. 5.2 The TED spread: December 2006–October 2009 (Federal Reserve Bank of St. Louis 2018)

First, the most important consequence of Bear Stearns' bailout was the establishment of an expectation among market participants that the Federal Reserve and US Treasury were willing to risk their own capital to avoid a chaotic unwinding of a systemically important financial institution. For instance, the Financial Crisis Inquiry Commission (FCIC) found that "the Bear episode...*set a precedent* for extraordinary government intervention" in financial markets (The Financial Crisis Inquiry Commission 2011, 292).[4]

Several financial market participants interviewed for *Social Finance* corroborated the FCIC's findings. A structured credit trader at one of Bear Stearns' peer investment banks claimed that Bear's bailout created a "precedent" for other financial institutions by telling the market that the government would "step in and prop up financial institutions" when needed (Sell-side structured credit trader 2018). According to a currency trader whose New York-based commercial bank served as a major counterparty to Bear Stearns, Bear's bailout created an "implicit understanding that banks would not go bankrupt." The currency trader also recalled that ABCP and repo counterparty money managers expressed to him that Bear's bailout convinced them that "there was an implicit safety net that large financial institutions would not fail." The trader remarked that in the minds of market participants, Bear Stearns became the baseline "worst case scenario for any bank," and that larger firms would receive comparable treatment from regulators if they ran into similar trouble (Sell-side foreign exchange trader 2018). Another interview subject said the Fed's intervention was a "huge relief to the market." The subject described the Fed's intervention as a "giant put option that the Federal government gave to the market" (Global macro hedge fund analyst 2018). A buy-side structured credit trader who worked at a peer investment bank of Bear Stearns' during the crisis opined that although most counterparties believed the Fed wanted to send a signal to markets that taxpayers would not bail out large financial institutions, Bear Stearns "forced regulators' hands" since Bear Stearns was even more systemically important than LTCM. The trader claimed that Bear "indicated a precedent" for other financial institutions, sowing a "perception that the government might just step in and prop up financial institutions regularly" (Buy-side structured credit trader 2018). Another sell-side trader who made bets on G7 short-term interest rates futures whose firm was a major counterparty to both Bear and Lehman Brothers said Bear Stearns showed his firm's management team that there was an "implicit understanding that there was a risk that a bank could fail, but even [if a bank were to fail], counterparties would be made whole" (Sell-side short-term interest rates trader 2018). Alan Greenspan echoed these traders and strategists' views, telling ABC's *This Week* talk show that "when Bear Stearns was bailed out, it drew a line under that level of firm, implying that anything that was larger than that firm was capable of getting federal assistance" (Zumbrun 2008). In the minds of counterparties, the Fed had become, via LTCM and Bear, a de facto lender of last resort in shadow banking markets.

Second, Bear Stearns' bailout signaled that short-term funding markets were a major vulnerability facing financial institutions, and therefore counterparties should more fully consider counterparty risks when trading in financial markets. As discussed in the preceding chapter, many large, interconnected bank and non-bank financial institutions, such as investment banks, commercial banks, insurance companies, among others, sponsored "structured investment vehicles" (SIVs) that issued ABCP and repo to finance purchases of risky ABS (see Fig. 1.2). SIVs carried two types of risks: credit risk, or the probability of defaults in their ABS portfolios, and roll over risk, or the risk that ABCP and repo counterparties would demand greater collateral or outright refuse to refinance SIVs' maturing obligations. During the crisis, these risks were inter-related: facing a maturity mismatch between short-term liabilities and long-term assets, banks were vulnerable to disruptions in the supply of interbank credit triggered by waning investor confidence due to fears of collapsing collateral values. In the wholesale funding markets, rumors of insolvency become self-fulfilling prophecies, wherein the market restricts credit to shadow banking conduits based on fears of insolvency, reifying funding problems that the market feared in the first place. This self-fulfilling, reflexive, and pro-cyclical dynamic of market confidence and bank solvency precipitated Bear Stearns' and sale in March 2008 (Jablecki and Machaj 2011).

Interviews conducted for *Social Finance* demonstrate that Bear Stearns caused counterparties to reassess their views of counterparty risk. A sell-side market analyst at a major North American financial institution whose trading desk saw about $250 billion in quarterly client orders described Bear Stearns' failure as "an absolute shock" that disproved the assumption that "everything works out in the world of fixed income." The subject recalled his bank scrutinizing its exposure to short-term funding risks after Bear Stearns. Prior to Bear, their firm believed that short-term funding markets did not "provide any meaningful risks, and certainly not systemic risks." Investment professionals did not have substantive expertise on short-term funding markets at his firm. Rather, a clerk who worked for the firm's primary investment professionals made trading decisions about short-term funding markets. The subject concluded that "this division of labor speaks to the flawed pre-crisis assumption that there was no counterparty risk in short-term funding markets" (Sell-side market analyst 2018).

Bear Stearns' swift demise also shows that using short-term, unsecured liabilities to accumulate long-term, risky assets is akin to "picking up nickels in front of a steam roller," since basing banks' long-term solvency on the caprice of investors left banks vulnerable to liquidity risk in the wholesale funding market (Duarte and Longstaff 2007). When Bear's collateral prices fell because of falling home prices and rising mortgage delinquencies, ABCP and repo investors demanded higher collateral (in the form of higher yields and greater repo "haircuts") to roll over Bear's maturing obligations. When investors denied Bear Stearns commercial paper and repo market access, Bear Stearns' liquidity position deteriorated in a matter of days, leading to its failure (Gorton and Metrick 2010).[5]

The speed by which Bear Stearns' creditors pulled their funds from the company illustrates how confidence in financial markets is not determined by individual risk calculations by shadow banking counterparties, but by the market's *conventional expectations* regarding second and third-order guesses about fellow investors' intentions. Bear also shows how counterparty confidence can shift rapidly. If creditors believe that a borrower will remain liquid and that *fellow market participants* hold similar beliefs, then speculative financing arrangements (in the Minsky sense) will remain liquid. If an individual investor believes that the rest of the market will continue to roll over maturing ABCP and repo obligations, then he too will continue to roll over banks' maturing ABCP and repo. If, on the other hand, an investor believes that *fellow market participants* believe that a bank might face funding pressures, then it may choose to refuse to roll over maturing obligations, even without a material change in the solvency of the SIV. Once the bank run was on, and once confidence yielded to fear, it was only a matter of days before Bear Stearns ran out of cash.

Third, Bear's failure also shows how credit ratings were enablers of pro-cyclical credit creation and triggers of financial distress. In theory, ratings were passive reflections of the likelihood of default of securities, such that the probability of default of a triple-A rated municipal bond issuer was the same as a triple-A rated mortgage-backed security. In practice, ratings were endogenous drivers of outcomes in financial markets, rather than passive abstractions of assets' material fundamentals. High ratings for ABS had a material effect on securities prices by allowing risk-averse pools of capital to invest in highly-rated, assets via ABCP and repo conduits. Since money market mutual funds faced restrictions on investing in ABCP and repos backed by risky collateral, high ratings allowed financial institutions to tap into a deep reservoir of risk-averse capital to finance their purchases of risky assets via SIV conduits. Likewise, banks' access to these wholesale funding markets (enabled by high ratings for their SIV collateral) led to higher demand for ABS, higher ABS prices, and lower yields, thus validating the perceived truth-value of ratings. This process meant that in the short run, high ratings were self-stabilizing and reified the very creditworthiness that they were meant to reflect. Moreover, many financial institutions used high ratings to justify their thin capital cushions to regulators, so high ratings allowed banks to make more loans, further fueling the credit availability in risky asset classes. Favorable bond ratings sowed financial fragility that ended up rendering large swaths of the global financial system insolvent when housing prices fell. To paraphrase Donald MacKenzie, ratings became "engines" that "drove" market prices, rather than being passive reflections of securities' underlying value (MacKenzie 2008). Bond ratings' institutionalization predicated market stability on the reliability of ratings as ultimate of value in markets. Bear Stearns benefitted from favorable ABS ratings and the ability to set their own internal ratings for capital adequacy during the boom years but suffered when the rating agencies downgraded their MBS during the crash. Moody's decision to downgrade several Bear Stearns-issued MBS sent the firm into terminal decline, leading to its sale to J.P. Morgan. Ratings were thus both an *amplifier* of pro-cyclical capital flows into ABS and a *trigger* of financial market instability via downgrades. The institutionalization of ratings into investors' decision-making calculi led bond ratings themselves to become causally tied to market outcomes. So, when rating agencies downgraded Bear Stearns' ABS, Bear Stearns' counterparties refused to roll over Bear's maturing ABCP and repo, leading to the bank run that caused Bear's bailout and sale to J.P. Morgan.

Summer 2008 provided a brief respite from Bear Stearns' turmoil, as concerns about bank solvency ebbed, financial institutions' CDS spreads fell, and America's fourteen biggest financial institutions raised roughly $140 billion in fresh capital. On March 27, 2008, the Federal Reserve created the Term Securities Lending Facility (TSLF), which allowed broker dealers and commercial banks exchange their housing agency debt for US Treasury bonds at one hundred percent of face value. The Fed would later revise the terms of the TSLF to accept all triple-A rated private-label ABS. The authorities also created the Primary Dealer Credit Facility (PDCF) to lend cash to primary dealers at interest rates comparable to those paid by commercial banks to borrow from the Fed's discount window. These programs provided investment banks with a liquidity lifeline should markets deny them access to fresh capital. Despite banks' initial enthusiasm for the TSLF and PDCF after Bear Stearns, their use of these programs "ceased completely" by late July, according to the FCIC. Banks refrained from using the TSLF and PDCF out of fear that their counterparties would construe accepting the Fed's capital as a sign of weakness, thus eroding the market's confidence in their solvency and hurting their market access (The Financial Crisis Inquiry Commission 2011, 292–295). While Bear's sale to J.P. Morgan and the Fed's emergency programs restored some confidence to financial institutions, signs of stress persisted in interbank funding markets, where the TED spread remained elevated at one hundred basis points, which was well above its pre-crisis average of thirty basis points.

Additionally, the Federal Housing Agencies, Fannie Mae and Freddie Mac, saw their stock prices decline throughout the summer 2008. Fannie and Freddie owned or securitized almost half of America's $12 trillion mortgage market and were valued as two of America's largest non-bank financial institutions, with a combined market capitalization of approximately $100 billion and total assets amounting to just under $2 trillion. Fannie and Freddie provided ample liquidity to the US secondary mortgage market by purchasing mortgages and repackaging them into re-saleable mortgage-backed securities. Because the market believed that the US government-backed Fannie and Freddie, the housing Agencies could borrow at below-market interest rates and then purchase mortgages from loan originators such as savings and loan banks. The Agencies would pool their purchased mortgages together and sell them to investors in the form of MBS. Starting in the 1980s, investment banks began experimenting with financial engineering based on Agency MBS in which they purchased MBS and sliced these securities in different risk categories for investors with different risk tolerances. Fed officials and regulators knew that the Agencies had little room to absorb falling asset prices, and the GSEs' primary regulator, James B. Lockhart, testified that the market's declining confidence in the GSEs had the potential to induce a "self-fulfilling credit crisis" against the companies.

Throughout summer 2008, with mortgage prices falling, defaults rising, and the Agencies writing down significant portions mortgage portfolio every quarter, confidence in the two companies reached new lows. With interest rates rising and ARM interest rates resetting to higher rates, and housing prices collapsing nationally, the housing Agencies began to face the skepticism of the market. As private capital dried up for new mortgages in 2006, the housing Agencies' share of new mortgages purchased rose from under fifty percent in 2005 and to seventy-five percent in 2007. In the first half of 2007, the cost of insuring Freddie Mac's debt was identical to the cost of insuring US government debt at the same maturity, reflecting the market's view that the GSEs' debt was tantamount to the US government's. As fears mounted throughout 2007 and into 2008, however, the spread between Freddie Mac and US

Treasury's CDS contracts rose to seventy-five basis points by summer 2008. The Agencies continued to book large losses and faced a buyers' strike in the debt market, as investors began to worry about the sanctity of the Agencies' implicit Federal guarantee, demanding higher collateral to finance the GSEs' short and long-term debt (The Financial Crisis Inquiry Commission 2011, 307–318).

Wanting to make the government's commitment to the companies clear, US Treasury Secretary Henry Paulson requested and received the right to inject capital in the GSEs from the US Congress and, if necessary, nationalize the nominally private corporations in July 2008 (Labaton 2008). The Housing and Economic Recovery Act (HERA) provided Paulson with a "bazooka" of financial firepower, authorizing the Treasury to inject capital into the GSEs and giving the Federal Housing Financing Agency (FHFA) the authority to place the companies into government conservatorship if necessary (The Financial Crisis Inquiry Commission 2011, 313–316). To alleviate the firms' funding pressures in repo markets, the Fed agreed to provide emergency, short-term liquidity to the Agencies. Paulson believed that HERA and his financial bazooka would provide a boon to market confidence, thus obviating the need to use his new authority to save the firms (*The Economist* 2008).

Despite the Treasury Secretary's leeway to do what he saw fit to manage the companies, the GSEs' stock prices continued to plummet throughout the summer. By the third quarter 2008, Fannie and Freddie had losses totaling nearly $50 billion. Foreign central banks stopped purchasing GSE securities, and the spread between the GSEs' preferred stock and Treasuries increased roughly four-fold from June through August. Facing falling share prices, rising borrowing costs, and soaring delinquencies in their mortgage portfolios, the housing Agencies turned to the Federal government for help. In August 2008, Fannie Mae told the US Treasury and the FHFA that it had no way of raising private capital to shore its capital base, given its mounting losses. Paulson and Lockhart, along with their colleagues at the Federal Reserve, decided to place the housing Agencies into government conservatorship on September 7, 2008, eight days before Lehman Brothers' bankruptcy.

When announcing the decision, Treasury Secretary Paulson assured reporters that he did not make this decision lightly. Paulson argued that a failure of the firms would be catastrophic for financial market stability. He described the housing giants as "so large and so interwoven" that bankruptcy "would directly and negatively impact household wealth" and would furthermore pose a significant drag on the real economy.

To Paulson, nationalizing the companies was a bitter pill to swallow. The Agencies did not become over-levered financial behemoths during his time at Treasury, nor did nationalizing the companies comport with Paulson's free-market tendencies (Paulson 2010, 2–6).

Still, when faced with the choice between a disorderly unwinding of a systemically important financial institution and a bailout, Fed and Treasury officials blinked, thus reinforcing the conventional expectation set by Bear that the Federal government would serve as liquidity providers of last resort to troubled financial institutions. Former Federal Reserve Bank of New York President (and later US Treasury Secretary) Timothy Geithner acknowledged as much when he told the FCIC that the housing Agencies were large sources of moral hazard in financial markets—a charge confirmed by their nationalization (Katz and Christie 2011).

Discussion and Conclusion

In all, regulators' repeated interventions in financial markets during LTCM, Bear, and the housing Agencies created a conventional expectation in financial markets that regulators would serve as liquidity providers of last resort in wholesale funding markets. Some firms became the victims of self-fulfilling credit crises, though ABCP and repo counterparty fears remained idiosyncratically isolated to specific institutions during this pre-Lehman period. One interview subject said Bear Stearns and the housing Agencies "emboldened" markets and gave them the relief that "if things really were to go downhill, the Federal government would be there." Therefore, even if counterparties failed, creditors would get bailed out. As a result, the interviewee believed Bear's bailout meant his firm's prime brokerage accounts and other short-term assets for which banks served as counterparties would be safe (Global macro hedge fund analyst 2018). Generalized contagion did not occur during these episodes because regulators intervened and eased credit conditions in interbank lending markets whenever a systemically important institution was on the brink of disorderly bankruptcy, thus preventing full-on bank runs against all ABCP and repo borrowers in the economy. If the market maintained confidence in this conventional expectation, the likelihood of system-wide bank runs in the wholesale funding markets remained low.

Even so, this convention became predicated upon the willingness of regulators to continue to backstop troubled financial institutions. If this convention were to fail, as it did following Lehman Brothers' bankruptcy, then markets could become unstable. The following chapter explains how Lehman Brothers' failure initiated a period of convention uncertainty and financial instability in markets. It argues that Lehman's failure can be conceptualized as a non-routine deviation from agents' convention-given expectations about regulators' willingness to provide de facto deposit insurance to shadow banking conduits. The evisceration of this conventional expectation initiated a period of convention uncertainty in financial markets, leading to acute financial instability and adverse selection problems in financial markets.

Notes

1. One historical footnote from the episode was that a consortium of investors, led by Warren Buffett, Goldman Sachs, and insurance giant AIG offered a bid for LTCM without any Fed involvement, though it was widely known at the time that LTCM's principals viewed the offer as considerably lower than the Fund's intrinsic value. Therefore, LTCM viewed this overture as a lowball offer. Dowd speculates that had the Fed not gotten involved in the negotiations, LTCM would have had no choice but to accept Buffett's below-market offer. For more, see Dowd (1999).
2. As Greenspan continued, "…of course, any time that there is a public involvement that softens the blow of private-sector losses – *even as obliquely as in this episode* – the issue of moral hazard arises…Over time, economic efficiency will be impaired as some uneconomic investments are undertaken under the implicit assumption that possible losses may be borne by the government." Emphasis added.
3. For two excellent retrospectives on the Bear Stearns bailout, see Cecchetti and Schoenholtz (2018) and Todd (2018).
4. Emphasis added.
5. The authors claim that this dynamic is fundamentally like a traditional bank run, only in the shadow banking market, it is wholesale lenders demanding their deposits, as opposed to retail depositors.

Works Cited

Anderson, Jenny. 2006. "Big Bonuses Seen Again for Wall St." *The New York Times*, November 7. Accessed March 20, 2018. http://www.nytimes.com/2006/11/07/business/07wall.html.

Bernanke, Ben S. 2007. "Testimony: The Economic Outlook." *Federal Reserve Board of Governors*. March 28. Accessed March 31, 2018. https://www.federalreserve.gov/newsevents/testimony/bernanke20070328a.htm.

———. 2008. "Testimony: Developments in the Financial Markets." *Federal Reserve Board of Governors*. April 3. Accessed March 31, 2018. https://www.federalreserve.gov/newsevents/testimony/bernanke20080403a.htm.

———. 2012. "Speech: Some Reflections on the Crisis and the Policy Response." *Federal Reserve Board of Governors*. April 13. Accessed March 31, 2018. https://www.federalreserve.gov/newsevents/speech/bernanke20120413a.htm.

Buy-side structured credit trader, interview by Neil Shenai. 2018. *Author Interview* (April 16).

Cecchetti, Stephen G., and Kermit L. Schoenholtz. 2018. "Ten Years After Bear." *Money and Banking*. March 12. Accessed June 5, 2018. https://www.moneyandbanking.com/commentary/2018/3/11/ten-years-after-bear.

Dowd, Kevin. 1999. "Too Big to Fail? Long-Term Capital Management and the Federal Reserve." *Cato Institute Briefing Papers* (53): 1–12.

Duarte, Jefferson, and Francis A. Longstaff. 2007. "Risk and Return in Fixed-Income Arbitrage: Nickels in Front of a Steamroller?" *Review of Financial Studies* 20 (3): 769–811.

Federal Reserve Bank of New York. n.d. "Maiden Lane Transactions." *Federal Reserve Bank of New York*. Accessed March 31, 2018. https://www.newyorkfed.org/markets/maidenlane.html.

Federal Reserve Bank of St. Louis. 2018. "Federal Reserve Economic Data database." *Federal Reserve Bank of St. Louis: Economic Research*. March 15. Accessed March 31, 2018. https://fred.stlouisfed.org/.

Fleming, Michael J., Warren B. Hrung, and Frank M. Keane. 2009. "The Term Securities Lending Facility: Origin, Design, and Effects." *Federal Reserve Bank of New York Current Issues in Economics and Finance* 15 (2): 1–11.

Former investment banker 2, interview by Neil Shenai. 2018. *Author Interview* (April 27).

Global macro hedge fund analyst, interview by Neil Shenai. 2018. *Author Interview* (February 15).

Gorton, Gary B., and Andrew Metrick. 2010. "Haircuts." *Federal Reserve Bank of St. Louis Review* 92 (6): 507–519.

Greenspan, Alan. 1998. "Testimony: Private-Sector Refinancing of the Large Hedge Fund, Long-Term Capital Management." *Federal Reserve Board of Governors*. October 1. Accessed March 31, 2018. https://www.federalreserve.gov/boarddocs/testimony/1998/19981001.htm.

Gross, Daniel. 2007. "Subprime Nonsense: The Fed Chairman and Treasury Secretary Say the Subprime Mess Has Been Contained. Are They Joking?" *Slate.com*. August 6. Accessed March 21, 2018. http://www.slate.com/articles/business/moneybox/2007/08/subprime_nonsense.html.

Haubrich, Joseph G. 2007. "Some Lessons on the Rescue of Long-Term Capital Management." *Federal Reserve Bank of Cleveland Policy Discussion Papers* 1–12.

Hedge fund macro analyst and G7 official, interview by Neil Shenai. 2018. *Author Interview* (February 25).
Jablecki, Juliusz, and Mateusz Machaj. 2011. "A Regulated Meltdown: The Basel Rules and Banks' Leverage." In *What Caused the Financial Crisis*, by Jeffrey Friedman, 200–227. Philadelphia: University of Pennsylvania Press.
Katz, Ian, and Rebecca Christie. 2011. "Geithner Called Housing Giants Biggest 'Moral Hazard'." *Bloomberg*. February 18. Accessed March 23, 2018. https://www.bloomberg.com/news/articles/2011-02-18/geithner-told-fcic-fannie-freddie-were-biggest-sources-of-moral-hazard-.
Labaton, Stephen. 2008. "Treasury Acts to Shore Up Fannie Mae and Freddie Mac." *The New York Times*, July 14. Accessed March 23, 2018. http://www.nytimes.com/2008/07/14/washington/14fannie.html.
Lowenstein, Roger. 2000. *When Genius Failed: The Rise and Fall of Long-Term Capital Management*. New York: Random House.
MacKenzie, Donald. 2008. *An Engine, Not a Camera: How Financial Models Shape Markets*. Cambridge: The MIT Press.
Paulson Jr., Henry M. 2010. *On the Brink: Inside the Race to Stop the Collapse of the Global Financial System*. New York: Business Plus.
Scholes, Myron S. 2000. "Crisis and Risk Management." *American Economic Review* 90 (2): 17–21.
Sell-side foreign exchange trader, interview by Neil Shenai. 2018. *Author Interview* (February 19).
Sell-side market analyst, interview by Neil Shenai. 2018. *Author Interview* (February 26).
Sell-side short-term interest rates trader, interview by Neil Shenai. 2018. *Author Interview* (April 4).
Sell-side structured credit trader, interview by Neil Shenai. 2018. *Author Interview* (February 12).
The Economist. 2008. "America's Mortgage Giants: Suffering a Seizure." *The Economist*, September 8. Accessed March 23, 2018. https://www.economist.com/node/12078933?story_id=12078933&source=features_box_main.
The Financial Crisis Inquiry Commission. 2011. *The Financial Crisis Inquiry Report: Final Report of the National Commission on the Causes of the Financial and Economic Crisis in the United States*. Washington: U.S. Government Printing Office.
Todd, Walker. 2018. "Rewarding Bad Behavior: The Bear Stearns Bailout." *Institute for New Economic Thinking*. March 12. Accessed June 5, 2018. https://www.ineteconomics.org/perspectives/blog/rewarding-bad-behavior-the-bear-stearns-bailout.
Zumbrun, Joshua. 2008. "Paulson's Line in the Sand." *Forbes*. September 15. Accessed March 23, 2018. https://www.forbes.com/2008/09/15/lehman-bernanke-paulson-biz-beltway-cx_jz_0915paulson.html#1148b9f32799.

CHAPTER 6

Markets After Lehman

INTRODUCTION

This chapter describes markets after the failure of Lehman Brothers. It argues that Lehman's failure negated the market's conventional expectation regarding regulators' willingness to backstop shadow banking conduits as established by prior market interventions. This convention uncertainty led to a panic in wholesale funding markets and transmitted financial contagion from shadow banks to the broader economy. Regulators' response to the crisis can be understood as a successful attempt to re-establish conventional equilibrium about their willingness to serve as liquidity providers of last resort. This chapter proposes that the United States' high degree of sovereign creditworthiness enabled regulators' forceful interventions, stabilizing short-term funding markets and ending the most acute phase of the global financial crisis.

FULL-BLOWN PANIC: THE MARKET AFTER LEHMAN BROTHERS AND AIG

After the failure of Bear Stearns in March 2008, regulators viewed investment bank Lehman Brothers as the "next big worry" facing financial markets (The Financial Crisis Inquiry Commission 2011, 325). Lehman Brothers, much like Bear Stearns, geared its business toward profiting from the early 2000s housing bubble and credit boom. It presided over the entire value chain of mortgage origination and securitization, including owning several retail mortgage brokers, earning fees for securitizing Agency and private label mortgage-backed securities (MBS), and investing in securitized assets via off-balance-sheet vehicles funded by asset-backed commercial paper (ABCP) and repurchase agreements ("repo").

In 2007, while the rest of Wall Street scaled back their ABS exposure, Lehman Brothers doubled down on real estate investment. In October 2007, Lehman purchased Archstone Smith, a firm that owned and leased about ninety thousand apartments across the United States. Lehman then adopted a "countercyclical growth strategy" and directed its traders to accumulate more real estate assets. In the eyes of Lehman's senior management, the firm was changing its business model from the "moving business" of brokering trades for third parties to the "storage business" of holding ABS in their own portfolio. Lehman's mortgage assets rose from about $67 billion in 2006 to $111 billion by the end of 2007 (The Financial Crisis Inquiry Commission 2011, 176–177).

As 2008 went on, markets grew skittish about Lehman Brothers' mortgage exposure, demanding greater compensation to insure Lehman's debt compared to its peer institutions. Many investors, including activist shareholder David Einhorn, claimed that Lehman failed to measure accurately the value of its mortgage assets. Einhorn told his investors that "there [was] good reason to question Lehman's fair value calculations" and that "greater transparency" of Lehman's mortgage holdings would "not inspire market confidence." Lehman's leadership nevertheless claimed that the firm had capital sufficient to cover any potential losses. The common market narrative was that "Lehman is just like Bear." Inside the firm, however, there was "zero belief Lehman was like Bear," according to a former Lehman Brothers investment banker. Senior management felt "strong and confident" about Lehman's cash position. The banker recalled a conversation with a senior executive comparing the financial media to terrorists, claiming the media was spreading rumors of Lehman's cash shortfall. The executive told the banker that Lehman cannot capitulate to the media, much like how the United States could not bow to the will of terrorists. The interview subject recalled views of senior management and staff at Lehman were split—some colleagues thought the firm's leadership understood the risks facing the firm, while others believed leadership was in a state of denial (Lehman Brothers banker 2 2018).

Facing uncertainty about Lehman's mortgage exposure, investors feared for the worst and demanded more collateral to continue rolling over Lehman's maturing ABCP and repo. Because Lehman depended on short-term borrowing to finance its long-term assets, regulators knew that Lehman's fortunes hinged on the confidence of its counterparties. The FCIC found that when "money market [mutual] funds, hedge funds, and investment banks believed Lehman's assets were worth less than Lehman's valuations, they would withdraw funds, demand more collateral, and curtail lending." As a result, withdrawn short-term credit "could force Lehman to sell its assets at fire-sale prices, wiping out capital and liquidity virtually overnight," especially because Bear Stearns "proved it could happen" just six months prior. Lehman's reluctance to revalue its mortgage assets and take credit write-downs while also refusing to reduce its reliance on short-term funding and raise capital damaged the firm's credibility and precipitated its bankruptcy.

In June 2008, Lehman's trading partners demanded higher collateral to trade with the firm, and the cost of insuring Lehman Brothers' debt via credit default swaps (CDS) rose from approximately 160 basis points in May 2008 to 350 basis points by mid-August (The Financial Crisis Inquiry Commission 2011, 324–328).[1] Lehman Brothers' C.E.O., Richard "Dick" Fuld requested that the Federal Reserve allow Lehman Brothers to become a bank holding company to gain access to the Fed's discount window, though Fed officials rejected his request as "gimmicky." Under pressure to raise capital and reassure investors, Dick Fuld sought a deal to shore up Lehman's capital base but could not agree on a fair valuation of the firm with Lehman's suitors. After news broke that Lehman's deal talks with Korea Development Bank soured, Lehman's stock price crashed 55% to $8 a share—less than 10% of its pre-crisis peak of above $80 a share in 2007. News of the failed talks caused Lehman's creditors to demand even more collateral from the firm, further depleting Lehman's dwindling cash reserves. On the Wednesday before its bankruptcy, Lehman Brothers announced a $3.9 billion loss, and money market mutual funds like Fidelity Investments pulled their capital from the firm. Entering the weekend of September 13, 2008, regulators knew that if they could not find a buyer for Lehman Brothers that weekend, the firm would not have enough cash to finance its operations by the time Asian markets opened early Monday morning. According to Lehman Brothers' bankruptcy estate, Lehman ended up posting $3.6 billion in collateral with J.P. Morgan in under the threat of withheld repo financing just days before its bankruptcy (The Financial Crisis Inquiry Commission 2011, 312–313). J.P. Morgan then became public enemy number one among the bank's bankers and traders (Lehman Brothers banker 2 2018).

On Friday, September 12, 2008, US Treasury Secretary Henry Paulson summoned the heads of America's biggest financial institutions to the Federal Reserve Bank of New York to discuss a plan to save Lehman to avoid a disorderly bankruptcy of the firm. Going into what became known as the "Lehman weekend," regulators believed that Bank of America was Lehman's most likely buyer. However, Merrill Lynch's C.E.O., John Thain, had plans of his own. Knowing that Merrill Lynch was next in line should Lehman Brothers go under, he positioned his firm as Bank of America's ultimate takeover target, selling the whole firm, including its coveted retail brokerage business, for forty billion dollars of Bank of America's common stock. The transaction dashed Lehman's hopes that Bank of America would purchase the firm.

Throughout the weekend deliberations, US Treasury Secretary Paulson insisted that the government would not help with Lehman. Some meeting participants, such as Sullivan & Cromwell bankruptcy attorney H. Rodgin Cohen, thought Paulson was posturing. According to Cohen, several bank chiefs believed that regulators were trying to play a game of "chicken" or "poker" with financial institutions to avoid having to risk taxpayer dollars to avert Lehman's bankruptcy. The FCIC confirmed Cohen's suspicion, claiming that since regulators took political "blowback" for the Bear Stearns bailout, they had to keep the potential of Federal support for a Lehman deal under strict confidentiality. According to the United Kingdom's former Chancellor of the Exchequer, Lord Alistair Darling, Paulson privately told him that regulators might have been willing to give a potential Lehman buyer, Barclays investment bank, "regulatory assistance to support a transaction if it was required." Paulson publicly claimed that banks had to arrange a private sector solution to bail out Lehman Brothers, since Federal assistance would not be forthcoming (The Financial Crisis Inquiry Commission 2011, 334).

Despite Bank of America's withdrawal from negotiations, by Saturday evening, September 13, it seemed Lehman had found a buyer in the British investment bank Barclays. To finance Barclays' purchase of Lehman, a private consortium of banks agreed to provide bridge financing for Lehman's forty to fifty billion dollars of mortgage assets to allow Barclays to purchase Lehman's broker-dealer unit. Even though Barclays, Lehman, and US regulators agreed to a deal in principle, England's

Financial Services Authority (FSA) refused to exempt Barclays from their requirement for a shareholder vote for such an acquisition. The FSA said that it would sanction the transaction if the Fed guaranteed Lehman's debts until the deal closed. Paulson's team demurred since such a guarantee would violate their policy of not using public funds to save Lehman and would leave regulators exposed to tens of billions of dollars of bad assets should the deal fail at the last minute. The FSA's reluctance to fast-track Barclays' acquisition of Lehman, coupled with the Federal Reserve and US Treasury's refusal to backstop Lehman's liabilities, killed the Barclays deal. With Barclays out of the running, there would be no buyer for Lehman Brothers. By Sunday night, Fuld convened his board of directors and, at the behest of regulators, filed for Chapter 11 bankruptcy protection early in the morning of September 15, 2008 (The Financial Crisis Inquiry Commission 2011, 335–339).

On the heels of Lehman Brothers' bankruptcy, regulators had to deal with insurance giant American International Group (AIG), which teetered on the brink of bankruptcy because of exposure to the US housing market. From 2001 to 2007, AIG's financial products group (AIG-FP) sold billions of dollars in credit default swap (CDS) protection on subprime ABS, and by 2007, AIG-FP sat on a portfolio of roughly $2.7 trillion notional CDS tied to the mortgage market. AIG also issued $6 billion in commercial paper liquidity puts on ABCP and repo issued by CDOs, thus insuring liquidity in a market for runnable, short-term capital. During the boom years, these businesses earned AIG a steady and seemingly low-risk income. Housing prices continued to rise, liquidity flowed into wholesale funding markets, and AIG earned profit by selling insurance on a doomsday scenario that its risk models anticipated would never occur (The Financial Crisis Inquiry Commission 2011, 139–142).

On September 12, 2008, the Friday before Lehman's bankruptcy, AIG faced a buyer's strike in the commercial paper and repo markets and struggled to raise the cash necessary to meet Wall Street's collateral calls. Facing obligations exceeding their $9 billion on hand, AIG asked the Federal Reserve Bank of New York for a loan under the Federal Reserve's 13(3) emergency lending authority. Privately, the Fed believed that such a loan might not be necessary since a consortium of banks had agreed in principle to provide bridge financing to AIG, but Lehman Brothers' bankruptcy caused AIG's emergency loan syndicate to fall apart. Rather than lending to AIG, syndicate banks hoarded cash to protect their own balance sheets. Without a private sector loan for

AIG, the Fed knew that it faced a choice between allowing the firm to go bankrupt or invoking its 13(3) authority to save the company. Fearing that a "a disorderly failure of AIG could add to already significant levels of financial market fragility and lead to substantially higher borrowing costs, reduced household wealth, and materially weaker economic performance" of the US economy, on Tuesday, September 16, 2008, the Fed made an $85 billion loan to AIG in exchange for preferred stock in AIG and its subsidiaries. In defending AIG's bailout just hours after allowing Lehman Brothers to go bankrupt, Fed Chairman Ben Bernanke told Congress that a disorderly bankruptcy of AIG would have been a devastating market blow to confidence in already-reeling commercial paper and money markets, which were experiencing full-on bank runs after Lehman's bankruptcy (The Financial Crisis Inquiry Commission 2011, 344–350). Regulators feared that an AIG bankruptcy would have disastrous consequences for the US economy, bankrupting state pensions, damaging AIG's counterparties, and shattering confidence in the entire financial system. Bernanke concluded that an AIG bankruptcy "could have resulted in a 1930s-style global financial and economic meltdown, with catastrophic implications for production, income, and jobs" (Bernanke 2009).

What does the rise, fall, and bailout of AIG tell us about the role of economic conventions in financial markets? There are two key takeaways.

First, AIG, much like Bear Stearns and Lehman Brothers, demonstrates the causal importance of credit ratings and conventional expectations as both *amplifiers* of pro-cyclical capital flows and *triggers* of financial instability. The FCIC found that "AIG's most valuable asset was its credit rating," which allowed the firm to "borrow cheaply and deploy the money in lucrative investments." Regulators permitted banks that purchased mortgage insurance from AIG to reserve less regulatory capital because they insured their mortgage exposure from a highly credible counterparty. Thus, AIG's triple-A rating endowed the firm with a "halo-effect" that helped it profit from insuring risky mortgages. During the boom years, AIG insured Wall Street's riskiest assets, in turn making the entire company (and by extension, the global financial system) appear safer (The Financial Crisis Inquiry Commission 2011, 139–142).

However, favorable bond ratings also contributed to AIG's financial fragility, since the terms of AIG's CDS contracts tied its collateral requirements to the firm's favorable credit rating. When the credit rating agencies (CRAs) downgraded AIG after Lehman Brothers' bankruptcy,

AIG had to meet numerous counterparty collateral calls simultaneously. The institutionalization of bond ratings into AIG's CDS made AIG vulnerable to downgrades when collateral prices declined, which went into overdrive after Lehman's bankruptcy. AIG is a case study in how institutionalized, ergodic conventions such as bond ratings can be both *amplifiers* of pro-cyclical capital flows into risky asset classes and *triggers* of instability within fragile financial systems.

In addition to using AIG-FP to make billions of dollars of bets against a collapse of the housing market via CDS, AIG also had a significant securities lending business, including repo. In 2007, AIG had nearly $90 billion in securities lending outstanding. AIG used securities lending to engage in shadow banking transactions by creating deposit-like liabilities for repo transactions and using their proceeds to intermediate credit for ABS borrowers. AIG suffered a classic run on the bank via their securities lending business as its mortgage losses mounted, in which counterparty fears of illiquidity proved self-fulfilling. This bank run dynamic fits with Keynesian notions about the importance of stable conventional expectations in maintaining the stability of fragile financing structures. From September 12 through September 30, 2008, AIG had to return nearly $24 billion in securities lending cash collateral to its counterparties. AIG's securities lending business boosted the firm's profits during the bubble years. But when markets turned, AIG could not meet its cash calls, in turn leading it to seek help from regulators (McDonald and Paulson 2014).

Second, AIG's fragility illustrates how risk models based on ergodic conventions can sow financial fragility. AIG-FP hired Yale University economist (and shadow banking expert) Gary Gorton as a consultant to build models to forecast potential losses in AIG's CDS portfolio. In December 2007, Gorton told AIG's investors that AIG's risk models were "very robust" and introduced "as little model risk as possible." Gorton mined historical data of real estate prices across the United States to forecast the likelihood of default in AIG's subprime MBS insurance business. According to one of AIG's pre-crisis SEC filings in 2006, AIG claimed that the likelihood of having to make simultaneous payouts on its entire mortgage portfolio remained "remote, even in severe recessionary market scenarios," based on the assumption that housing prices would not decline nationally. Even if there were a housing bubble, AIG told its investors that housing prices would plateau, rather than fall across the board (Mollenkamp et al. 2008). As the FCIC found,

AIG-FP "predicted with 99.85 [percent] confidence that there would be no realized economic loss on the safest portions of the collateralized debt obligations (CDOs) on which they wrote CDS protection, and failed to make any provisions whatsoever for declines in value – or unrealized losses – a decision that would prove fatal…" (The Financial Crisis Inquiry Commission 2011, 140). By basing their provisions on historical default and home price data, AIG predicated its solvency on the reliability of their risk models. These models underestimated the likelihood of home prices declining nationally and left AIG vulnerable to creditor panics when the housing bubble burst.

Immediately after Lehman's bankruptcy and bailout of AIG, the market experienced a "flight to quality," as money poured out of wholesale funding markets, causing healthy, non-financial companies to have trouble raising money via commercial paper and repo. Trading in entire derivatives markets ceased. Stock prices collapsed as equity volatility surged. Federal Reserve Chairman Ben Bernanke testified to the FCIC that he "honestly believe[d] that September and October of 2008 was the worst financial crisis in global history…" (The Financial Crisis Inquiry Commission 2011, 354).

How does *Social Finance*'s theoretical framework explain this post-Lehman market dynamic?

The bankruptcy of Lehman Brothers and bailout for AIG negated the market's conventional expectation that regulators would serve as deposit guarantors in wholesale funding markets. Absent this de facto shadow banking deposit insurance, shadow banks experienced runs as depositors such as money market mutual funds refused to roll over maturing short-term debt. According to Charles Doran, "nonlinearities in the reality one is trying to predict" undermine the reliability of conventions-based expectations of the future. Doran defines nonlinearity as a "discontinuity" that "signals a total break with the past" (Doran 1999, 15–20). As argued by Chapter 2, shocks to convention-given expectations can catalyze convention uncertainty (proposition 3). Given sufficient financial fragility, uncertainty causes market participants to revert to first principles of survival, disrupting the market's normal price discovery mechanism and triggering financial instability (proposition 4). In this case, the shock of having to cope with defied expectations that counterparties would not always be saved catalyzed convention uncertainty about regulators' willingness to serve as lenders of last resort in markets. There are two sources of evidence that Lehman's bankruptcy defied the market's conventional expectations, which in turn drove broader market instability.

First, regulators' may have deliberately wanted to send a signal to markets that they would not continue to bail out troubled financial institutions based on their belief that the market had come to expect continuing support. At the beginning of the Lehman weekend, Treasury Secretary Paulson told the bank chiefs in attendance that the Fed would not provide "any form of extraordinary credit support" to save Lehman (The Financial Crisis Inquiry Commission 2011, 334). As the *Wall Street Journal* surmised on the eve of Lehman's bankruptcy, Lehman presented regulators with a 'Catch-22': "in rescuing those businesses to prevent chaos in the markets, the government *may have created the expectation* that it would be a major financial player in other distressed situations." As a result, Lehman served as a "line in the sand" regarding future bailouts (Moore 2008).[2] According to one popular account of the crisis, US Treasury Secretary Henry Paulson told President George W. Bush that "allowing Lehman to fail would send a strong signal to the market that his administration wasn't in the business of bailing out Wall Street firms any longer" (Sorkin 2009, 374). Minutes from the Federal Open Market Committee's September 16, 2008 meeting reveal that Federal Reserve Bank of St. Louis President James Bullard opined that "by denying funding to Lehman suitors, the Fed has begun to reestablish the idea that markets should not expect help at each difficult juncture." Federal Reserve Bank of Richmond President Jeffrey Lacker concurred, noting that Lehman's failure's "silver lining" was "enhance[ing] the credibility of any commitment that [regulators] make in the future to be willing to let an institution fail and to risk such disruption again." Federal Reserve Bank of Boston President Eric Rosengren said regulators had "taken a bet" that the market could sort itself out (Federal Open Market Committee 2008b). Based on these accounts, it follows that regulators' desire to contravene the perception that they would bail out troubled firms (i.e., moral hazard) may have motivated their decision to let Lehman Brothers go bankrupt.

Second, several market participants interviewed for this book agreed that Lehman's bankruptcy negated whatever preconceptions they had about regulators' willingness to bail out troubled Wall Street firms, in turn confusing markets about which firms would be saved and which would fail. A sell-side structured credit trader whose firm regularly traded against Lehman said Lehman's bankruptcy "sent a signal" to the market that "counterparties could fail; there was definitely counterparty risk; and the government wanted banks to start pricing this risk accordingly" (Sell-side structured credit trader 2018). Another interview subject described Lehman Brothers as "speaking to how complicated modern institutions could be." As a result, "markets had no idea whether regulators had the ability to bail out Lehman, let alone the willingness" (Sell-side market analyst 2018). A buy-side structured credit trader said that counterparty credit fears surged after Lehman failed, which "threw a lot of pricing off." The government's decision to "let Lehman go but not others" created "confusion" for markets (Buy-side structured credit trader 2018). A former hedge fund macroeconomic strategist and current G7 finance ministry official said markets interpreted regulators' actions as "making capricious and hard to predict decisions" that were "at best a higher order of uncertainty in terms of policy reaction function." To the strategist, the biggest issue was regulators' inconsistent treatment of Bear Stearns and Lehman Brothers. Therefore, the strategist said the failure of Lehman induced his $2 billion hedge fund to pull its prime brokerage accounts from Morgan Stanley, based on the logic that since counterparties could now fail, his firm was best off going with those firms with the best balance sheets (Hedge fund macro analyst and G7 official 2018).

The most important, proximate effect of Lehman's bankruptcy was undermining confidence in the wholesale funding market by leading to a surge in counterparty risk. This uncertainty triggered a bank run in both commercial paper and repo markets. When the Reserve Primary Fund, a money market mutual fund that invested in about $785 million of Lehman's commercial paper, "broke the buck" of $1.00 net asset value, this event was the first time a money market mutual fund refused redemptions and broke par value since 1994 (Gullapalli et al. 2008). This credit event caused a broad-based run across all commercial paper and repo markets, leading to a rapid reassessment of commercial paper creditworthiness after Lehman's failure (Kacperczyk and Schnabl 2010, 41). Lehman Brothers' bankruptcy altered the market's risk perception of ABCP, thus triggering a bank run throughout the commercial paper markets. From September 10 to October 22, 2008, the total amount of financial commercial paper outstanding fell roughly thirty percent as commercial paper yields rose. Money market mutual funds boycotted all commercial paper issuers, even those with no connection to Lehman Brothers, which initiated "a broad-based run on commercial paper markets," as former Federal Reserve Bank of New York President and US Treasury Secretary Timothy Geithner told the FCIC. Investors withdrew some $450 billion from prime money market funds, and to meet the rush of redemptions, money market mutual funds sold their illiquid investments, though "there was little market to speak of" and "dealers weren't even picking up their phones," according to the FCIC (The Financial Crisis Inquiry Commission 2011, 358).

Repo markets experienced similar stresses. As Gary Gorton and Andrew Metrick found, the average repo "haircut" (or discount to face value accepted of repo collateral) on structured debt jumped from 25 to 43% after Lehman's bankruptcy, reflecting the fact that "repo depositors did not know which securitized banks were most likely to fail or whether the Fed would let them fail." Lehman's failure caused repo counterparties to assume that shadow banking collateral was *information-sensitive*, since regulators knew more about their willingness to backstop troubled counterparties than did their wholesale lenders. When counterparties lost confidence in the collateral backing repo transactions, they demanded greater repo haircuts as a hedge against the information asymmetry created by this convention uncertainty (Gorton and Metrick 2010, 512–513). Rising repo haircuts are to shadow banks as depositor withdrawals are to traditional banks. When faced with haircuts, financial institutions sell risky assets to make up for their funding shortfall. The collective effect of rising haircuts for all repo issuers for all risky assets was a *generalized banking panic* in which many large, interconnected financial institutions sold the same assets at the same time. As a result, collateral prices fell further, rendering shadow banks (and their sponsoring parents) illiquid and potentially insolvent (Gorton 2009, 512–513).

Interbank lending markets exhibited similar signs of stress. The one-month LIBOR-Overnight indexed swap (OIS) spread, a commonly accepted measure of bank counterparty risk that measures the cost of interbank lending at LIBOR relative interbank lending via the federal funds market, increased from roughly 100 basis points before Lehman to 360 basis points by October 10, 2008. The spread between three-month dollar LIBOR and three-month US Treasury bills, known as the "TED spread," increased from approximately 200 basis points pre-Lehman to 460 basis points by mid-October. As a sign of credit rationing in commercial paper markets, financial commercial paper rates spiked from about 2.40% before Lehman to just over 4.00% afterward (see Fig. 6.1).

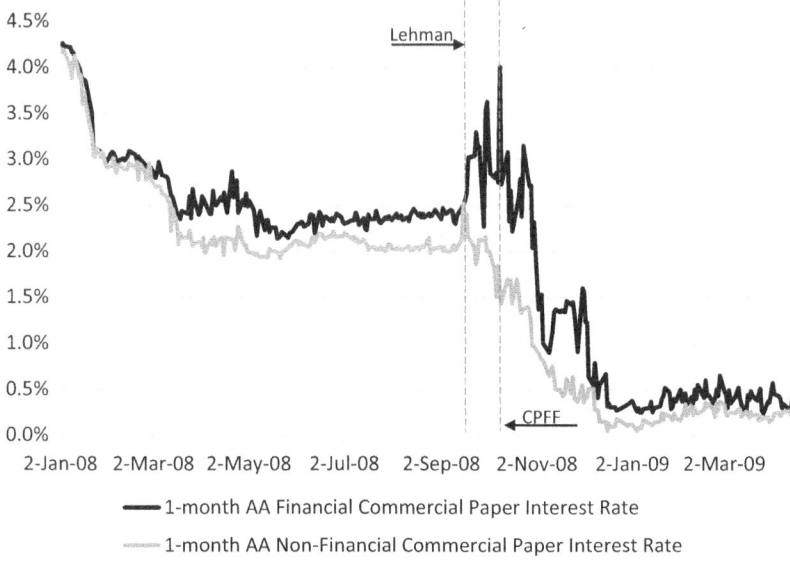

Fig. 6.1 Financial and non-financial commercial paper rates after Lehman (Federal Reserve Economic Data)

This run on commercial paper catalyzed financial market risk to broader market credit rationing.

These pressures resulted in a massive rise in perceived counterparty risks, which created a self-fulfilling panic among shadow banks that broke only after regulators intervened to prop up the system. A sell-side foreign exchange trader noted that prior to Lehman, most of his counterparties believed that banks failed due to idiosyncratic risks. After Lehman and AIG occurred, market participants realized that "every institution could be in trouble." It was thus rational to "assume the worst of one another," which led to "insane" volatility and widening bid-ask spreads on illiquid assets (Sell-side foreign exchange trader 2018). A former management consultant and current private equity investor recalled many of his clients saw their working capital financing "dry up," making it difficult for firms to operate due to a lack of liquidity. The subject's clients had to make difficult operational choices amid broader credit rationing, which created novel stresses for CFOs and CEOs who had yet to live through a full economic cycle, let alone a systemic crisis (Former consultant and private equity investor 2018). Another interview subject said that after Lehman's bankruptcy, "complacency about counterparty risk was gone" and that his hedge fund had to play a "three-dimensional game" in which they considered both counterparty and political risk that some counterparties would fail while others would not, which exacerbated market uncertainty. The subject remembered that the "interim period where there was no clarity after Lehman" as being the most stressful period during the global financial crisis, with questions swirling about whether the entire financial system was insolvent. The subject recalled that his firm spent time analyzing "who was next" after Lehman and his management team expressing confusion about regulators' reaction function (Global macro hedge fund analyst 2018). As a sign of this uncertainty about counterparty risk, credit spreads among the last two standing investment banks, Goldman Sachs and Morgan Stanley, also widened. On Friday, September 12, 2008, it cost 182 basis points to insure Goldman Sachs' five-year debt. By Wednesday, September 17, it cost roughly 550 basis points for the same protection. Morgan Stanley's five-year CDS insurance cost surged from 250 basis points pre-Lehman to 850 basis points after Lehman's bankruptcy as well.

After the fall of Lehman Brothers, the market exhibited several signs of the flight to quality because of convention uncertainty, in which investors sold risky assets and purchased money and money-like equivalents. As Keynes described, "partly on reasonable and partly on instinctive grounds, our desire to hold Money as a store of wealth is a barometer of *the degree of our distrust of our own calculations and conventions concerning the future.*" Further, money "operates…at a deeper level of our motivation. It takes charge at the moments when the higher, more precarious conventions have weakened." This quality of money reflects the fact that "the possession of actual money lulls our disquietude; and the premium which we require to make us part with money is the measure of the degree of our disquietude" (Keynes 1937, 216).[3] In other words, Keynes believed that money demand and its equivalents surged during periods of convention uncertainty. The FCIC describes this tendency as the "flight to quality," which, in the context of the global financial crisis, meant that ABCP and repo investors pulled their funds out of shadow banking conduits and purchased perceived safe-havens like US Treasury securities (The Financial Crisis Inquiry Commission 2011, 252). Yields on the riskiest corporate bonds, those rated CCC and higher by the CRAs, shot up from roughly 9 to 16%. The foreign exchange value of the dollar rose approximately 10% in the month after Lehman's bankruptcy, while four-week Treasury bill interest rates fell from 1.5% before Lehman to 0% afterward (see Fig. 6.2). Public equity markets reeled, and stock market volatility surged. The VIX, or "fear index," which measures the implied volatility of options on the stock performance of Standard & Poor's 500 companies, rose almost 200% immediately after the fall of Lehman. A former investment banker and G7 finance ministry official said that before the crisis, "everybody assumed a dollar would be worth a dollar" in ABCP and repo markets. After Lehman, "there was a fear that wherever you put your cash, it might not be there for you to get back." Lehman's failure "opened up a fault line" that made markets realize that "widely held assumptions [of counterparty solvency] were no longer valid," which induced the market's flight to quality (Former investment banker 2018).

Convention uncertainty also made it difficult for buyers and sellers to agree upon the value of illiquid and non-transparent ABS. Some markets were "completely locked" and "some things couldn't trade at all," as J.P.

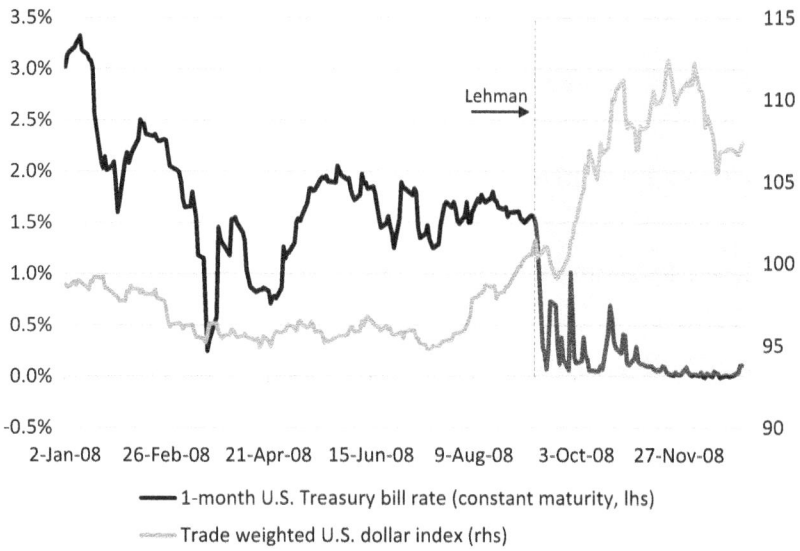

Fig. 6.2 Post-Lehman flight to quality: the dollar and short-term interest rates (Federal Reserve Economic Data)

Morgan Chief Executive Jamie Dimon told the FCIC (The Financial Crisis Inquiry Commission 2011, 353). Stephen Morris and Hyun Song Shin argue that the breakdown of "market confidence" led to an adverse selection problem in financial markets. These authors claim that markets will function normally as long as there is "common understanding" about potential losses in an asset class. When markets lack a common understanding of securities values, then adverse selection problems emerge and trading stops (Morris and Shin 2012). Economic conventions provided this social basis of knowledge in financial markets. The over-the-counter derivatives market came to a "grinding halt" after Lehman's bankruptcy, which illustrates the relationship between an absence of convention-given common understanding and adverse selection in financial markets (The Financial Crisis Inquiry Commission 2011, 364).

Several traders interviewed for this book corroborated the FCIC's findings. One former Lehman Brothers investment banker recalled that "fear and uncertainty" dominated the market during this period. The banker said that it was hard to value assets because there was a perception in markets that certain key insiders (e.g. regulators) had information not otherwise available to market participants. Therefore, it became much harder to trade securities in this environment (Lehman Brothers banker 2018). Another structured credit trader observed that Lehman's bankruptcy "threw a lot of pricing off," and that so-called market fundamentals depended on market confidence, which was absent during the market turmoil. The trader argued that market prices "just didn't make sense mathematically," and recalled seeing fifteen standard deviation events occur daily. Implied default rates on derivatives appeared "astronomical," and prices seemed disconnected from fundamental value. Structured credit markets suffered from a "lack of conviction" because there were no value anchors upon which traders could base their decisions. Lehman and AIG "changed everything" because "suddenly, [traders] had to guess the intentions of regulators. Since there were no clear guidelines about who would fail and who regulators would save, everybody just assumed the worst." Allowing Lehman to fail and bailing out AIG initiated a bank run against all financial institutions that ended only after US authorities guaranteed the solvency of all systemically important financial institutions, as argued in the subsequent section. Lehman and AIG began a period of profound uncertainty in financial markets, in which "every market price *became a call option on a firm's survival*" (Buy-side structured credit trader 2018).[4] A sell-side short-term interest rate futures trader at a major North American financial institution added that Lehman presented a "completely unknown risk [to] the market." As a result, "people did not know what to do. There was no historical basis upon which you could judge what made sense and what did not," and the market was paralyzed. It became difficult to unwind trades facing troubled counterparties. His firm tried to unwind trades at any price, often selling positions for less than their perceived fundamental value due to fears of counterparty risk. The trader recalled that Keynesian beauty contest dynamics "tended to get exaggerated during times of volatility" because market participants have fewer value anchors (Sell-side short-term interest rates trader 2018).

The results of these selected market data and interviews show that the failure of Lehman Brothers catalyzed a generalized bank run in the wholesale funding market, which had a profound impact on shadow banks and the market generally. Lehman's bankruptcy invalidated the market's *conventional expectations* that regulators would serve as liquidity providers of last resort in wholesale funding markets. AIG signaled that some firms would receive bailouts and others would fail, confusing market participants further. Trying to guess the caprice of regulators introduced novel stress among counterparties, causing banks' ABCP and repo collateral to become information-sensitive while also invalidating the market's common understanding of the potential losses in ABS. Generalized convention uncertainty took hold. Wholesale funding markets experienced bank runs and trading in some derivatives markets ceased. Equity volatility surged, and investors partook in a flight to quality. Stock prices fell, and the long-term solvency of all systemically important financial institutions came into question.

Many of these outcomes adhere to J.M. Keynes and James Crotty's hypotheses about convention uncertainty and financial stability. Keynes claimed that money demand would surge under conditions of convention uncertainty, which is exactly what happened when the dollar's foreign exchange value appreciated and short-term interest rates plummeted (Keynes 1937, 216). As Crotty describes, "on…occasions when the consensus forecast turns out to be disastrously mistaken, the irreducible ignorance of the collective wisdom will be made painfully manifest to all agents, the convention will collapse, and the confidence in the ability to forecast the future that is built on that convention will shatter." This selection seems apt to describe financial markets after market participants realized that they were "disastrously mistaken" regarding regulators' intentions to save troubled counterparties. Lehman's bankruptcy caused wholesale funding market counterparties' conventional expectations of regulators' lender of last resort function to "collapse," and confidence in their future forecasts to "shatter" (Crotty 1994, 125).

Responding to the Crisis and Restoring Convention Certainty

After the bailout of AIG, regulators realized that they had a big problem on their hands. Liquidity was pouring out of money markets and into safe haven Treasury securities, while non-financial corporations struggled to raise cash in short-term money markets. Bank share prices fell, and the cost of insuring their debt via CDS rose. Stock market volatility surged. Financial institutions had to sell large portfolios of risky assets *en masse* to keep up with margin and collateral calls, which further depressed asset prices and exacerbated banks' already-dire liquidity and solvency issues. Throughout the crisis, regulators worked around the clock to prevent other systemically important financial institutions from failing, deploying trillions of dollars of support to the financial system. Their response to the crisis sought to achieve three interrelated goals: stemming the shadow bank runs, recapitalizing financial institutions, and removing bad assets from bank balance sheets.

Regulators first focused on stopping the shadow banking runs in the ABCP and repo markets. On September 19, 2008, just days after Lehman's bankruptcy and after the Reserve Primary Fund "broke the buck," the Federal Reserve created the Asset-Backed Commercial Paper Money Market Mutual Fund Liquidity Facility (AMLF) under their emergency lending provision of the Federal Reserve Act. The AMLF allowed depository institutions to borrow from the Fed to repurchase their own ABCP, allowing money market mutual funds to redeem commercial paper at par value. When announcing the AMLF, the Federal Reserve stated that illiquidity in money markets and high redemptions meant that in the absence of Federal involvement, more money market mutual funds would "break the buck" of a $1.00 net asset value, further exacerbating funding pressures in the money markets (The Federal Reserve 2008). By creating the AMLF, the Fed essentially extended deposit insurance to ABCP counterparties, helping to stabilize short-term funding markets for banks that sponsored structures to take advantage of low ABCP rates to accumulate risky assets. This program also helped preserve the moneyness of ABCP.

The authorities also launched the Commercial Paper Funding Facility (CPFF), which came into effect on October 7, 2008, and provided a backstop to "eligible issuers" of short-term debt, extending unlimited commercial paper insurance to all financial and non-financial commercial paper issuers. The Federal Reserve Bank of New York limited eligibility of this program to issuers who had been active issuers of commercial paper during January through August 2008. They also mandated that the commercial paper be rated at least A-/A3 by two of the three major CRAs. Much like Walter Bagehot would have prescribed, the CPFF lent freely only to solvent institutions with high-quality collateral and at a penalty rate (the program carried a 0.1% participation fee for issuers) (Federal Reserve Bank of New York 2009), (Bagehot [1873] 1962, 22–26). After the announcement of this program, 1-month AA financial commercial paper interest rates fell from about 4.00% on October 7, 2009, to less than 1% by early November, 2008 (see Fig. 6.1). The program also alleviated contagion-induced funding pressures for non-financial companies, allowing the Fed to extend sovereign credit to companies such as General Electric, Harley-Davidson, Inc., McDonalds Corporation, and Verizon (Federal Reserve Board of Governors 2016). Much like the AMLF, the CPFF was a form of deposit insurance designed to improve confidence in short-term funding markets.

Other measures adopted in September and October 2008 to improve confidence in financial institutions included the US Treasury's Temporary Guarantee Program for Money Market Funds, in which the US Treasury guaranteed $1.00 par net asset value of money market mutual funds using capital in the Exchange Stabilization Fund (US Department of the Treasury 2008).[5] Also, the Federal Deposit Insurance Corporation launched the Temporary Liquidity Guarantee Program, which extended FDIC insurance to some senior unsecured debt issued by qualified financial institutions (Gray 2008). At its peak use, this program guaranteed nearly $350 billion in debt from 122 entities (Federal Deposit Insurance Corporation 2013). One week after the launch of the Temporary Liquidity Guarantee Program, the Fed rolled out the Money Market Investor Funding Facility (MMIFF) to purchase assets from US money market mutual funds and provide them with liquidity in case they faced redemptions or credit risks (Federal Reserve Board of Governors 2010).

A second plank of regulators' plan to save the US financial system was to recapitalize financial institutions while establishing credible standards for capital shortfalls. Less than one week after Lehman Brothers declared bankruptcy, the Fed allowed Morgan Stanley and Goldman Sachs to become bank holding companies, thereby granting the firms access to the Fed's discount window. By turning America's last remaining investment banks into commercial banks, regulators gave Morgan Stanley and Goldman Sachs a critical lifeline of liquidity support. The FOMC slashed the target federal funds rate to 0%, further easing interbank funding pressures. Some companies received special attention from regulators during this period as well. For instance, on November 23, 2008, the US Treasury and Federal Reserve backstopped over $300 billion of real estate assets on Citigroup's balance sheet.

US Treasury Secretary Henry Paulson eventually convinced the US Congress (after they initially refused to pass the bill) to pass the $700 billion Troubled Asset Relief Program (TARP), which was designed to purchase bad assets from financial institutions but morphed into a recapitalization program after regulators realized that asset purchases would take too long to work themselves through the financial system. So, on October 28, 2008, the US Treasury purchased some $125 billion in preferred stock from nine US financial institutions. On November 14, 2008, the Treasury purchased another $33.5 billion worth of preferred shares from twenty-one banks, and on November 17, 2008, TARP funding was extended to insurance companies as well.

A third plank of regulators' strategy was removing the bad assets from bank balance sheets while transparently disclosing potential capital shortfalls. To that end, the Federal Reserve ended up purchasing some $1.5 trillion in various assets, including ABCP, MBS, repo, among countless other securities. The Federal Reserve became the US economy's repository of risky financial assets, and the Fed's balance sheet remains well above its pre-crisis level to this day (see Figs. 6.3 and 6.6). In mid-2009, the Treasury and Federal Reserve orchestrated the Public–Private Investment Program (PPIP), designed to remove $30 billion of legacy assets off the balance sheets of financial institutions (The Financial Crisis Inquiry Commission 2011, 353–382). The Federal Reserve also conducted a series of stress tests of nineteen bank holding companies to assess their total tier one capital shortfalls under different adverse macroeconomic scenarios. Regulators used the results of the test to guide their recapitalization plans for banks. The market widely viewed the stress

Global financial crisis locus of financial support

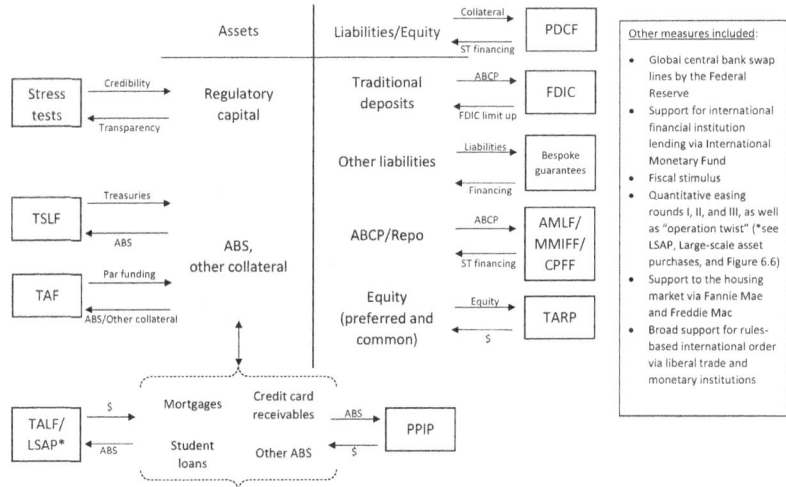

Fig. 6.3 Global financial crisis locus of financial support

tests as a success because the Fed's underlying assumptions were deemed credible. As a result, by understanding the full extent of banks' capital shortfalls in a worst-case scenario, private markets could be confident about bank health when injecting new capital into the banks. The tests also helped the market distinguish between strong and weak financial institutions (Federal Reserve Board of Governors 2009; Geithner n.d.).

One interview subject claimed that interventions quelled market concerns about counterparty risk, recalling that interventions helped "back [the system] away from the abyss" (Sell-side foreign exchange trader 2018). A structured credit trader agreed with this sentiment and said that once the Fed intervened, counterparty risk diminished and returned shadow banking markets to normal. They added that the period when they could not predict which banks would survive was the most stressful in markets (Sell-side structured credit trader 2018). Another hedge fund analyst remembered that government interventions "arrested the sentiment that the financial system could collapse," recalling that before the launch of these programs, there was a "significant fear that [the] entire financial system was going to collapse, with ATMs running out of cash, and companies like [General Electric] unable to make payroll" (Hedge fund macro analyst and G7 official 2018). A former investment banker and G7 finance ministry official noted that the most effective interventions included the FOMC cutting the target federal funds rate to 0% and other short-term capital fixes, which "essentially gave unlimited free money to banks." Alleviating bank funding pressure "had the best impact on markets." Unlike other interview respondents, the former investment banker saw value in the authorities' firm-level interventions, claiming that "individual patch-ups of bank balance sheets helped ensure that regulators would rehabilitate counterparties when they ran into trouble, thus reducing [counterparty] fears" (Former investment banker 2018).

In hindsight, regulators' interventions prevented America's financial institutions from falling into a disorderly bankruptcy. For instance, the AMLF, CPFF, and MMIFF succeeded in diminishing funding pressures in the interbank lending market. By mid-November 2008, one-month dollar LIBOR-OIS, the TED spread, and investment bank CDS spreads fell to about half of their pre-Lehman highs. However, idiosyncratic concerns about specific banks, such as Bank of America and Citigroup, persisted throughout early 2009. Equity prices continued their slide until March 2009, while risky bond yields fell and hit their pre-crisis levels by summer 2009. The crisis left lasting scars on the real economy as well. The United States' unemployment rate increased to above 10% as firms shed jobs to cut costs given rising macroeconomic uncertainty. From September 2008 to April 2009, the US economy lost roughly 680,000 jobs per month, while growth contracted in the fourth quarter of 2008 and first and second quarters of 2009 (see Figs. 6.4 and 6.5). Despite the considerable real economy fallout and damage to market confidence, regulators' interventions succeeded in stemming the shadow banking bank run that accelerated after the failure of Lehman Brothers.

The bank bailouts also illustrate the plasticity of institutions during crises and the causal role of economic conventions held by regulators during crisis periods. Matthias Matthijs defines a crisis as "a moment of decisive intervention in the process of institutional change when contradictions in the system are generally acknowledged" (Matthijs 2011, 25). By this definition, the shadow banking run that began in early 2008 and accelerated after the failure of Lehman Brothers qualifies as a crisis. In this case, the contradiction acknowledged was confusion over regulators' willingness to serve as lenders of last resort among shadow banking conduits. Regulators' "decisive

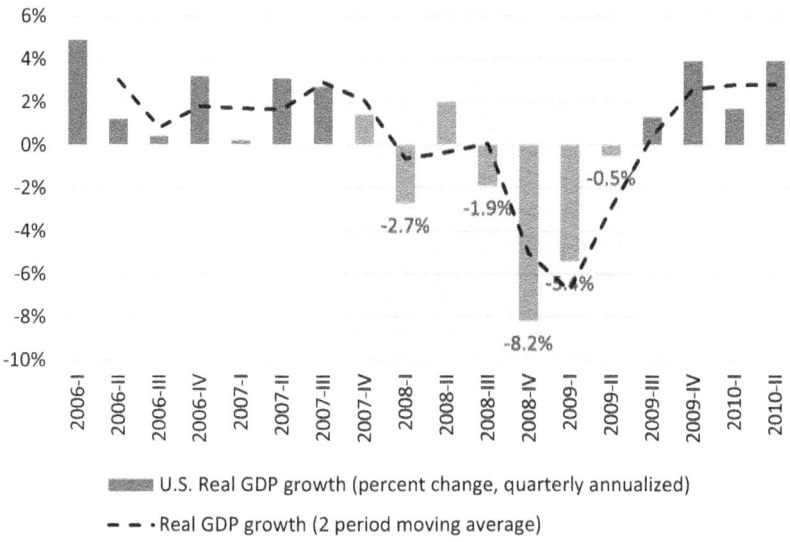

Fig. 6.4 US GDP growth: 2006–2011 (Federal Reserve Economic Data)

intervention" was their various support programs announced to stem the shadow banking bank run and provide de facto deposit insurance to shadow banking depositors. Regulators' response to the crisis can also be understood as an example of the influence of ergodicity conventions, specifically informing regulators' fears of repeating the Great Depression. Immediately after the failure of Lehman Brothers, regulators realized that bank runs in the ABCP and repo markets, interbank funding pressures, collapsing asset prices, and rising stock market volatility, posed a catastrophic risk to the US economy. Allowing the market to clear on its own led regulators to fear that they might have to endure the bankruptcy of the entire global financial system and drastic fall in economic activity, well below the economy's productive potential.

Although there was heterogeneity of beliefs among regulators regarding the structural causes of the crisis, there was a consensus among the Federal Reserve and the US Treasury that it was essential to prevent further bankruptcies of systemically important financial institutions after Lehman's failure lest the US economy experience another Great Depression. For instance, Federal Reserve Chairman Ben Bernanke

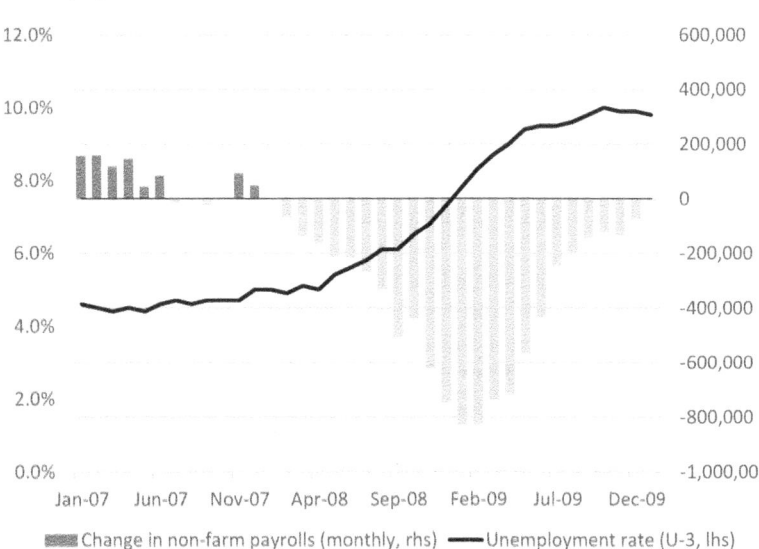

Fig. 6.5 US unemployment rate and job creation: 2007–2009 (Federal Reserve Economic Data)

claimed that the lessons of the US economy in the 1930s had "been learned" and that during the global financial crisis, regulators' repeated financial market interventions spared the global economy "an even worse cataclysm that could have rivaled or surpassed the Great Depression." Bernanke argued that the Great Depression occurred because of bad policy choices on behalf of regulators, characterizing policy choices of the 1930s as "[running] the gamut from passivity to timidity." In contrast, he and his fellow policymakers "acted sooner and with greater force than in the 1930s." The biggest lesson Bernanke took from the Great Depression was that a greater sense of urgency by regulators to stem bank runs could have avoided a domino effect of cascading defaults across the global financial system. As has been argued throughout this book, Bernanke also viewed shadow banking as banking per se, and found that the US financial system "experienced the equivalent of runs on the network of nonbank financial institutions that has come to be called the shadow banking system." It was imperative to Bernanke to stop these shadow banking runs, since he knew that they could spiral out of control and cause a steep contraction of credit with disastrous real economy consequences (Bernanke 2010). Bernanke's background as a scholar of the Great Depression influenced his thinking and predisposed him to responding to the threat of bank runs and contagion. However, his decisions were by no means pre-ordained and historically path dependent. Rather, Bernanke's socialization, both as an academic and policymaker, made him more likely to buy into the Great Depression as a salient narrative about the consequences of not responding forcefully to the crisis.

Other Fed officials voiced similar concerns about inaction leading to a deeper depression as well, following Bernanke's lead. For instance, Federal Reserve Bank of Chicago President Charles Evans told the FOMC during the June 24–25, 2008 meeting that "many of the actions [the Fed] has taken are defenses against" nonmonetary risks of another Great Depression (Federal Open Market Committee 2008a). Federal Reserve Bank of Richmond President Jeffrey Lacker noted at the October 28–29 meeting based on his "reading of the Great Depression," the main policy lesson is that central banks should cut interest rates and keep them low (Federal Open Market Committee 2008c).

Additionally, the success of regulators' response to the shadow banking bank runs reveals much about the market's conventions about regulators. As argued previously, one of the reasons why ABCP and repo counterparties ran on shadow banking conduits was because the failure of Lehman Brothers revealed that regulators were willing to go all the way and allow some financial institutions to fail while bailing out others, and the Reserve Primary Fund's "breaking the buck" further exacerbated the market's waning confidence. In response to the shadow banking runs, regulators sought to re-establish conventional expectations that regulators would serve as liquidity providers of last resort in financial markets. Regulators were successful in restoring confidence to the banks because they effectively guaranteed the face value of all money market instruments, thus extending de facto deposit insurance to the shadow banking market. By directing the FDIC to backstop bank and non-bank short-term borrowing, the federal government extended public credit to the financial system's private liabilities. Because the market deemed regulators' commitment credible, and because the market held America's sovereign credit in high esteem, regulators were able to halt the run on shadow banking conduits.

This *domestic credibility transfer* of sovereign credit to private liabilities reflects many conventional processes at play in the market. As Jonathan Kirshner finds, capital market liberalization introduces new constraints on national regulators, wherein the market punished policies it deemed illegitimate with capital outflows and rewarded legitimate policies with capital inflows and lower borrowing costs (Kirshner 2003, 665). In this case, whether banks were truly insolvent was beside the point—what mattered was the market's perceptions of bank solvency, which in turn had implications for bank solvency in self-fulfilling ways: those financial institutions that the market deemed creditworthy by their access (both potential and realized) to sovereign credit gained market access. Because support to the financial system was widespread, regulators' interventions improved systemic confidence. For instance, one interview subject emphasized the difficulty of dis-embedding liquidity and solvency during a crisis. The subject emphasized that even today, it is unclear whether Lehman was simply illiquid rather than insolvent. Therefore, the provision of public support to banks via liquidity support and asset reflation enhanced banks' perceived and realized solvency, which depended on conventional processes, specifically credibility transfer between banks' private liabilities and public balance sheets (Sell-side market analyst 2018).

The question, then, is why did the market view regulators as particularly creditworthy? The answer to this question exceeds the scope of this book, though scholars point out that America's relative creditworthiness relates to the fact that America has never defaulted on its debt and that the dollar is the premier the global reserve asset (and thus faced structurally higher demand and thus lower borrowing costs than other currencies) (Calleo 1992; Eichengreen 2011; Wolf 2014). Together, these factors explain why regulators had *intervention capacity* to restore confidence to America's financial system and were able to engage in credibility transfer of public credit to the shadow banking system's private liabilities. Interview subjects universally agreed the Fed and Treasury's interventions helped stem the banking panic, and none of them expressed concern about the sovereign capacity of the United States to stem the crisis. A few interview subjects noted the Federal Reserve's coordinated swap lines with multiple central banks as being a positive signal for global market health, leading one subject to conclude that the swaps communicated that the Fed "was willing to provide as much financing as the market needs" (Sell-side structured credit trader 2018).[6] So not only did the United States' authorities have *intervention capacity* to stem the panic domestically, but the United States' global response provided a semblance of *international credibility transfer* that restored stability to global markets.[7]

Discussion

Some of the scholarship produced after the global financial crisis has criticized the policy choices made by regulators during the fog of uncertainty of the crisis. This section briefly summarizes these critiques and responds to them using insights informed by this book's theoretical framework. Common criticisms of regulators' crisis response include: letting Lehman Brothers fail was a mistake; the crisis response was illegitimate and illegal; regulators did not do enough to help homeowners; and post-crisis stabilization policy was tepid, with premature austerity.

First, regulators' decision to let Lehman Brothers fail has been one of the most hotly contested choices made during the global financial crisis. According to Fed Chairman Ben Bernanke and US Treasury Secretary Timothy Geithner, the Fed did not have the legal recourse to lend to Lehman during a bank run because it was unclear whether Lehman had sufficient collateral against which the Fed could lend (Stewart and Eavis 2014). According to Geithner, Lehman "looked insolvent in almost any state of the world" and therefore a bailout of Lehman would have simply "financed a run on an unsalvageable institution" (Geithner 2014, 207). Lawrence Ball rejects this view and claims that the Fed had ample recourse to lend to Lehman. Based on detailed accounts of recently released meeting transcripts of regulators' pre-Lehman deliberations, Ball concludes that the Fed's stated reason for letting Lehman fail (a lack of collateral and absence of regulatory authority) is false. Ball argues that there was "no evidence…[regulators]…examined the adequacy of Lehman's collateral, or that legal barriers deterred [regulators] from assisting" Lehman. In fact, Lehman simply faced a liquidity crisis, and had sufficient collateral to warrant a bailout. Ball speculated that had the Fed availed the PDCF to Lehman Brothers that was used to lend to Morgan Stanley and Goldman Sachs after Lehman's bankruptcy, then Lehman "probably could have survived" (Ball 2016, 2–3).

There are several responses to Ball's critique that follow from this book's theoretical framework. It is not obvious that Lehman Brothers was solvent on the eve of its bankruptcy. Recall that during a crisis, liquidity and solvency are interrelated. When market confidence goes and asset price values fall below equilibrium value due to liquidity scarcity, even healthy financial institutions might appear insolvent. Assessing Lehman Brothers' solvency after the fact in the wake of regulators' extraordinary interventions in markets suffers from several logical pitfalls. Regulators did not have perfect foresight into the long-term value of Lehman's collateral when Lehman failed. Therefore, it is unfair to judge regulators' misappraisal on long-term estimates of Lehman's assets on the eve of the crisis, when they and the rest of the market suffered from acute convention uncertainty. Many ex-post accounts of Lehman's solvency also suffer from circular reasoning, since it is unclear whether regulators could have obtained emergency powers to save the broader financial system absent the exigency caused by Lehman Brothers' bankruptcy. Former US Treasury Secretary Henry Paulson acknowledged that Lehman's bankruptcy was a wake-up call to the market and to politicians, which created a sense of urgency to solve the crisis (Ryssdal 2018). Paulson's view comports with Matthias Matthijs' argument that crises create unique windows of opportunity for policy entrepreneurs to push for radical policy change. Lehman could thus be interpreted as a costly but necessary sacrifice to increase the plasticity of America's economic governance institutions, in turn broadening the scope of regulators' potential crisis responses. Even accepting that letting Lehman fail was a mistake, regulators deserve credit for recognizing their error and rapidly reversing course. Emergency lending programs that regulators denied to Lehman, such as access to the Fed's discount window, were quickly extended to Lehman's rivals Morgan Stanley and Goldman Sachs after Lehman declared bankruptcy. Policymakers learned from their mistakes from Lehman and reversed course rapidly. Given the difficulties of operating in an uncertain environment with its attendant stresses, regulators deserve credit for relaxing their stringent views when events belied their expectations.

A second common critique of regulators' response to the crisis was that regulators did not do enough to provide foreclosure relief to homeowners. One of the best examples of this debate took place on Jon Stewart's *Comedy Central* television program *The Daily Show*. Stewart had key crisis player Timothy Geithner on set and challenged him for regulators' perceived favoritism to banks over homeowners. Stewart claimed that regulators failed to provide principal forgiveness and loan modifications to homeowners, in turn exacerbating the toll of the financial market downturn on the real economy. As a result, banks foreclosed on borrowers who lacked the recourse to continue paying their mortgages, while regulators gave trillions of dollars in support to financial institutions, with little of this aid trickling down to individual homeowners. Millions of Americans lost their homes, while bankers paid themselves seven-figure bonuses (Stewart 2014).

There are several responses to this line of criticism. First is the question of regulators' priorities and maximizing the impact of each dollar spent on the bailout. In a perfect world, regulators could have mobilized the resources necessary to provide mass foreclosure relief to homeowners, but regulators' first—and correct—priority was halting the shadow banking bank runs that accelerated after the failure of Lehman Brothers. If regulators had to make difficult tradeoffs about where to allocate their scarce political capital and human resources during the fog of crisis, then they made the right decision to focus on the primary locus of financial fragility during the crisis. It is hard to imagine that foreclosure relief in September 2008 would have alleviated General Electric's short-term funding pressures, for instance, or stopped clients from pulling their money from the major broker-dealers. Second, this book's account of the global financial crisis is that the crisis was caused by fragility, of which the housing bubble played just one part. Although commentators tend to blame the bubble asset class for crises, Minsky finds that asset price bubbles are necessary but insufficient conditions for systemic financial crises. Focusing on end-borrowers when faced with a bank run would have led to an incomplete crisis response since the most important priority for regulators was restoring confidence in financial institutions. A response to this line of reasoning is that housing relief and emergency lending to banks are not mutually exclusive targets. But consider that regulators were severely constrained in their ability to request resources from Congress during the crisis. For instance, TARP failed its first Congressional vote. Given the general hostility of Congress to any bailouts, regulators had to pick their political battles and opted for resources to save truly systemic financial institutions, rather than potentially foreclosed homeowners. Additionally, the process of combing through individual mortgages and conducting a full credit analysis of each borrower to determine needs would have been too much for regulators to handle while balancing other goals. Third, by preventing a second Great Depression and worse real economy downturn due to the post-Lehman shadow banking runs, regulators helped homeowners stay in their homes. The Federal Reserve's monetary policy reduced interest rates and boosted asset prices. The US Treasury's placement of Fannie Mae and Freddie Mac into receivership and Federal Reserve's consecutive rounds of asset purchases via quantitative easing also eased financing conditions (see Fig. 6.6). These actions provided advantageous financing and home buying conditions for consumers, helping homeowners on the margins avoid losing their homes. And by preventing the collapse of the global payments system through their interventions, regulators avoided a much worse fate for all borrowers in the global economy, including homeowners.

A third critique of regulators' response to the crisis is that regulators' interventions were politically illegitimate and, worse, potentially illegal. In a wide-ranging and convincing discussion of the legal bases of the Federal Reserve and US Treasury's crisis response, Philip Wallach finds that regulators were not concerned with the legality of their actions during the crisis. Worse, by skirting rule of law constraints on their actions, regulators corroded the legitimacy of the same economic institutions

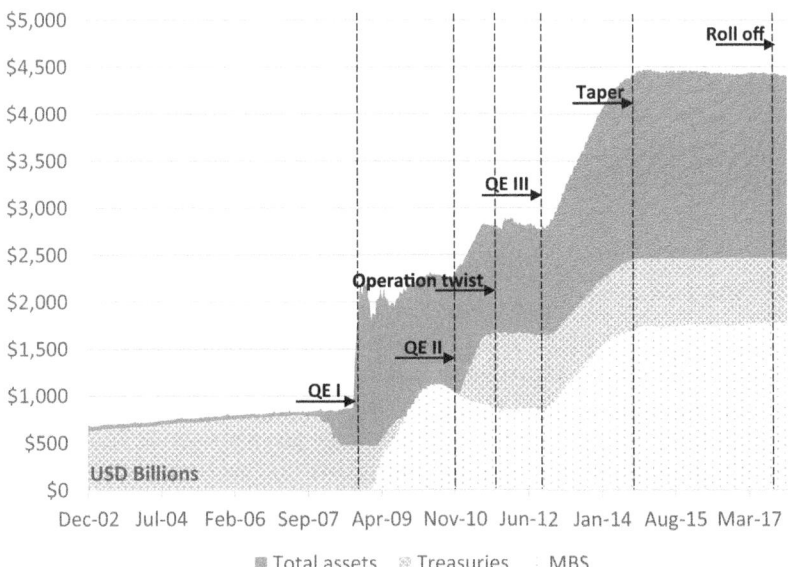

Fig. 6.6 Federal Reserve balance sheet: 2002–2018 (Federal Reserve Economic Data)

and policy interventions that were aimed at stabilizing the economy and averting an even worse economic collapse (Wallach 2015). *Social Finance* does not contest Wallach's account. However, the fact that regulators were willing and capable to work around legal limitations on their actions is consistent with *Social Finance*'s theoretical framework, especially Charles Doran and constructivists' findings on the plasticity of institutions during crises, specifically that crisis dynamics relax constraints on elite intervention in the economy. The crisis may also illustrate a political tradeoff between legitimacy of interventions and expediency and intervention scope. The Federal Reserve and US Treasury Department very well could have expended countless hours trying to vet each potential policy proposal through appropriate legal channels, with full US government interagency coordination and ample Congressional oversight. It is reasonable to assume that such a course would have taken additional time and diluted regulators' ideal responses to the crisis. Therefore, opting for the legitimate path during a crisis could have blunted the scope and size of regulators' interventions, thus hampering the efficacy of the crisis response. Economic institutions took a damaging hit to their credibility due to the perception that financial interests had captured regulators and as a result, the regulatory response coddled banks at the expense of individual homeowners. But US regulators do not have a legitimacy mandate, and it is the job of politicians to narrate their policies to the body politic to couch crises actions in legitimacy. Additionally, because regulators spared the public a counterfactual scenario in which regulators opted not to bail out the financial system, or instead sought emergency powers from Congress at every turn, there is scant public evidence that the crisis response was necessary and effective for the broader political consciousness. This is a political problem and one that will continue to plague crisis fighters. One potential solution to the concern over legitimacy is focusing on creating crisis response mechanisms before a crisis strikes. Doing so would require significant foresight on behalf of regulators. Creating such mechanisms that could then be activated during the crisis interval may blunt some of the illegitimacy concerns voiced by the critics of the crisis response, particularly if such facilities had built in oversight features.

Fourth, many critiques of the crisis response argue that regulators' post-crisis stabilization policy was tepid, with premature austerity. Mark Blyth describes austerity as a deliberate attempt at internal devaluation in which states cut government expenditure to reduce wages and restore competitiveness. As Blyth argues in *Austerity: The History of a Dangerous Idea*, austerity does not work and misplaces the blame for the private sector's bad decisions on governments. Through a detailed history of the idea of austerity, Blyth shows how austerity exacerbates economic downturns and sometimes leads to fascism, as illustrated by pre-World War II Germany and Japan (Blyth 2015). Some of the crisis' biggest players agreed with Blyth's assessment. For instance, Timothy Geithner described the fiscal consolidation that took place beginning in 2010 as "a serious and frustrating self-inflicted wound" that "sapped the strength" of the recovery" (Geithner 2014, 499–500). Given the dissatisfaction with austerity after the crisis, why did this policy gain such prominence, particularly in the United States where fiscal space was ample? Recall that *Social Finance* argued that policymakers will respond to crises using preexisting ideational scripts available to them. The absence of a concerted push against austerity and in favor of counter-cyclical fiscal spending demonstrates that policymakers may have lacked a cogent set of economic ideas that could successfully bring together anti-austerity political coalitions and that policymakers did not have the ammunition to respond rhetorically to calls for austerity. Therefore, some of the blame for the economy's premature turn to austerity rests with the intellectual progenitors of the anti-austerity movement. Academics should actively think about a coherent set of economic ideas that can stand up to the intuitive appeal of austerity politics so that politicians can be equipped with tools necessary to push back against premature austerity after crises.

Conclusion

Chapter 5 and this chapter described the establishment, nullification, and re-establishment of the market's *conventional expectation* that regulators would serve as liquidity providers of last resort in shadow banking markets. Chapter 5 began by describing how regulators' repeated interventions during systemic events, including the failure of hedge fund Long-Term Capital Management in 1998, sale of investment bank Bear Stearns to J.P. Morgan in March 2008, and nationalization of the Federal housing giants Fannie Mae and Freddie Mac established a belief among market participants that regulators would intervene whenever a counterparty was on the brink of a creditor panic. The chapter then argued that the failure of Lehman Brothers in September 2008 negated this expectation and ushered in a period of deep uncertainty in markets as market participants tried to divine the intentions of regulators. The bankruptcy of Lehman Brothers constituted a deviation from convention-given expectations which, coupled with the system's underlying fragility, led to a run on all short-term funding markets, as predicted by propositions three and four of *Social Finance*. Regulators' response to the crisis is best understood as a function of their conventions of ergodicity, specifically their fears of repeating the Great Depression. Bailouts succeeded in stabilizing short-term funding markets because regulators were able to convince the market of their credible commitment to the shadow banking system regarding their capacity to serve as liquidity providers of last resort in wholesale funding markets. The United States' sovereign creditworthiness enhanced US regulators' intervention capacity to extend public credit guarantees to private liabilities, thus alleviating funding pressures in shadow banking markets, allowing regulators to re-establish conventional equilibrium in markets.

Notes

1. In this context, "higher collateral" implies greater repo haircuts and higher interest rates on ABCP.
2. Emphasis added.
3. Emphasis added.
4. Emphasis added.
5. For additional background on the Exchange Stabilization Fund, see Henning (1999) and Geithner (2014, 49–52).
6. The United States' willingness to serve as an international lender of last resort is consistent with Charles Kindleberger's description of hegemonic role during crises, see Kindleberger (2013). For a modern account applying Kindleberger and others to the global financial crisis, see Drezner (2014).
7. For a primer on the Fed's foreign exchange swaps, see Fleming and Klagge (2010).

Works Cited

Bagehot, Walter. [1873] 1962. *Lombard Street: A Description of the Money Market*. Westport: Hyperion Press.
Ball, Lawrence. 2016. "The Fed and Lehman Brothers." *NBER Monetary Economics Working Paper Series*, 1–218. National Bureau of Economic Research.

Bernanke, Ben S. 2009. "Testimony: American International Group." *Federal Reserve Board of Governors*. March 24. Accessed March 24, 2018. http://www.federalreserve.gov/newsevents/testimony/bernanke20090324a.htm.

———. 2010. "Speech: Economic Policy: Lessons from History." *Federal Reserve Board of Governors*. April 8. Accessed March 26, 2018. https://www.federalreserve.gov/newsevents/speech/bernanke20100408a.htm.

Blyth, Mark. 2015. *Austerity: The History of a Dangerous Idea*. Oxford: Oxford University Press.

Buy-side structured credit trader, interview by Neil Shenai. 2018. *Author Interview* (April 16).

Calleo, David P. 1992. *The Bankrupting of America: How the Federal Budget Is Impoverishing the Nation*. New York: Avon Books.

Crotty, James. 1994. "Are Keynesian Uncertainty and Macrotheory Incompatible? Conventional Decision Making, Institutional Structures and Conditional Stability in Keynesian Macromodels." In *New Perspectives in Monetary Macroeconomics: Explorations in the Tradition of Hyman Minsky*, by G. Dymski and R. Pollin (eds.), 105–142. Ann Arbor: University of Michigan Press.

Doran, Charles F. 1999. "Why Forecasts Fail: The Limits and Potential of Forecasting in International Relations and Economics." *International Studies Review* 1 (2): 11–41.

Drezner, Daniel W. 2014. *The System Worked: How the World Stopped Another Great Depression*. Oxford: Oxford University Press.

Eichengreen, Barry. 2011. *Exorbitant Privilege: The Rise and Fall of the Dollar and the Future of the International Monetary System*. Oxford: Oxford University Press.

Federal Deposit Insurance Corporation. 2013. "Temporary Liquidity Guarantee Program." *Federal Deposit Insurance Corporation*. February 27. Accessed April 20, 2018. https://www.fdic.gov/regulations/resources/tlgp/.

Federal Open Market Committee. 2008a. "Transcript of the Federal Open Market Committee." *The Federal Reserve Board*. June 24–25. Accessed May 1, 2018. https://www.federalreserve.gov/monetarypolicy/files/FOMC20080625meeting.pdf.

———. 2008b. "Transcript of the Federal Open Market Committee." *The Federal Reserve Board*. September 16. Accessed April 19, 2018. https://www.federalreserve.gov/monetarypolicy/files/FOMC20080916meeting.pdf.

———. 2008c. "Transcript of the Federal Open Market Committee." *The Federal Reserve Board*. October 28–29. Accessed May 1, 2018. https://www.federalreserve.gov/monetarypolicy/files/FOMC20081029meeting.pdf.

Federal Reserve Bank of New York. 2009. "Commercial Paper Funding Facility: Frequently Asked Questions." *Federal Reserve Bank of New York*. October 19.

Accessed March 25, 2018. http://www.newyorkfed.org/markets/cpff_faq.html.

Federal Reserve Board of Governors. 2009. "Supervisory Capital Assessment Program: Design and Implementation." *Federal Reserve Board of Governors.* April 24. Accessed April 1, 2018. https://www.federalreserve.gov/newsevents/pressreleases/files/bcreg20090424a1.pdf.

———. 2010. "Money Market Investor Funding Facility." *Federal Reserve Board of Governors.* February 5. https://www.federalreserve.gov/monetarypolicy/mmiff.htm.

———. 2016. "Regulatory Reform." *Commercial Paper Funding Facility (CPFF).* February 12. Accessed March 25, 2018. https://www.federalreserve.gov/regreform/reform-cpff.htm.

Fleming, Michael J., and Nicholas J. Klagge. 2010. "The Federal Reserve's Foreign Exchange Swap Lines." *Current Issues in Economics and Finance* 16 (4): 1–7.

Former consultant and private equity investor, interview by Neil Shenai. 2018. *Author Interview* (March 24).

Former investment banker, interview by Neil Shenai. 2018. *Author Interview* (April 18).

Geithner, Timothy F. n.d. "Lecture: The Stress Test." *Coursera.* Accessed March 31, 2018. https://www.coursera.org/learn/global-financial-crisis/lecture/Fb3Jc/lecture-the-stress-test.

———. 2014. *Stress Test: Reflections on Financial Crises.* New York: Crown Publishers.

Global macro hedge fund analyst, interview by Neil Shenai. 2018. *Author Interview* (February 15).

Gorton, Gary B. 2009. "Slapped in the Face by the Invisible Hand: Banking and the Panic of 2007." *Federal Reserve Bank of Atlanta's 2009 Financial Markets Conference: Financial Innovation and Crisis,* 1–52. Atlanta: Federal Reserve Bank of Atlanta.

Gorton, Gary B., and Andrew Metrick. 2010. "Haircuts." *Federal Reserve Bank of St. Louis Review* 92 (6): 507–519.

Gray, Andrew. 2008. "FDIC Announces Plan to Free Up Bank Liquidity: Creates New Program to Guarantee Bank Debt and Fully Insure Non-interest Bearing Deposit Transaction Accounts." *Federal Deposit Insurance Corporation.* October 14. Accessed March 31, 2018. https://www.fdic.gov/news/news/press/2008/pr08100.html.

Gullapalli, Diya, Shefali Anand, and Daisey Maxey. 2008. "Money Fund, Hurt by Debt Tied to Lehman, Breaks the Buck." *The Wall Street Journal.* September 17. Accessed March 24, 2018. https://www.wsj.com/articles/SB122160102128644897.

Hedge fund macro analyst and G7 official, interview by Neil Shenai. 2018. *Author Interview* (February 26).

Henning, C. Randall. 1999. *The Exchange Stabilization Fund: Slush Money or War Chest?* Washington: Institute for International Economics.

Kacperczyk, Marcin, and Philipp Schnabl. 2010. "When Safe Proved Risky: Commercial Paper During the Financial Crisis of 2007–2009." *Journal of Economic Perspectives* 24 (1): 29–50.

Keynes, John M. 1937. "The General Theory of Employment." *The Quarterly Journal of Economics* 51 (2): 209–223.

Kindleberger, Charles P. 2013. *The World in Depression: 1929–1939.* Oakland: University of California Press.

Kirshner, Jonathan. 2003. "Money Is Politics." *Review of International Political Economy* 10 (4): 645–660.

Lehman Brothers banker, interview by Neil Shenai. 2018. *Author Interview* (March 3).

Lehman Brothers banker 2, interview by Neil Shenai. 2018. *Author Interview* (March 25).

Matthijs, Matthias M. 2011. *Ideas and Economic Crises in Britain from Attlee to Blair (1945–2005).* London: Routledge.

McDonald, Robert, and Anna Paulson. 2014. "AIG in Hindsight." *Federal Reserve Bank of Chicago Working Paper Series* (7): 1–55.

Mollenkamp, Carrick, Serena Ng, Liam Plevan, and Randall Smith. 2008. "Behind AIG's Fall, Risk Models Failed to Pass Real-World Test." *The Wall Street Journal.* October 31. Accessed March 24, 2018. https://www.wsj.com/articles/SB122538449722784635.

Moore, Heidi N. 2008. "Lehman Brothers, Moral Hazard and Who's Next." *The Wall Street Journal.* September 14. Accessed March 31, 2018. https://blogs.wsj.com/deals/2008/09/14/lehman-brothers-moral-hazard-and-whos-next/.

Morris, Stephen, and Hyun Song Shin. 2012. "Contagious Adverse Selection." *American Economic Journal: Macroeconomics* 4 (1): 1–21.

Ryssdal, Kai. 2018. *Bernanke, Geithner and Paulson: The Full Interview* (March).

Sell-side foreign exchange trader, interview by Neil Shenai. 2018. *Author Interview* (February 19).

Sell-side market analyst, interview by Neil Shenai. 2018. *Author Interview* (February 26).

Sell-side short-term interest rates trader, interview by Neil Shenai. 2018. *Author Interview* (April 4).

Sell-side structured credit trader, interview by Neil Shenai. 2018. *Author Interview* (February 12).

Sorkin, Aaron Ross. 2009. *Too Big to Fail.* New York: Penguin.

Stewart, James B., and Peter Eavis. 2014. "Revisiting the Lehman Brothers Bailout That Never Was." *The New York Times.* September 29. Accessed March 29, 2018. https://www.nytimes.com/2014/09/30/business/revisiting-the-lehman-brothers-bailout-that-never-was.html.

Stewart, Jon. 2014. *Timothy Geithner Extended Interview*. Television Interview. May 21. http://www.cc.com/video-clips/qd03iv/the-daily-show-with-jon-stewart-exclusive—timothy-geithner-extended-interview-pt–1.

The Federal Reserve. 2008. "Asset Backed Commercial Paper (ABCP) Money Market Mutual Fund (MMMF) Liquidity Facility." *Federal Reserve Discount Window: Payment System Risk*. September 22. Accessed March 25, 2018. https://www.frbdiscountwindow.org/Home/GeneralPages/Asset-Backed-Commercial-Paper-ABCP-Money-Market-Mutual-Fund-MMMF-Liquidity-Facility-AMLF-or-the-Facility-#f7.

The Financial Crisis Inquiry Commission. 2011. *The Financial Crisis Inquiry Report: Final Report of the National Commission on the Causes of the Financial and Economic Crisis in the United States*. Washington, DC: U.S. Government Printing Office.

U.S. Department of the Treasury. 2008. "Treasury Announces Temporary Guarantee Program for Money Market Funds." *U.S. Department of the Treasury*. September 29. Accessed April 20, 2018. https://www.treasury.gov/press-center/press-releases/Pages/hp1161.aspx.

Wallach, Philip A. 2015. *To the Edge: Legality, Legitmacy, and the Responses to the 2008 Financial Crisis*. Washington, DC: Brookings Institution Press.

Wolf, Martin. 2014. *The Shifts and the Shocks: What We've Learned—And Have Still to Learn—From the Financial Crisis*. New York: Penguin.

CHAPTER 7

Conclusions and Extensions

Based on this book's core arguments and findings, what conclusions can we draw about the role of economic conventions in financial markets? This chapter summarizes *Social Finance's* ontological and theoretical implications and main empirical findings. It also touches upon the policy implications of the book. It then discusses the limitations of the study and concludes with avenues of further research.

THEORETICAL IMPLICATIONS: TAKING CONVENTIONS SERIOUSLY IN THE STORY OF FINANCIAL INSTABILITY

Primarily, this book sought to understand the relationship between economic conventions and financial stability. There are two theoretical takeaways from *Social Finance*.

First, this book contended that while Charles Kindleberger and Hyman Minsky provide a plausible heuristic model of financial instability, their model suffers from the fact that it understates the causal importance of economic ideas as drivers of stability and instability in asset markets. By drawing on insights from J.M. Keynes, Charles Doran, and economic constructivists, this book attempted to bring economic conventions "back into" the Post-Keynesian model of financial crises. This book explained the sociological micro-foundations of Post-Keynesianism and showed how incorporating economic conventions into the study of financial instability could lead to a better model of financial crises. It problematized and identified the sources of stability in the Post-Keynesian model, arguing that economic conventions are responsible both for stabilizing markets and sowing epistemic blindness to fragility prior to crises. Conventions triggered Minsky's endogenous dynamics of stability transitioning to fragility over time while lulling market participants into ignoring signs of precrisis fragility and impending financial collapse. This book provided a framework of understanding how stable (but fragile) systems erupt into crisis by drawing on Charles Doran's theory of crises in international relations. Financial panics followed from a discontinuity in expectations that invalidated agents' conventions and caused convention uncertainty. This convention uncertainty, set against a backdrop of financial fragility, precipitated panics. It also described the ideational constraints on elite intervention in the economy during crisis periods as informed by political economy scholarship. Elite responses to financial instability depend on their unique socialization and the market's latitude given to regulators to intervene in their financial systems (i.e. what *Social Finance* terms *intervention capacity*).

Second, *Social Finance* supports the argument, often made by international relations and political economy constructivists, that ideational scholarship occupies a unique ontology of investigating outcomes in complex social systems such as markets. This book adopted a *strongly constitutive* standard of causality, rejecting Humean linear causality in favor of a more probabilistic or emergent causal standard. Linear causality (i.e. X produces Y) is problematic in financial markets because the variables under investigation, X and Y (such as prices and fundamental value), are mutually constituted and recursive (Lebow 2009, 4–6) and (Soros 2003). Most mainstream accounts of markets tend to be static, linear, treat change as exogenous, and see outcomes as normally distributed (Blyth 2011, 84–86). This book challenges these contentions on a theoretical level and showed that misplaced belief in linear causality in markets actually can generate the very fragility that leads to systemic crises. Risk models built on the assumption of asset price distribution normality, central bankers that believed that the greater risk to the US economy was a Japanese-style deflation rather than a chaotic unwinding of a decade-long debt-fueled credit binge and housing bubble, and bond ratings that ignored the possibility of home prices declining nationally all show that the narratives that agents invent to guide their behavior generate the very stability that they end up taking for granted while also ensuring that they are surprised when outcomes belie convention-given expectations.

EMPIRICAL IMPLICATIONS: THE ROLE OF CONVENTIONS IN SOWING FRAGILITY AND TRIGGERING BANK-RUNS DURING THE GLOBAL FINANCIAL CRISIS

Empirically, this book used its conventions-based theoretical framework to explain central banking and shadow banking prior to and during the global financial crisis. Chapter 3 described how economic conventions led the Federal Reserve's interest rate setting body, the Federal Open Market Committee (FOMC), to cut short-term interest rates and keep them low, thus inducing an unsustainable increase in housing prices and the proliferation of fragile financing arrangements. The chapter used process-tracing techniques and counter-factual analysis to illustrate how Japan's historical experience with deflation, the construction of the Fed's inflation metrics via the CPI and PCE deflator, and the Greenspan Doctrine ideology that held that it was better to "clean up" after a bubble burst rather than to "lean against" its inflation explain the FOMC's rationale for cutting interest rates and keeping them low in the early 2000s. Central bankers' decisions follow from their economic ideas. Monetary policy can therefore be understood as both historically contingent and agency-driven. The chapter then tied accommodative monetary policy to Minsky's drivers of fragility, linking low short-term interest rates to the upward-sloping interest rate term structure that emerged in the US economy during the early 2000s. Different conventions may have led to different monetary policy choices, possibly limiting the inflation of the housing bubble.

Chapter 4 then described how economic conventions drove the rise of America's fragile financial system that emerged in tandem with the inflating housing bubble from 2001 to 2006. It detailed the mechanics of shadow banking, or off-balance sheet, market-based financial intermediation, in which various wholesale "depositors" made loans to "borrowers" via asset-backed commercial paper (ABCP), repurchase agreements ("repo"), and asset-backed securities (ABS). Building on the work of Viral Acharya, Gary Gorton, Perry Mehrling, Andrew Metrick, Zoltan Pozsar, and others, the chapter explained how banks' precrisis capital inadequacy was a function of their economic conventions of *ergodicity* incorporated into their risk models and regulatory capital rules. Bank risk models such as value-at-risk institutionalized ergodic conventions regarding market volatility, correlation risk, and normally distributed asset price returns, and thus made banks vulnerable to capital shortfalls when housing prices fell. Moreover, this book found that institutionalized conventions of *expert opinion* via bond ratings had a pro-cyclical effect on capital flows into risky asset classes. The credit rating agencies (CRAs) were important cogs in enabling banks to manufacture "information insensitive" collateral for shadow banking depositors. Together, banks' internal risk models and bond ratings illustrate how economic conventions can be causal drivers of stability and fragility in the financial system, since banks' stability depended on the continued truth-value of these economic conventions.

Chapters 4, 5, and 6 also examined the role of *conventional expectations* in shadow banking markets and demonstrated how the most acute phase of the global financial crisis was best understood as a generalized shadow banking run accelerated by the failure of Lehman Brothers. Chapter 5 drew on findings from elite interviews with market participants and other primary source material to show that regulators' repeated interventions in financial markets from Long-Term Capital Management (LTCM) in 1998, Bear Stearns in March 2008, and the government-sponsored housing giants in September 2008, created a *conventional expectation* that regulators would serve as *liquidity providers of last resort* for shadow banking conduits in wholesale funding markets. This convention explains why bank runs prior to Lehman were idiosyncratic, or isolated to specific firms, rather than generalized, or across all shadow banking conduits and short-term funding markets. Chapter 6 then explored how the failure of Lehman Brothers eviscerated this convention and initiated a bank run against all ABCP and repo markets. It cited market data to show how Lehman's failure precipitated a *flight to quality* in financial markets, just as Keynes would have predicted, as agents coped with the stress of convention uncertainty. This chapter described how conventions held by regulators shaped their response to the crisis. Regulators' fears of initiating a "second Great Depression" colored their thinking and made them much more likely to issue unconditional bailouts to the entire financial system, thereby offering deposit insurance to shadow banking markets and stemming the ABCP and repo bank runs after Lehman. Chapter 6 also described how regulators' *intervention capacity* depended on the market's belief in the United States' sovereign creditworthiness, enabling regulators to use *credibility transfer* to stem the panic in short-term funding markets. This book's final empirical chapter illustrates the importance of economic conventions during crisis periods, showing that conventions held by elites and the market's conventions about regulators shape responses to crisis.

Policy Implications: Thinking About Crisis Causes, Mitigation, and Prevention

There are several policy implications that follow from *Social Finance*'s analysis, which open several avenues of future research.

First, *Social Finance* helps practitioners identify the conditions of fragility in financial markets. Per Minsky, economic fragility follows from an upward sloping yield curve, bank risk tolerance, short-term runnable capital, and credit risks in long-term assets. A financial crisis can occur if financial institutions are willing to issue short-term runnable capital to accumulate risky long-term assets to engage in interest rate term structure arbitrage via credit, liquidity, and maturity transformation. Credit risks are thus a necessary but insufficient condition for systemic crises. The presence of a lender of last resort influences the stability of fragile financing structures amid mounting credit risks. If the lender of last resort is willing to extend sovereign credit to runnable capital, and the market deems the sovereign credible, then this action obviates the need for creditors to run while regulators have scope to stem a panic. Critically, the lender of last resort must be viewed as sufficiently creditworthy, such that their *intervention capacity* crosses the necessary threshold to provide insurance to the financial system. Future financial risks can be identified by applying this book's augmented Minsky rubric to financial instability and studying the underlying economic conventions that, when defied, can trigger runs. International financial stability efforts should also focus on building counter-cyclical *credibility transfer* devices such as precautionary international credit lines while boosting the autonomy and financial firepower of domestic lender of last resort authorities.

Second, once a crisis starts, regulators should focus on the entire locus of fragility to stem the panic. One of the main critiques of US regulators' response to the global financial crisis was their inability or lack of willingness to provide mortgage relief to underwater homeowners. Surely this action could have dulled the pain of the crisis. But as Minsky argues and as this book showed, credit risks are just one area of fragility and are thus necessary but insufficient conditions for crises. In contrast, regulators in the United States adopted a multifaced response to deal with the crisis by addressing bank runs in short-term funding markets, rehabilitating banks via transparency exercises such as the stress tests and recapitalization, and reflating asset prices via accommodative monetary policy. It is not a coincidence that these actions focused on Minsky's areas of fragility in markets. Researchers can do more work on analyzing historic crises responses via this Minsky rubric to study the relative importance of addressing each underlying aspect of precrisis fragility once a crisis strikes.

Third, the ability of authorities to respond to a crisis depends on their *intervention capacity*, which follows from both their ability and willingness to deploy sovereign resources to stem a crisis. Despite the United States government's reputation for legislative deadlock, the global financial crisis showed that US institutions had the capacity to adapt to rapidly changing financial circumstances, as evidenced by the passage of the Troubled Asset Relief Program (TARP) and expansion of Federal Reserve and US Treasury emergency lending programs during the crisis. Of course, these actions toed the line of legality and eroded the public legitimacy of America's economic regulatory institutions. Part of this legitimacy cost is unavoidable—during a systemic crisis, all options seem terrible, and often the only way to save the financial system is to accept collateral beneficiaries of market intervention in exchange for market stability. But economic technocrats ought to consider bolstering their intervention capacity during non-emergency periods. *Counter-cyclical legitimation* of emergency powers may involve building up intervention buffers during periods of robust economic growth, establishing precautionary international credit lines and credibly committing to the pro-market precepts of these credit lines (e.g. Flexible Credit Lines from the International Monetary Fund, see IMF Staff 2018), and economic technocrats building political support for robust controls against financial market risk, even as the memory of past crises fades and political economy forces lean against the erosion of margins of safety in the financial system.[1] Governments can ensure they themselves are not the drivers of fragility by running countercyclical fiscal policies, refinancing their debt to have a long weighted average maturity, building up their financial sector supervisory capacities, developing a robust domestic market for government securities, and ensuring central bank independence with a clear and credible inflation target with a floating exchange rate regime to act as a buffer against external shocks and facilitate macroeconomic adjustment. An avenue of future research motivated by this policy lesson is to study the best practices on how to build the latitude of regulators to respond to financial distress.

Fourth, it helps to have agents who remember the lessons of history and are willing to act despite populist political pressure. In this sense, the United States got lucky by having a strong bench of political and technocratic talent that recognized the exigency of the shadow banking runs and was willing to make the hard choices to stem the panic. Building a class of crisis fighters may include a greater emphasis on the history of financial instability and signs of impending financial distress in economics Ph.D. programs and public policy schools. Career staff at finance ministries, central banks, and the international financial institutions should also emphasize this institutional memory and lessons learned to junior staff. The United States also benefitted from the leadership of Presidents George W. Bush and Barack Obama, neither of whom opted to politicize the crisis response (even in exchange for easy and cheap political points). Rather, by all accounts, the Obama transition team worked together with the outgoing Bush team and worked to ensure that the agreed-upon strategy continued credibly despite a political transition between two rival political parties. For instance, one senior Democratic congressional staffer with work experience on presidential campaigns recalled that at the height of the crisis around October 2008, the campaign "realized it had won" and as a result, the policy staff on President Obama's campaign decided to "play the crisis politically in a straight forward way" to focus on governing and not "politicizing the response" (Senior Congressional staffer 2018). Obama's decision to keep Federal Reserve Chairman Ben Bernanke in his post and to promote Federal Reserve Bank of New York President Timothy Geithner to Treasury Secretary provided much-needed continuity to the crisis response, even at a potential political cost.[2]

Fifth, the global financial crisis and its aftermath demonstrate the *time-inconsistency problem* of financial sector regulation after a crisis. Under such conditions, the maximum amount of leverage that regulators hold over the financial system coincides at the point of the crisis when sentiment is most depressed and banks are weakest and in greatest need of government support. But this moment is also precisely when regulators' stringent interventions—say by firing bank leadership, bailing in creditors, wiping out shareholders, and putting restrictions on leverage and high-risk activities—would damage banks and potentially prevent their recovery. After a crisis passes, at which point banks are healthy enough to absorb new regulations and restrictions on their activity, the political exigency of re-regulating the financial system has often diminished. A Congressional staffer interviewed for *Social Finance* agreed that the US Treasury and Federal Reserve, as well as other regulatory and legal bodies such as the Department of Justice, had "massive leeway" to re-regulate the financial sector in the United States during fall 2008. He noted that "any time you deal with the financial industry, there are big headwinds. They are competent and well-funded. So, there was a sense that you only had one shot to regulate the financial sector and could only do so without hurting banks' ability to originate credit." Therefore, the staffer surmised that "once you move beyond the initial crisis period it becomes harder to regulate the banks," partially because "pro-financial services representatives are over-represented on the main banking and financial services committees." Another issue with re-regulating the financial sector is that "financial stability does not have a natural constituency," which is compounded by the fact that there is only a "small class of people in Congress who understand these issues well" (Senior Congressional staffer 2018). Subsequent scholarship can focus on the political economy dynamics of financial sector regulation after crises intervals, problematizing the time-inconsistency of financial sector regulation. Such research would have policy implications for Post-Keynesian notions on the reduction of the "cushions of safety" in financial markets during a crisis (Kregel 2008).

LIMITATIONS: WHAT *SOCIAL FINANCE* DOES AND DOES NOT DO

There is no perfect theory, and the present study is not without its limitations. This section responds to some of the potential critiques of the book's ontology, theoretical insights, and empirical conclusions. This section tries to be charitable to potential critiques, while responding to them in turn.

One of the major critiques of *Social Finance* is its elevation of agency-based explanations of crises over structural variables. Central to any theory of the social sciences is an epistemological, ontological, and methodological posture about the role of agency in complex systems. One of the most contested issues in the social sciences is the "agency and structure" debate (Dessler 1989; Wendt 1987). On one end of the spectrum, pure agency-based approaches elevate the decision-making of specific actors as important causal determinants of outcomes. Agency-based accounts of financial crises tend to focus on the decisions of elites in shaping financial institutions' risk tolerance, monetary policy, and political preferences for deregulation, to name a few examples. Implicit in such agency-based views is that actors make choices based on their own volition. For this reason, different animating ideas or social constructs may have led to different choices on behalf of key agents, thus leading to different outcomes.

Purely structural arguments are on the other end of the spectrum. Rather than focusing on the idiosyncratic cognition of specific agents in explaining outcomes, structural theories treat the existence of self-interested, rational agents as given and study the constraints and incentives that shape agent behavior. According to a purely structural account of the global financial crisis, the economic conventions held by central bankers, financial institutions, market participants, and policymakers were *epiphenomenal* to structural factors like factor endowments, global imbalances, banks' institutionally determined mono-focus on bottom-line profits, and politicians' goal-oriented electioneering, among many others. The specific features of such structural arguments are not important to the present study. Rather, structural arguments tend to elevate non-agency-based explanations of outcomes over alternatives.

At first blush, this book seems to confirm the argument, often made by ideational scholarship, that ideas matter because structures do not come with "instruction sheets" that tell agents how to act in complex environments (Blyth 2003). This book's strongly constitutive causal standard claims that economic conventions imbue factor endowments, market prices, interest rates, asset classes, and other "material fundamentals" with meaning to agents. Economic conventions provide the researcher with a lens for understanding agent behavior that "would make little sense without them," as Abdelal et al. argue (Abdelal et al.

2010, 17). In addition, an honest reading of the facts surrounding agent behavior during the crisis should prompt even the staunchest structuralist to accept that during crisis periods, agency can matter. There was nothing structurally pre-ordained about Bear Stearns' bailout and Lehman's bankruptcy, other than the inter-subjective constructs guiding regulators' behavior. Can one say for certain that different central bankers, each with their own unique socialization distinct from Alan Greenspan and Ben Bernanke would have made the *exact same decisions* in comparable circumstances? Perhaps an anti-bailout central banker might have refrained from extending sovereign credit to America's financial system after Lehman Brothers. While researchers do not have the luxury of running a controlled experiment to test this proposition and provide a definitive answer, this book presented evidence that market actors exhibited agency regarding the social construction of their governing economic conventions, such that different economic conventions might have led to different outcomes in the US economy.

A second potential limitation of the study is that it did not address the conventions behind other material causes of the crisis. Two potential alternative explanations deserve discussion, including the populist credit expansion by the government-sponsored enterprises (GSEs) and global macroeconomic imbalances. These other causes include populist credit expansion on behalf of Fannie Mae and Freddie Mac and global imbalances fueled by surplus saving countries such as China, Japan, Germany, and commodity exporting states, which might have depressed long-term real interest rates in the United States. Certainly, Fannie Mae and Freddie Mac added *incremental* demand to the housing market, using their quasi-government status to purchase and securitize mortgages (Acharya et al. 2011).[3] Nevertheless, there are reasons to believe that the GSEs were not decisive factors in the inflation of the housing bubble, including that numerous countries experienced housing bubbles during the 2000s without government-sponsored housing finance. As Acharya et al. argue and Andrew Lo summarizes, it may be best to think of the GSEs as supercharged hedge funds that took outsized housing market risks (Lo 2012, 167). The GSEs therefore likely added incremental housing demand and marginal fuel to the fire but were not central players in the shadow banking bank runs that translated the deflating housing bubble to broader market instability.

Global imbalances could have been important co-determinants of the housing bubble, as far as capital inflows from abroad depressed interest rates and added demand to the housing market. But America's current account deficit, which peaked around 5.8% of GDP in 2006, was not large enough to account for the surge in demand for housing assets in the US economy before the crisis. Moreover, the United States ran a current account deficit from the early 1980s onward, so it is hard to see how the current account deficit suddenly became a problem and critical driver fragility only during the early 2000s. A bigger determinant of financial fragility may have been the *gross* cross-border capital flows prior to the global financial crisis. Using Bank for International Settlements data, Hyun Song Shin argues convincingly that the European banking system was a big driver of market fragility prior to the crisis. He found that European global banks tapped US wholesale funding markets to then reinvest their proceeds into higher-yielding dollar assets (principally private label mortgage-backed securities), much like US financial institutions did prior to the crisis. Regulatory arbitrage drove European bank involvement in the United States, rather than low net national savings in the United States relative to its trading partners (Song Shin 2011). Certainly, global flows did interact with the US economy prior to the global financial crisis, but these flows reflected realities associated with the drivers of fragility discussed at length in this book, including the rise of wholesale funding markets and securitization, as well as bank undercapitalization prior to the crisis.

A third potential limitation of this book was the quality and quantity of evidence it cited when trying to demonstrate its causal propositions. *Social Finance* marshaled a variety of qualitative and quantitative data to make its argument that scholars and practitioners need to take economic conventions seriously as causal drivers of financial instability. Nevertheless, more work can and should be done. With adequate research access, it would be possible to analyze the specific shadow banking mechanisms within financial institutions to understand how and why banks' capital commitment committees agreed to adopt such structures prior to the global financial crisis. Further interviews with shadow banking counterparties, particularly the management committees of hedge funds and money market mutual funds, could also enhance readers' understanding of the liability side of shadow banks. Granted, there is only so much one can do when completing a research monograph, and banks are understandably reluctant to allow researchers into their institutions to ask the tough questions about their own pre-crisis foibles. Luckily, numerous other actors had access to such data, which is why this book borrowed liberally from the findings of the Federal Reserve, the Financial Crisis Inquiry Commission, and the US Department of the Treasury. Still, more evidence could be gathered with proper institutional access, and subsequent work can build upon the empirical work and evidence presented by *Social Finance*.

ADDITIONAL AVENUES FOR FURTHER RESEARCH

Below are five avenues of further research that can build on the insights put forth by *Social Finance*. While by no means exhaustive, these areas could prove fruitful for scholars interested continuing the study between economic ideas and financial stability.

First, future work can apply *Social Finance*'s conventions-based theoretical framework to different cases of financial market instability. This book focused on a "single-n" case study of the global financial crisis. While its core theoretical propositions are generalizable and non-case specific, further scholarship can test its applicability to novel cases. For example, consider how *Social Finance*'s conventions-based theoretical framework can explain the Asian financial crisis of the late 1990s and the 2010s European sovereign debt crisis.

In the case of the Asian financial crisis, the researcher could begin by studying how the epistemic consensus of capital account liberalization among technocrats in the 1990s created incentives for financial institutions and governments to borrow in short-term funding markets to accumulate higher-yielding domestic assets to capture the difference in yield between short-term and long-term debt via credit, currency, liquidity, and maturity transformation, just as Minsky would have predicted. These choices would have created a "double mismatch" of both currency and maturity of financial institutions' liabilities. The accumulation of large, foreign exchange-denominated, short-term debt, made financial institutions and governments vulnerable to *rollover risk* in global capital markets and *credit risk* if the value of their assets fell. The devaluation of the Thai baht in 1997 exposed this underlying fragility, triggering capital flight out of Southeast Asian economies. This crisis trigger was a non-routine deviation from agents' convention-given expectations that exchange rates would remain credibly defended and fixed, in turn catalyzing convention uncertainty and causing a flight to quality out of risky developing country capital markets and into perceived safe havens like US Treasuries, much as the Minsky/Doran model of conditional non-rationality described. The IMF and US Treasury-led bailouts were regulators' attempt to restore convention certainty to financial markets in exchange for painful (and in hindsight, counterproductive) structural reforms. The specific course of regulatory actions taken by the global financial safety net involved *credibility transfer* to improve confidence in perceived risky economies. Even if the structural reforms pursued were counterproductive, they may have followed from the elevation of certain conventions (i.e. a free market ideology or ridding Asian economies of "crony capitalism") over alternatives.[4]

Applying *Social Finance*'s theory to the European sovereign debt crisis, the researcher could start analyzing the crisis following the adoption of the euro, the European common currency, which led several current account surplus "core" European economies to lend to current account deficit "peripheral" economies, converging bond yields and making it appear as though Greek debt was materially tantamount to Germany's. As the global financial crisis spread, European banks and investors de-risked their portfolios, pulling money out of peripheral economies and creating funding pressures among over-levered European economies. Some countries were fiscally profligate during the boom years, such as Greece, while others simply suffered from the cyclical effects of asset price declines, slowing growth, declining tax revenues, and overall adverse fiscal dynamics. Much of the pain of the European sovereign debt crisis traces to policy choices made in Berlin and Brussels, particularly calls for fiscal austerity in peripheral economies. After several missteps, the crisis reached a turning point when European Central Bank President Mario Draghi vowed in 2012 to do "whatever it takes" to save the euro, putting a floor on peripheral bond prices and spurring a gradual recovery in borrowing costs. European quantitative easing launched in 2015 also helped reduce financial pressures in the Eurozone, further compressing yields and helping European growth.[5]

Much of the European sovereign debt crisis played out according to Minsky and *Social Finance*'s rubric of financial instability, with several inter-related conventional processes at play. Core European banks had an upward-sloping interest rate term structure because deposit rates in Europe were lower than yields on peripheral debt. As a result, core European banks could borrow deposits and use them to fund credit, liquidity, and maturity transformation trades via purchases of peripheral debt from Portugal, Ireland, Italy, Greece, and Spain. European banking rules permitted banks to accumulate exposure to peripheral economies as well, allowing a pool of willing lenders to sponsor debt accumulation. European banks and other international investors in peripheral debt served as counterparties willing to permit debt accumulation but were also sources of runnable capital once financing conditions tightened and credit risks materialized. The introduction of the euro also enabled a pool of borrowers willing to emit risky debt. The peripheral economies took advantage of lax financing conditions offered by euro membership to fund current account deficits vis-à-vis more competitive members such as Germany. Draghi's vow to do "whatever it takes" to save the Euro served as an effective mechanism of credibility transfer, while quantitative easing finally started to reflate European assets and underpin a broad-based (albeit fragile) recovery in output for European economies.

Second, future work can study the relationship between antecedent crisis resolutions and subsequent market displacements. For instance, the primary policy response of many Southeast Asian states after the Asian financial crisis was a de facto policy of dollar accumulation to buffer their economies in case of capital flight. Countries such as China, Hong Kong, Indonesia, South Korea, Thailand, and Vietnam managed their nominal exchange rates to spur export-led growth and accumulate foreign exchange reserves. These countries re-invested their foreign exchange into US capital markets, thus depressing long-term interest rates and fueling the housing bubble. Excess savings from North and Southeast Asia lowered interest rates and caused an increase in demand for risky assets by financial institutions.[6] Several empirical studies demonstrate that foreign capital flows did indeed affect borrowing costs in the US economy, which summarily impacted borrowing decisions in the US housing market. Economists estimate that foreign capital inflows accounted for a roughly fifty to one hundred basis point fall in US Treasury bond yields from 2004 and 2006 (Warnock and Warnock 2009). Considering that many of the riskiest mortgages issued during the housing bubble were "adjustable rate," it is conceivable that falling interest rates did have a disproportionate effect on the incentives facing prospective homeowners in the United States, encouraging home construction and fueling the housing bubble. William Miles argued that long-term interest rates—those that global imbalances would be most likely to influence—had independent predictive power over housing prices (Miles 2015). Maurice Obstfeld and Kenneth Rogoff found that low interest rates, touched off by the acceleration in dollar recycling from abroad, "fed into a powerful multiplier mechanism" that entrenched "unrealistic expectations" and "asset-market distortions" in the US housing finance market (Obstfeld and Rogoff 2009, 25). This analysis is not to argue that all financial crises are path dependent and follow from prior crisis resolutions or that foreign savings and investment decisions *caused* the housing bubble. Rather, researchers should consider that the policy responses to today's problems might induce future displacements. More work can be done to identify the causal links between antecedent crisis resolutions and subsequent displacements, as well as the impact of crisis resolutions on economic conventions and how those conventions relate to subsequent fragility.

A third avenue of research opened by this book is studying the role of *ideational transfer among borrowers* during crisis periods. This line of research supports this book's ontology of strongly constitutive causality that problematizes the false dichotomy between ideational and material factors in asset markets. For instance, during the height of the global financial crisis, South Korea experienced acute capital outflows, likely due to the flight to quality in asset markets after Lehman's failure. South Korean markets stabilized when the United States struck a $30 billion notional currency swap arrangement with the Bank of Korea, which in turn stemmed the capital flight and stabilized Korean markets. Korea also signed several other currency swap arrangements with other foreign central banks. Yet Korea drew down on less than ten percent of their swap line with the United States, with comparable levels of utilization for other swap agreements with other foreign central banks (Chung 2010). Thus, the real impact of the currency swap arrangements was that they provided a form of *ideational transfer* between the sovereign creditworthiness of the United States and third parties. As this episode from the global financial crisis shows, during crisis moments, the distinction between material and ideational factors is moot, since conventions are so in flux and subject to considerable uncertainty that *notions* of fundamental value *become* fundamental value in a self-fulfilling manner. Future work should study in-crisis credibility transfer dynamic.

Fourth, another related but distinct avenue of research opened by *Social Finance* is a broader discussion of other economic ideas and market outcomes, particularly the role of norms. Finnemore and Sikkink define a norm as "a standard of appropriate behavior for actors with a given identity" (Finnemore and Sikkink 1998). The economy is an example of a domain dominated by many normative frameworks that imbue agent behavior with meaning. For instance, the norm of homeownership could explain the rise of government-sponsored housing finance in the United States. Notions of "housing as the American dream" and the "ownership society" are understudied as causal drivers of populist credit expansion in the United States from 1930 to 2008. Nevertheless, the US economy experienced a bipartisan push to expand homeownership from the Great Depression onward, culminating in the nationalization of Fannie Mae and Freddie Mac in September 2008 (Acharya et al. 2011).[7]

Fifth, this book provides a predictive framework for anticipating future financial instability. If it is accepted that the systematic failure of agents' taken-for-granted conventions catalyzes convention uncertainty and thus financial market instability, then it is possible to appraise the vulnerability of our most taken-for-granted conventions when judging the likelihood of financial market instability. For instance, in today's post-crisis environment, there exist some risks to the global recovery, including the risk of America ceasing to provide its litany of global public goods that guarantee a liberal trade and monetary order, a potential hard economic landing in China, the build-up of debt in emerging markets during the period of easy monetary conditions, the possible looming threat of inflation, and the haphazard erosion of financial sector regulation that could unleash speculative financial forces and fragility. While the primary goal of *Social Finance* is not to speculate on future risks, this book's theoretical framework can at least tell us that if we want to understand the nature of future systemic crises, it helps to examine the potential fragility of our most taken-for-granted beliefs that stand as the premises for other, second and third-order investment hypotheses. By identifying the areas where these conditions exist, along with the conventions upon these conditions rely, one can work backwards into stress testing the governing economic conventions in markets and speculate on the robustness of the system to the failure of these conventions.

Notes

1. Thomas Palley presents a convincing theory of a Minsky "super-cycle" that describes how both regulatory relaxation and increased risk-taking typify the erosions of the margins of safety of economies prior to systemic crises. He argues that regulatory relaxation follows from

regulatory capture, or the idea that financial interests influence political regulatory processes, regulatory relapse, or fading memories of prior crises among regulators, and regulatory escape, which describes the creation of new financial technologies that fall outside of pre-established regulatory boundaries. Increased risk-taking by entrepreneurs, financial institutions, and firms follows from financial innovation, memory loss of past crises, and data hysteresis (in the Keynesian sense). For more, see Palley (2011).
2. In his biography, Timothy Geithner acknowledged that President Barack Obama's nomination as Treasury Secretary tied the Obama Administration to several Bush-era crisis policies, see Geithner (2014, 251).
3. Also see the dissent in the *Financial Crisis Inquiry Report* (The Financial Crisis Inquiry Commission 2011). For a few other interesting volumes on the symbiosis between international savers, particularly in China, and current account deficit countries like the United States (with an attendant focus on interest rates and other asset market developments) see Schwartz (2009), Wolf (2008, 2014). For a solid ex-post account on global imbalances after the global financial crisis, see Eichengreen (2014).
4. For some background on the Asian financial crisis from which this section drew, see Jackson (1999), Woo et al. (2000), and Stiglitz (2003).
5. For a good summary of the Euro crisis, see Jones (2014), Matthijs and Blyth (2015, especially chapters 1 and 2), Sandbu (2016), and Stiglitz (2016).
6. Raghuram Rajan refers to this tendency of market participants to purchase riskier assets when benchmark interest rates fall as "risk shifting." Most investment managers, including insurance companies, mutual funds, and pension funds, face fixed liability structures and floating asset bases. To see why risk shifting is a rational response for investors in an environment of falling benchmark interest rates, consider the example of an insurance company that guarantees policyholders a return of six percent per annum in an environment of falling interest rates. Faced with this differential between promised returns and investment income, fund managers will tend to prefer riskier assets (and get compensated for doing so via higher yields) to match asset returns with liability promises. If enough actors engage in risk shifting, interest rates on risky assets will fall, thus boosting pro-cyclical asset market conditions in risky asset classes. For more on risk shifting, see Rajan (2006).
7. For a timely volume on how homeownership became central to the United States' domestic political economy since the 1930s, see Thurston (2018).

WORKS CITED

Abdelal, Rawi, Mark Blyth, and Craig Parsons. 2010. *Constructing the International Economy*. Ithaca: Cornell University Press.

Acharya, Viral V., Matthew Richardson, Stijn Van Nieuwerburgh, and Lawrence J. White. 2011. *Guaranteed to Fail: Fannie Mae, Freddie Mac, and the Debacle of Mortgage Finance*. Princeton: Princeton University Press.

Blyth, Mark. 2011. "Ideas, Uncertainty and Evolution." In *Ideas and Politics in Social Science Research*, by Robert Cox and Daniel Beland (eds.), 83–101. Oxford: Oxford University Press.

Blyth, Mark. 2003. "Structures Do Not Come with an Instruction Sheet: Interests, Ideas, and Progress in Political Science." *Perspectives on Politics* 1 (4): 695–706.

Chung, Hee Chun. 2010. "The Bank of Korea's Policy Response to the Global Financial Crisis." *BIS Research Papers* (54): 1–10.

Dessler, David. 1989. "What's at Stake in the Agent-Structure Debate?" *International Organizatoin* 43 (3): 441–473.

Eichengreen, Barry. 2014. "A Requiem for Global Imbalances." *Project Syndicate*. January 13. Accessed March 27, 2018. https://www.project-syndicate.org/commentary/barry-eichengreen-notes-that-a-decade-after-external-imbalances-emerged-as-a-supposed-threat-to-the-global-economy–the-problem-has-disappeared?barrier=accessreg.

Finnemore, Martha, and Kathryn Sikkink. 1998. "International Norm Dynamics and Political Change." *International Organization* 52 (4): 887–917.

Geithner, Timothy F. 2014. *Stress Test: Reflections on Financial Crises*. New York: Broadway Books.

IMF Staff. 2018. "IMF Flexible Credit Line (FCL)." *International Monetary Fund*. March 8. Accessed May 10, 2018. https://www.imf.org/en/About/Factsheets/Sheets/2016/08/01/20/40/Flexible-Credit-Line.

Jackson, Karl. 1999. *Asian Contagion: The Causes and Consequences of a Financial Crisis*. Boulder: Westview Press.

Jones, Erik. 2014. *The Year the European Crisis Ended*. Basingstroke: Palgrave.

Kregel, Jan. 2008. "Minsky's Cushions of Safety: Systemic Risk and the Crisis in the U.S. Subprime Mortgage Market." *Levy Economics Institute: Economics Public Policy Brief Archive*.

Lebow, R. Ned. 2009. "Constitutive Causality: Imagined Spaces and Political Practices." *Millenium: Journal of International Studies* 38 (2): 211–239.

Lo, Andrew W. 2012. "Reading About the Financial Crisis: A Twenty-One-Book Review." *Journal of Economic Literature* 50 (1): 151–178.

Matthijs, Matthias, and Mark Blyth. 2015. *The Future of the Euro*. Oxford: Oxford University Press.

Miles, William. 2015. "The Housing Bubble: Monetary Policy or Global Imbalances." https://ssrn.com/abstract=2031729.

Obstfeld, Maurice, and Kenneth Rogoff. 2009. "Global Imbalances and the Financial Crisis: Products of Common Causes." *Federal Reserve Bank of San Francisco Asia Economic Policy Conference*. Santa Barbara. 1–70.

Palley, Thomas I. 2011. "A Theory of Minsky Super-Cycles and Financial Crises." *Contributions to Political Economy* 30 (1): 31–46.

Rajan, Raghuram G. 2006. "Monetary Policy and Incentives." *International Monetary Fund*. June 8. Accessed March 27, 2018. http://www.imf.org/external/np/speeches/2006/060806.htm.

Sandbu, Martin. 2016. *Europe's Orphan: The Future of the Euro and the Politics of Debt*. Princeton: Princeton University Press.

Schwartz, Herman. 2009. *Subprime Nation: American Power, Global Capital, and the Housing Bubble*. Ithaca: Cornell University Press.

Senior Congressional staffer, Interview by Neil Shenai. 2018. *Author Interview* (April 5).

Song Shin, Hyun. 2011. "Global Banking Glut and Loan Risk Premium." *12th Jacques Polak Annual Research Conference*. Washington: International Monetary Fund. 1–48.

Soros, George. 2003. *The Alchemy of Finance*. Hoboken: Wiley.

Stiglitz, Joseph. 2003. *Globalization and Its Discontents*. New York: W. W. Norton.

———. 2016. *The Euro: How a Common Currency Threatens the Future of Europe*. New York: W. W. Norton.

The Financial Crisis Inquiry Commission. 2011. *The Financial Crisis Inquiry Report: Final Report of the National Commission on the Causes of the Financial and Economic Crisis in the United States*. Washington, DC: U.S. Government Printing Office.

Thurston, Chloe. 2018. *At the Boundaries of Homeownership: Credit, Discrimination, and the American State*. Cambridge: Cambridge University Press.

Warnock, Francis E., and Veronica Cacdac Warnock. 2009. "International Capital Flows and U.S. Interest Rates." *Journal of International Money and Finance* 28: 903–919.

Wendt, Alexander E. 1987. "The Agent-Structure Problem in International Relations Theory." *International Organization* 41 (3): 335–370.

Wolf, Martin. 2008. *Fixing Global Finance*. Baltimore: Johns Hopkins University Press.

———. 2014. *The Shifts and the Shocks: What We've Learned—And Have Still to Learn—From the Financial Crisis*. New York: Penguin.

Woo, Wing Thye, Jeffrey D. Sachs, and Klaus Schwab. 2000. *The Asian Financial Crisis: Lessons for a Resilient Asia*. Cambridge: Cambridge University Press.

Interview Appendix

The empirical chapters of *Social Finance* incorporate the results of interviews with market participants to illustrate the analytical utility of the book's causal propositions via a case study of shadow banking during the global financial crisis. This interview appendix presents an overview of the interview data and methods of this book.

Social Finance draws on the results of sixteen interviews with fifteen market participants, including ten professionals from market-making (i.e. "sell-side") institutions; five institutional investors (i.e. the "buy-side"); as well as several economic technocrats, predominately located in North American and European financial centers such as London, Los Angeles, New York City, and Toronto. In total, the interviewees oversaw nearly $2 trillion in annual order flows and managed nearly $160 billion in assets during the crisis. Nearly all subjects had direct exposure to securities transactions during the crisis with specific expertise in shadow banking conduits, auction-rate securities, convertible securities, mortgage-backed securities and related derivatives, short-term funding markets, namely asset-backed commercial paper and repurchase agreements, structured credit products, and US Treasury securities, among many other asset classes. Moreover, all market interview subjects received Financial Industry Regulatory Authority certifications and international equivalents, while several held doctorates in economics and finance from top programs and Certified Financial Analyst designations. One exception was a United States Congressional staffer who did not have a market-facing role but advised presidential campaigns and thus understood the political dynamics of crisis responses based on first-hand experience. This interlocutor provided additional political context for the crisis response, as detailed in Chapter 6.

Interviews were conducted over two periods, including the first quarter of 2013 and from December 2017 through May 2018. Respondents interviewed in 2013 were reinterviewed again during the second period and were made familiar with the scope of the book's research, with a focus on similarities and differences from the doctoral dissertation upon which this book was based. Most interviews lasted about sixty minutes and took place via voice telephone calls. While it would have been preferable to conduct interviews in person, practical constraints (namely geographic distance and the author having a full-time nonacademic job based in Mexico City, Mexico) prohibited face-to-face interviews in many cases. As a result, subjects' body language and other non-verbal cues were not interpreted nor recorded for any interviews. Simultaneous notes were taken throughout.

Interviews were conducted in a "semi-structured" format, in which the interview questions promoted a free-flowing discussion about several topics related to the global financial crisis. Rapport-building techniques for each interview included asking interviewees about their backgrounds in markets and discussing recent market themes related to global macroeconomic trend strategies. Nearly all interview subjects expressed humility about their ability to answer the prepared questions and some sought reassurance that their views would not be fact checked or otherwise evaluated for correctness and historical accuracy. During the interview, subject-provided answers were briefly restated to check for author comprehension. Interview subjects received a list of fixed questions up to two weeks prior to the official interview, presented in Table A.1. Questions were geared toward asking easier questions first to promote candor and rapport (Leech 2002). All interview subjects received the chance to review their responses for the final version of the manuscript. Only one subject proactively requested to see their interview transcripts. All interview subjects also signed permissions release forms prior to being interviewed, which were also transmitted to the publisher with the final manuscript.

Social Finance employed a "snowball" or chain referral sampling technique of soliciting additional interview leads from an initial set of interview subjects. This method helped increase the response rate of potential interviewees and allowed the author to build a network of

Table A.1 Interview questions for *Social Finance*

Interview questions for *Social Finance*

Your answers to the below questions might be referenced in a forthcoming book entitled *Social Finance: Shadow Banking During the Global Financial Crisis* (Palgrave, 2018). You will have full discretion about how you are referenced in the book (e.g. buy-side strategist, sell-side trader, G20 financial regulator, etc.). If there is anybody else you think I should interview, please let me know at the end of our interview. Thank you for agreeing to help my research. If you have any questions, email {personal e-mail redacted}

Shadow banking:
- How did the functioning of shadow banking (i.e. ABCP and repo) conduits evolve in the periods prior to, during, and after the global financial crisis? What accounts for the rapid rise of ABCP and repo prior to the global financial crisis? What role did foreign (i.e. non-US) flows play in facilitating and/or destabilizing this system?
- On what basis did you/your clients/shadow banking counterparties decide to roll over maturing ABCP and repo throughout the global financial crisis?
- Some analysts argue that counterparties "ran" on shadow banking conduits during the global financial crisis. Do you agree with this assessment? What determined counterparty confidence in conduits?

Regime changes:
- Were there critical junctures during the global financial crisis? Feel free to define critical junctures as you see fit
- How did the failure of Lehman Brothers change your outlook for financial markets, particularly related to the stability of financial institutions, during the global financial crisis?

Rating agencies/market functioning/valuation:
- How did credit ratings factor into your trading decisions and valuation of market assets before, during, and after the global financial crisis? Did ratings action change how you/your investors decided to allocate capital?
- How did you value assets during periods of heightened market volatility, particularly after the failure of Lehman Brothers? What happened to bid-ask spreads after Lehman?
- What role did other market participants' opinions play, if at all, in your decision-making and valuation decisions? Were valuation models based on historical price performance useful after the failure of Lehman Brothers? How about other authoritative market participants—did you pay attention to what other investors were doing when valuing assets?
- Why did Lehman's failure trigger financial dislocation? What were the signs and market indicators of financial dislocation, in your view?

Crisis response:
- What role did regulators' interventions (or lack thereof) play in maintaining confidence in shadow banking conduits? Did regulators' disparate treatment of Bear Stearns and Lehman Brothers influence your market views? Why or why not?
- Were regulators successful at restoring market stability? Why or why not? If so, how? If not, why not?
- Were there any intervention typologies that were more effective than others? Explain
- How has shadow banking regulation evolved since the global financial crisis?

Author as source

highly knowledgeable interview subjects. Moreover, snowball sampling allows the interviewer to study the interaction among different key players in the social network of study. In the case of this book, asking market participants to refer trading partners builds a base of knowledge where the whole is greater than the sum of the parts of individual interviews (Biernacki and Waldorf 1981). One risk of such a technique is getting stuck inside of a closed network of like-minded individuals, which diminishes the representativeness of the interview sample. To mitigate this risk, initial subjects were selected from a diverse pool of respondents whose firms were representative of the diversity of major players in financial markets, including market makers, buy-side investors, and regulators. Compliance controls limited interactions with financial market participants currently employed by major sell-side institutions. Six potential interviewees agreed to be interviewed completely off the record but demurred when asked to sign the publisher's release for inclusion in the final manuscript. The author had background conversations with these individuals but did not include official findings of interviews in the final manuscript. The fact that some subjects currently employed by sell-side financial institutions could not be interviewed for compliance reasons, in addition to the book's snowball interview technique, may have introduced selection bias into the study. This concern is a common risk associated with interviewing market participants: intuitively, the "winners" will be more likely to discuss trading strategies and outcomes than "losers," who may have been kicked out of the market due to competitive pressures. Correcting for selection bias is challenging in interview research with circumspect subjects, though one hedge against this bias is using a variety of complementary data sources, as this book attempts to do.

This book's interview results presentation draws on an interview reporting technique suggested by Erik Bleich and Robert Pekkanen (Bleich and Pekkanen 2013). These authors identify three common difficulties associated with interview research, including: (1) putting together a representative sample of subjects; (2) information quality; and (3) interviewer bias. It is impossible to completely mitigate these risks. However, the size and scope of assets transacted and managed by *Social Finance*'s interview respondents imply that respondents' views were, at a minimum, representative of a large swath of markets. More likely, it is logical that respondents at sell-side institutions and larger funds had an informational advantage over other respondents from smaller institutions, since market-making and price setting in key crisis-related asset classes had oligopolistic and monopsonistic qualities. As a result, these market participants may offer especially credible insights into the inner working of markets during stressful periods. Interviews conducted with smaller firms, including private equity funds and hedge funds, further complement the views of subjects from bigger institutions, thus helping to mitigate sampling and representativeness issues.

Information quality refers to problems when interviews do not yield accurate results, possibly due to respondents' poor memory of past events, reticence about sensitive market topics, or attempts to deliberately mislead the researcher. Information quality issues can be mitigated by sampling a diverse array of market participants and stress testing outlier results against the average. Moreover, *Social Finance* attempted to corroborate or disprove interview results using other source material, including on-the-record statements by central crisis players under subpoena (e.g. for the Financial Crisis Inquiry Commission) and secondary accounts of market sentiment.

Interviewer bias refers to cases in which the interviewer omits disconformity interview data in favor of his preferred explanation for outcomes. Again, drawing on a wide array of potential evidence helps mitigate this risk. Furthermore, this interview appendix includes a table of interview data that presents interview results rigorously. Table A.2 provides more information on each interview subject to allow the reader to judge the representativeness and accuracy of interview responses for themselves. This exhibit allows the reader to vet and arrive at his own conclusions about interview data quality.

Interview subjects are classified into categories based on their role in financial markets during the financial crisis. Primary interview role categories include sell-side professionals, or those working at major financial institutions that made markets in financial assets and sponsored shadow banking conduits; buy-side professionals from firms that served as counterparties for major financial institutions and made directional bets on asset price changes; regulators of financial institutions; and policymakers involved in financial regulation process. Some interview subjects were out of finance during the crisis but nevertheless had extensive contact with key agents studied. Therefore, the results of their interviews were included in the book. Table A.2 lists secondary roles if current positions provide additional background information on interview subjects. For instance, several subjects worked at financial institutions during the crisis but moved on to roles in regulation.

Table A.2 Interview methods table

Interviewee[a]	Primary role during crisis[b]	Secondary role[c]	Primary/secondary frames	Assets/order flows[d]	Length and medium	Referral	Most recent interview date
Buy-side structured credit trader	Sell-side structured credit trader, primarily structuring and market-making in collateralized loan obligations	Buy-side structured credit trader	Sell-side/buy-side	$20 billion assets under management during crisis	120 minutes, voice calls	Self	April 16, 2018
Former consultant and private equity investor	Private equity investor	Management consultant for top-3 firm	Buy-side	$4 billion under management	50 minutes, voice call	Self	March 24, 2018
Former investment banker	Investment banker at Lehman Brothers peer institution	G7 finance ministry official	Sell-side/policy	$60 billion notional in annual deals in 2007	50 minutes, voice call	Self	April 18, 2018
Former investment banker 2	Investment banker at major North America financial institution	Private equity investor	Sell-side/buy-side	$20 billion notional in annual deals in 2007	45 minutes, voice call	Self	April 27, 2018
Global macro hedge fund analyst	Global macro hedge fund analyst	G7 finance ministry official	Buy-side/policy	$3 billion	60 minutes, voice call	Self	February 15, 2018

(continued)

INTERVIEW APPENDIX 217

Table A.2 (continued)

Interviewee[a]	Primary role during crisis[b]	Secondary role[c]	Primary/secondary frames	Assets/order flows[d]	Length and medium	Referral	Most recent interview date
Global market strategist	Global market strategist for money manager	Independent consultant	Buy-side	$100 billion under management during the crisis	45 minutes, voice call	Self	May 6, 2018
Hedge fund macro analyst and G7 official	Global macro hedge fund analyst with purview of global commodities, currencies, equities, and interest rates	G7 finance ministry official	Buy-side/policy	$2 billion	60 minutes, voice call	Self	February 25, 2018
Hedge fund manager	Hedge fund manager	Buy-side interest rate trader	Buy-side/sell-side	$30 billion in assets under management during crisis	55 minutes, voice call	Sell-side market analyst	May 2, 2018
Lehman Brothers banker 1	Lehman Brothers banker with experience in both industry and product groups	Management consultant for top-3 firm; hedge fund investor; entrepreneur	Sell-side/buy-side	$25 billion in deals originated annually	60 minutes, voice call	Self	March 3, 2018

(continued)

218 INTERVIEW APPENDIX

Table A.2 (continued)

Interviewee[a]	Primary role during crisis[b]	Secondary role[c]	Primary/secondary frames	Assets/order flows[d]	Length and medium	Referral	Most recent interview date
Lehman Brothers banker 2	Lehman Brothers banker	Equity research analyst at globally systemically important financial institution	Sell-side	Declined to answer	60 minutes, voice call	Self	March 25, 2018
Sell-side fixed-income strategist	Sell-side fixed-income strategist at major North American financial institution	Former G20 finance ministry official	Sell-side/policy	$100 billion in monthly order flows (notional)	55 minutes, voice call	Self	April 20, 2018
Sell-side foreign exchange trader	Sell-side foreign exchange trader at UK-based investment bank; focus on G7 currencies	Global macro hedge fund portfolio manager trading across asset classes	Sell-side/buy-side	> $100 billion in annual order flows	60 minutes, voice call	Sell-side structured credit trader	February 19, 2018
Sell-side market analyst	Sell-side market analyst at major North American financial institution, focused on US Treasury bond market and agency securities	N/A	Sell-side	$800 billion in annual order flows (notional)	60 minutes, voice call	Lehman Brothers banker 2	February 26, 2018

(continued)

Table A.2 (continued)

Interviewee[a]	Primary role during crisis[b]	Secondary role[c]	Primary/secondary frames	Assets/order flows[d]	Length and medium	Referral	Most recent interview date
Sell-side short-term interest rates trader	Sell-side short-term interest rate futures trader at major North American financial institution; engaged in both market-making and propriety trading prior to Volcker rule	N/A	Sell-side/buy-side	Did not remember	60 minutes, voice call	Self	April 4, 2018
Sell-side structured credit trader	Sell-side structured credit (primarily synthetic collateralized debt obligations) market maker at top-3 US universal bank by assets (offered services in both commercial and investment banking)	Market-maker in US interest rates products at major UK-based bank	Sell-side	$650 billion in annual order flows (notional)	60 minutes, voice call	Self	February 12, 2018
Senior Congressional staff	Senior Congressional staffer	Presidential campaign advisor	Policy	N/A	60 minutes, voice call	Self	April 5, 2018

[a] Pseudonyms and identifiers in text chosen at request of interview subjects
[b] Primary role self-reported; if subject changed jobs during 2007–2009 period, role presented corresponds to role that encompassed majority of the crisis
[c] Roles prior to and after role during crisis
[d] Self-reported during crisis, fact checked via public documents when possible. Downwardly estimated when hard to confirm based on peer institutions
Author as source
Note All interviews transcribed simultaneously via computer. In some cases, the author asked interview subjects for further follow-up information via e-mail

WORKS CITED

Biernacki, Patrick, and Dan Waldorf. 1981. "Snowball Sampling: Problems and Techniques of Chain Referral Sampling." *Sociological Methods and Research* 10 (2): 141–163.

Bleich, Erik, and Robert Pekkanen. 2013. "How to Report Interview Data." In *Interview Research in Political Science*, by Layna Mosley (ed.), 84–108. Ithaca: Cornell University Press.

Leech, Beth L. 2002. "Asking Questions: Techniques for Semistructured Interviews." *Political Science and Politics* 35 (4): 665–668.

Index

A

Abacus 2007-AC1, 122. *See also* Goldman Sachs
Abdelal, Rawi, 23, 46, 47, 50, 66, 119, 121, 199–200
Accommodative monetary policy
  and other asset prices, 74, 78, 196
  and the housing bubble, 74, 84, 193
  economic conventions behind, 73
Adjustable-rate mortgage, 138
  and FOMC monetary policy, 80
  and the housing bubble, 80, 204
Advanced internal ratings-based approach, 114. *See also* Value-at-risk
Agency vs. structure debate, 199
Akerlof, George, 37, 55, 63, 118
American International Group
  credit rating, 55, 117
  ergodic risk models, 56, 62. *See also* Gorton, Gary
  financial products group, 159
Asian financial crisis, 116, 202, 204, 207
  Potential application of *Social Finance* theoretical framework to, 18
  Relationship to antecedent crises resolutions, 204
Asset-backed commercial paper
  and bank capital requirements, 128
  run on during global financial crisis, 2, 15
  support to during global financial crisis, 111
Asset-backed commercial paper and repurchase agreements, 63, 125, 211
Asset-Backed Commercial Paper Money Market Mutual Fund Liquidity Facility (AMLF), 171, 172, 175
Asset-backed securities, 10, 50, 62, 95, 103, 125, 193. *See also* Securitization
  and pareto optimality, 107
  stabilization programs during global financial crisis, 16
Asymmetric information, 21, 37, 55
Austerity, 66, 67, 180, 184, 185, 203
Avenues for further research, 202

B

Bailouts. *See* Regulators' response to the crisis
Ball, Lawrence, 180
Bank capital requirements, 49, 113. *See also* Basel accords
　and value-at-risk, 49
　capital quantification problem, 112
　prior to global financial crisis, 112
Barclays, 158, 159
Basel accords, 113
Basel Committee on Banking Supervision, 113
Bear Stearns
　mortgage exposure, 160
　precedent for future bailouts, 147, 163
　sale to J.P. Morgan, 2, 14, 137, 140, 142, 147, 148
Benefits of *Social Finance*, 15
Bernanke, Ben S., 1, 76, 81, 82, 86, 97, 136, 139, 141, 142, 160, 162, 176–178, 180, 197, 200
　historic memories of Great Depression, 15
Blyth, Mark, 8, 32, 35, 40, 45, 46, 50, 51, 55–57, 64, 66, 108, 119, 112, 116, 119, 121, 184, 185, 192, 199, 207
BNP Paribas, 1, 138
Bond ratings
　and AIG, 160, 161
　and Bear Stearns' sale to J.P. Morgan, 147
　and epistemic blindness, 122
　and information asymmetry, 14
　as conventions, 104, 121, 194
Bubbles, 65, 98
　as necessary but insufficient conditions for systemic crises, 106
Bureau of Labor Statistics, 87–90
Bush, George W., 163, 197

C

Capital flows, 50, 124, 147, 160, 161, 194, 201, 204
Case study method
　limitations, 191
　pathway case definition, 60
Citigroup, 55, 127, 138, 173, 175
Cohen, H. Rodgin, 158
Colander, David, 30, 31, 37, 63–65, 115
Collateral, 186
　and shadow banking conduits, 10, 13, 14, 108, 120, 165, 194
　See also Information-insensitivity
Collateralized debt obligations, 106, 138, 162, 219
Conditional non-rationality, 43, 45, 203
Constitutive causality, 57, 62, 205
　applied to economic ideas, 47
　vs. linear causality, 192
Consumer price index, 87, 97
　and housing, 87
Conventional expectations
　and Bear Stearns sale, 14, 142
　and conduit stability, 12, 19, 49, 133
　and Lehman Brothers bankruptcy, 2, 14
　and rollover risk, 49
　and stability of shadow banking conduits, 12, 49, 53, 54, 64, 104, 110, 155, 194
Conventions
　and blindness, 9
　and stability, 19, 29, 41, 51, 192, 194
　and uncertainty mitigation, 9, 51
　as constraints on elite intervention, 55, 192
　convention uncertainty, 9, 14, 21, 44, 46, 52–55, 61, 126, 133,

151, 155, 162, 165, 167, 168, 170, 181, 192, 194, 202, 206
defined, 48
ergodicity; and bond ratings, 51, 161
expert opinion, 13, 17, 40, 41, 49, 94, 105, 118, 125, 194
types, 5, 40, 48
Counter-cyclical legitimation, 196
Counter-factual analysis, 58, 59, 62, 91, 94, 193
Counterparty confidence, 6, 146, 213
Counterparty risk, 14, 113, 115, 138, 139, 145, 164, 165, 167, 170, 174
Credibility transfer, 6, 56, 179, 180, 195, 203–205
Credit, liquidity, and maturity transformation, 2, 11, 12, 73, 103, 104, 109, 195, 203
Credit default swap, 115, 138, 159
Credit rating agencies, 13, 117, 125, 127, 138, 160
Credit ratings. *See* Bond ratings
Credit transformation, 34
Crotty, James, 6, 23, 41, 42, 45, 48, 52, 113, 170, 171

D

Data hysteresis, 124
Deflation, 6, 49, 51, 73–75, 83–86, 92–95, 192, 193
Deposit insurance, 3, 6, 10, 12, 14, 15, 20, 35, 51, 52, 56, 105, 108, 110, 120, 125, 126, 151, 162, 171, 172, 178, 194
Domestic credibility transfer, 179
Doran, Charles. *See* Power cycle theory
Dow, Sheila, 42, 48, 53, 63
Dynamic stochastic general equilibrium models

influence over thinking of financial crises, 29

E

Economic constructivism, 4, 5, 8, 17, 29, 39, 46, 47, 61, 67
on crises, 17, 39
ontology. *See* Constitutive causality
Efficient markets hypothesis, 92
Einhorn, David, 156
Empirical implications of *Social Finance*, 10, 15, 51, 56, 58, 59, 73, 202, 211
Epistemic blindness
due to conventions, 50, 117, 192
in the Post-Keynesian model, 5, 16, 37, 192
Equilibrium bias. *See* Expert opinion
Ergodicity
and economic conventions, 17, 48, 193
definition, 48
Evans, Charles, 178
Evidentiary standards, 94. *See also* Operationalization
Exchange stabilization fund, 172, 186
Expectations
and conventions, 5, 9, 19, 41, 51, 62, 66, 104, 110, 128, 133, 134, 146, 160–162, 170, 171, 178, 192, 194
defied expectations and shocks, 21, 54, 162
in Doran's model, 7, 43
Expert opinion
and bond ratings, 49, 104, 125, 194

F

Fallacy of composition, 30, 67

Fannie Mae. *See* Government-sponsored enterprises
Federal funds rate, 74–79, 82, 173, 175
 and correlation to housing prices, 76
 and housing-related interest rates, 74
Federal Housing Financing Agency, 149
Federal Open Market Committee (FOMC), 48–49, 51, 59, 74–76, 79–84, 86–89, 91, 93–97, 96, 163, 173, 175, 178, 193
Federal Reserve Bank of Boston, 163
Federal Reserve Bank of Chicago, 178
Federal Reserve Bank of Kansas City, 1, 92. *See also* Jackson Hole Economic Policy Symposium
Federal Reserve Bank of New York, 3, 134, 136, 137, 141, 150, 159, 165, 172
Federal Reserve Bank of Richmond, 163, 178
Federal Reserve Board of Governors 13(3) emergency lending authority, 159
Financial crisis
 and conventions, 12, 48, 94, 199
 regulators' response, 55, 56, 178, 186
Financial Crisis Inquiry Commission, 37, 117, 143, 202
Financial Services Authority, 159
Financial stability, 2, 9, 16, 19, 29, 38, 41, 45, 48, 57, 65, 120, 133, 134, 139, 170, 191, 195, 198, 202
 and convention stability, 9, 19, 48
Fisher relationship, 85
Fitch, 117–119
Fixed income arbitrage, 135. *See also* Long-Term Capital Management
Flight to quality, 9, 18, 21, 32, 53, 55, 59, 133, 135, 162, 167, 168, 194, 202, 205
 as a sign of convention uncertainty, 133, 167
Forecasting future financial instability, 17
Fragility, 2–5, 9, 12–15, 17–21, 24, 30, 32, 33, 35–38, 41, 48–51, 53, 62, 63, 73, 74, 82, 83, 93, 95, 97, 103–106, 111, 115, 117, 124, 125, 127, 133, 147, 160–162, 182, 186, 192–197, 201, 202, 205, 206
Freddie Mac. *See* Government-sponsored enterprises
Fuld, Richard, 157, 159. *See also* Lehman Brothers

G
GDP volatility. *See* Great moderation
Geithner, Timothy, 3, 150, 165, 180, 181, 185, 197, 207
Global macroeconomic imbalances, 80, 200
 as a driver of the housing bubble, 82
Goldman Sachs, 122, 138, 142, 151, 167, 173, 180, 181
Gorton, Gary, 2, 10, 11, 23, 24, 34, 52, 103, 106–110, 120, 126, 127, 146, 161, 165, 193
 and AIG, 161
Government-sponsored enterprises, 95, 127, 200
Great Depression, 2, 15, 18, 22, 24, 56, 176–178, 182, 186, 194, 206
 historic memories and global financial crisis response, 15
Great moderation
 evidence of, 84
 influence on pre-crisis monetary policy, 85
Greenspan, Alan, 12
 on Fannie Mae and Freddie Mac, 14, 51, 140